THE
ENCHANTED GROUND

THE ENCHANTED GROUND

Americans in Italy, 1760-1980

by ERIK AMFITHEATROF

LITTLE, BROWN AND COMPANY

Boston · Toronto

FIRST EDITION

The author is grateful to the Massachusetts Historical Society and the
Houghton Library, Harvard University for permission to quote
from letters in their collections.

Library of Congress Cataloging in Publication Data

Amfitheatrof, Erik.
  The enchanted ground.

  Includes index.
  1. Americans in Italy—History. I. Title.
DG457.A75A43 945'.00451 80-18438
ISBN 0-316-03700-1

MV

Designed by Janis Capone

*Published simultaneously in Canada
by Little, Brown & Company (Canada) Limited*

PRINTED IN THE UNITED STATES OF AMERICA

To Stefania

ACKNOWLEDGMENTS

great many people have helped me in researching this book. Though any errors are entirely mine, I wish to express my deepest gratitude to the people listed here. They are distinguished in their own right and have no need of my naming them, but I would be remiss in not doing so.

I owe special thanks to Donatella Ortona Ferrario and to Stephanie Abarbanel for their invaluable research and ideas; to the On. Susanna Agnelli for her recollections and thoughts, and for graciously making time available to this undertaking; to Marchesa Iris Origo, whose own books on Italy are an exciting discovery for any reader; to Henry Cabot Lodge, formerly the President's special representative to the Vatican; to Cardinal John Wright, for his delightful recollections and the loan of useful books; to John Navone, friend and wise counsel; to Prince Guglielmo "Bill" Rospigliosi for his valuable assistance; to Gore Vidal, who on several occasions contributed ideas and suggestions; to Countess Alicia Spalding Paolozzi for her gracious hospitality and kind help; to David Lees, friend and matchmaker; to Bill and Beverly Pepper, who contributed their thoughts and experiences; to Duchess Terry Canevaro, who generously shared her recollections; to Princess Letizia Ludovisi-Boncompagni, for her gracious help; to Mrs. Mercedes Huntington, for her kind hospitality at Bellosguardo; to Contessa Laura Camerana and Marchesa Clara Ferrero di Ventimiglia, for their generous assistance; to General Mark Clark, who graciously found time to speak to me during his commemorative visit to Rome; to

Harry Brewster, who is of this book; to Enrico and Peany Middleton, for their hospitality and valuable help; to Federico Fellini, whose words match his pictures; to Marchese Emilio Pucci, for making his valuable time available and contributing his recollections and ideas; to Baron Giovanni Battista Rubin de Cervin, director of the wonderful Naval Museum in Venice, and to Pietro Breda; to John Walker, for his valuable and generous help; to Claire Sterling, who generously assisted in dotting the i's; to Aileen Branca, whose wonderful stories remain a fond memory; to Maggie Furguson, for recollections generously shared; to Gianfranco Corsini, for his valuable help; to Francis McCool, S.J.

I am deeply beholden also to a number of people at the American Academy, principally to Professor Henry Millon and to Professor John H. D'Arms, to Mrs. Christine Young and Lucilla Marino. The use of the academy's splendid library was an invaluable service, and I wish to express my gratitude here. I am deeply grateful, also, to Dott.sa Alessandra Sordi, director of the Nelson Gay Memorial Library at Rome's Palazzo Antici Mattei. With her abundant and gracious help, I was able to read many hard-to-obtain books in that library. I also wish to thank Professor Craig Smythe, Fiorella Gioffredi Superbi, and Susan Arcamone for their kind assistance at I Tatti; and I am beholden for generous help to Baron Cecil Anrep; to Madame Michele Rivas; to Alexandra Tirindelli; to various friends in the Foreign Service; to P. M. Pasinetti; to Dr. Edward F. Parker and Dr. Peter C. Graffagnino, who served their country and fellow human beings as wartime surgeons in Italy; to Dr. Jack Pryor and his brilliant wife, Olga; to Robert Edwards; to Senator Bob Dole; to Luigi Barzini, Jr.; to the late Professor John McAndrew; to Professor Frank Brown and Professor Kyle Phillips, Jr.; to Claudio and Nelsa Emmer; to Bruna Sevini of USIS in Rome; to Sam Steinman; to Hank Werba; to my sister Stella, noblest Roman of the family; and to Julia Banfi.

I am indebted to the staff of Harvard's Houghton Library and the staff of the Massachusetts Historical Society for their valuable assistance; to Bianca Spantigatti Gabbrielli, Aldo Durazzo, and Velio Cioni, who helped to assemble pictures; to Renata dal Zotto, Karen Craft, Letizia Allegri, and Margaret Wright, who typed the manuscript at various stages; to my colleagues at Time Inc., and particularly to Jerry Korn, who gave me a leave of absence to start the book, and to Murray Gart and Dick Duncan, who kept me in

Rome long enough to get it done; to Don Neff, traveler in Arcadia, Ann Natanson, whose valuable counsel is always precious to me; and to Countess Logan Lessona.

I wish to express my deep gratitude to two people at Little, Brown. The first is Llewellyn Howland III, former editor, who wanted this book written. And the second is Robert Emmett Ginna, Jr., the present editor in chief, who encouraged me to persevere. Special thanks are due to Christina Potter for her many helpful contributions.

My wife, Elvira, as always, participated more than words can here express.

I naturally read a good many books in researching this one. Many of them proved unusually enjoyable as well as useful. To anyone interested in the life of Margaret Fuller, I strongly recommend Jay Deiss's excellent biography, and I recommend just as strongly Francis Steegmuller's *The Two Lives of James Jackson Jarves* to anyone interested in Jarves. For the flavor of Americans in the old-time Italy, one could hardly do better than to read Henry James's *William Wetmore Story and His Friends*. Van Wyck Brooks's *The Dream of Arcadia* and Professor Baker's *The Fortunate Pilgrims* are both very enjoyable and useful surveys of American artists and scholars in Italy. Louise Hall Tharp's *Mrs. Jack* is a useful biography of Isabella Stewart Gardner, and I would highly recommend Iris Origo's books to anyone interested in Italy, particularly her elegant autobiography, *Images and Shadows*. Robert Katz's *The Fall of the House of Savoy* is an excellent and very readable account of Italy's modern monarchs. Mary McCarthy's *The Stones of Florence* and *Venice Observed* are spirited, penetrating portraits of these cities and their people. Finally, in fiction, Irwin Shaw's *Two Weeks in Another Town* conveys the flavor of Hollywood on the Tiber in the 1960s, while Herman Wouk's *The Winds of War* has an arresting portrait of a Berenson-like sage.

FOREWORD

In the winter of 1943–1944, Frank Holden was picked up for questioning by the Gestapo. They thought he was a spy. Though he was all of sixty-five, a tall, elegantly casual gentleman with a great mane of ivory hair who helped himself along with a handsome Bond Street cane, in their punctilious eyes it was inconceivable that an American citizen should have quietly inhabited his Italian villa all through the war without even reporting once a week to the authorities.

The Italian police in the Ligurian town of Levanto, where Frank Holden had his villa, had never been troubled by his presence. With the incomparable Italian gift of treating familiar individuals, even enemy aliens, with respectful intimacy, they had regularly sipped a cappuccino with this tart, grumbly Yankee and shared his neutral sighs over the war and its cruel toll. To the Gestapo, this fraternization between policemen and a potential spy was inconceivable. They took the old gentleman up the coast to one of their detention centers and grilled him. But then, because he was so obviously not a secret agent, just an expatriate, they released him and allowed him to hike back almost a hundred miles to Levanto with the aid of his elegant, English walking stick.

A few weeks later Frank Holden stood on the terrace of his villa and watched with sorely mixed emotions as P-47 Thunderbolts flown by American boys plastered hell out of the town where he had lived for over twenty years, trying to hit a slender, arched railroad culvert carrying the tracks that connected Genoa to the north with the naval base of La Spezia, some twenty miles to the south.

Born on Staten Island, Frank Holden had gone to work at eighteen in a mechanical design studio near the Battery. After a few years he was hired by General Electric, in Schenectady, New York, where he designed electric meters and gauges. His way of inventing things was eccentric at a time when romantic individualism was still respectable in American business. Once the spirit was upon him, he would lock up his office, put on a white hat, shoulder a backpack, and go walking for a couple of weeks through the towns and hills of New England, often striding as far north as the White Mountains of New Hampshire. As ideas came to him, he would jot them down in his notebook, and on his return he would test them in the lab and transform the best of them into patented inventions. By the time he was thirty Frank Holden was rich, holding patents to some homely but vital pieces of industrial equipment, such as the gas meter.

Around the turn of the century, Frank Holden began to chafe at the increasingly regulated life inside the American corporation. The inventor's buttoned-down bosses did not approve of his impromptu disappearances and two-week absences. They curbed him, but he was the kind of Yankee not easily curbed. A shy, truculent six-footer with a strong, sharply chiseled face and a dry, caustic sense of humor, he was still a bachelor and couldn't be worried about mortgages and such. Besides, every gas meter brought him a fraction of a cent. He chucked the corporation, went to London, and set himself up as a consultant.

His business took him to the Continent, and in the Milanese home of a representative of the Swiss firm of Brown Boveri he met the woman of his life. A small-nosed, sharp-voiced woman whose mother was English, Mary Pandiani had grown up in England during the final years of Queen Victoria's reign. Frank married her after a long courtship and took her to live in London. She would tongue-lash him daily while adoring his masculine independence of spirit; it was this combination, apparently, that he had sought for so long.

In the 1920s, however, the couple gravitated back to Italy. Mary Holden's elder sister Nelly had married another Anglo-Italian, an electrical engineer named Guido Semenza. A slender, almost frail man but a beaver in his work, Semenza had also been professionally successful and had bought a hillside villa at Levanto, on the Ligurian coast. The Holdens found Levanto so congenial that they too acquired a villa there.

Though Levanto was one of Italy's first beach resorts, it remained fundamentally a Ligurian fishing village. It was very pretty, set in a crescent-shaped bay with pine-green hills rising behind. The pastel houses had green blinds and occasional false windows painted on a side wall in the Genoese style. At sunset, the fishermen would drag their colorful boats to the water's edge, light their big, mushroom-shaped, kerosene lamps bolted to the stern, and spend the night bobbing on the horizon like stars fallen onto the surface of the sea. At dawn they would row back into the bay, extinguish their lamps, and spread their silvery catch on the beach, where the maids from the villas could buy the freshest fish in their world for their signori. Life was sweet and easygoing. During his service as minister to France, Thomas Jefferson had walked through parts of Liguria in 1878 and had written in his journal that "if any person wished to retire from his acquaintances and live absolutely unknown, and yet in the midst of physical enjoyments, it should be in some of the little villages of this coast where air, water, and earth concur to offer what each has most precious."

In the 1920s, technology had not yet changed the pace of life in Levanto. The engineers could enjoy the simple beauty of a fishing town before the momentum of industrialization, of which they were proponents and servants, smudged its picturesque charm.

The Holdens were not really isolated in Levanto. Upper-class Florentine families came for holidays; British and American families would appear in late spring and settle into their villas until September, when schools started again and it was time to sail home on a luxury liner. Even in the winter, Frank Holden could enjoy the company of local expatriates, including that of a huge, white-bearded Russian writer, Alexander Amfitheatrof, who had been exiled after the revolution of 1905 and told retrospectively funny stories about Siberia. He had D. H. Lawrence to lunch and put up Jan Masaryk when the famous Czech patriot was being hunted by the police.

In the late 1920s, Daniele Amfitheatrof, the writer's son, and May Semenza, one of the electrical engineer's four daughters, married and went to the United States to live while the original American in the family, Frank Holden, stayed on in Levanto through

World War II to experience his nasty brush with the SS. At that, he was lucky. I am the son of Daniele and May, and I never knew two of my Italian uncles, Robbie Lepetit and Giangio Banfi, who perished in German concentration camps for having joined the Resistance during those final demonic months of the war.

My great regret in writing this book is that Uncle Frank is no longer alive. By the time I had returned from my American upbringing to inspect and cherish those mingled family roots at Levanto, Frank was well into his eighties. Once or twice I unwillingly did my family duty and called at his large, marble-floored villa at five in the afternoon for a tea ceremony almost as elaborate as that of the Japanese. Silent maids would appear (one of them black-eyed and very pretty) with a succession of silver platters bearing cakes and biscuits of all sizes and shapes. The conversation was proper and nostalgic, as the Holdens recalled bygone times and incidents from their years in London and Levanto or, in Frank's case funny anecdotes from his years with G.E. Frank's speech, however, had become slow and hard to follow. Even the New England witticisms that rumbled softly from his lips were so rusty as to be incomprehensible. There was so much he could have told me, for he had lived the expatriate experience at the twilight of an era when the hills of Florence and the Roman palazzi were full of Americans, when it was considered controversial and even sinful to steal away to Italy as so many upper-class Americans did and flaunt one's individualism in the extravagant setting of an Italian villa.

The urge that drove Americans to Italy, and what they experienced there, is the subject of this book. I have tried to cast as wide a net as possible, catching up everyone from the starry-eyed adventurers when the United States was barely a nation to the Hollywood stars who paced the Via Veneto like so many Byrons and Shelleys in that golden cusp between the fifties and the sixties. My hope is that future American tourists to Italy will read this book. It may not help them to know that Thomas Jefferson crossed the Alps into Italy on muleback, thinking hard about Hannibal, or that some of the American ladies tucked away in those Florentine villas, like Mabel Dodge, were liberated well ahead of their time, but the aim of any social history is to instruct as well as to entertain. Americans have sought many things from Italy over the past two centuries and that, most of all, is the story these pages tell.

Rome
1979

THE
ENCHANTED GROUND

CHAPTER ONE

In 1805, Washington Irving arrived in Rome. Packed off to Europe for his health, the future writer had spent several months wandering through Sicily on foot with a couple of U.S. Marine Corps officers (from the crew of a warship berthed at Messina for action against the Tripoli pirates). He and the two young officers enjoyed themselves hugely, whether sleeping on the floor of a peasant hut or whirling aristocratic ladies around the ballroom floor of a rococo Bourbon palazzo. Every step of the journey, Irving wrote, had been "enchanted ground."

In Rome, Irving fell in with his namesake Washington Allston, the gifted and sensitive painter from South Carolina. The two of them would roam through the Villa Borghese gardens nearly every day and go on long walking trips to places like Tivoli. Irving, liking this upper-class bohemian life, began toying with the idea of becoming an artist like Allston rather than going home again "to the dry study of the law." There was not much of a painter in him, probably, but he was swayed toward art by the sheer good time he was having and by the idea that Allston would stay in Italy, "surrounded by masterpieces of art, by classic and historic monuments, by men of congenial minds and tastes, engaged like him in the constant study of the sublime and the beautiful."

The temptation of Italy was to remain a constant theme for Americans of the nineteenth century; a dream for many, distant and beguiling; an undertow drawing the new citizen of the New World

3

back to the biblical stained-glass oldness of a Mediterranean time and coloring, to art, to the stones of history. American travelers in Italy found the pace slow, the people friendly, the sun sensuous and enervating. Others found intellectual stimulation, physical challenge. Women in particular, like Elizabeth Sedgwich, became ardent supporters of the Italian patriots fighting for the independence and unification of their divided country. A number of American visitors, male and female, settled in Italy and never, or rarely, returned to their native land. Because Italy had acquired, in the Renaissance, a gothic romance aura of sinfulness and lust, the relatives back home were usually scandalized when Uncle Edward or Aunt Sally sank into expatriation in a Tuscan villa or a Roman palazzo and stubbornly turned away from the challenges of nation-building. Remote scandals involving Edward's boys or Sally's middle-aged Italian lover would be embroidered into family history. Part of Italy's fascination for Protestant Americans was that its morals had seemingly worn away like a decayed marble surface. The New Yorker Theodore Fay put his readers on guard when they took their Grand Tours, warning that an upright Yankee would feel "for the first time, perchance, ashamed that he is *man!*"

Most Americans were skeptical of the country, wary of its morals, and in love with the ruins and the picture galleries. The roster of those who spent a few months in Rome or Florence includes the intellectual aristocracy of New England, men such as Harvard's Charles Eliot Norton, journalists, bankers — even politicians like the unlucky James Garfield, who declared ebulliently after a visit to Rome that it would be "my country forevermore." Nearly every American painter from West and Copley to Samuel F. B. Morse, the inventor of the telegraph, spent a year or two copying Old Masters. Writers, of course, were regular pilgrims, including Hawthorne, Emerson, Richard Henry Dana (who is buried near Keats in Rome's little Protestant cemetery), James, Melville, Twain, Longfellow, and James Fenimore Cooper.

Cooper, almost as famous in Europe for *The Last of the Mohicans* as Hemingway would be in the twentieth century after *The Sun Also Rises,* was one of the first American men of letters to popularize for Americans the idea of Italy as a land of sensuous whim and arcadian charm, thus a temporary retreat from the severity of New England Calvinism. "There is no place," he wrote to a friend, "where mere living is such a luxury." He had arrived with his numerous family in 1828, during the travel boom that followed the eclipse of Napoleon and almost fifteen years of constant warfare. At Leghorn the writer chartered a felucca — a yacht-sized boat with a lateen sail — and sailed it down to Sorrento, where he settled his numerous brood in a castle said to be the birthplace of the poet Tasso. Cooper, who had been a U.S. Navy officer in the war of 1812 and knew how to handle ships, took his family sailing in the Bay of Naples and wrote much of *The Water-Witch* during those months in Sorrento. Later, the Coopers settled for a season in Florence, where the writer befriended one of the first American sculptors to try to make a go of it in Italy, Horatio Greenough. Greenough was not doing very well, and Cooper generously helped him out with some life-saving loans. The Coopers drifted up to Paris next, but Fenimore did not like France and would grumble to friends, "Ah, Italy, it sticks in my ribs like a second wife."

There was something about Italy before the Industrial Revolution that charmed half the world. Dickens spent a season in Florence and Rome and wrote a book about it. Liszt lived in Rome for a while, the Brownings in Florence, and Dostoyevsky wrote most of *The Idiot* there. Madame de Staël wrote her novel *Corinne* in Rome, modeling her hero on a young American from Charleston, South Carolina. He was John Izard Middleton, a grandson of one of the signers of the Declaration of Independence, who happened to be in Rome at the same time. It was he who founded the tradition of American scholarship in Italy by walking on foot through the then-wild parts of the Campagna outside Rome and the countryside near Naples, sketching the ruins and the colorfully dressed peasants. The ruins were perfectly *au naturel*. Nobody had dug them out, tidied them up. They came out of the ground like some kind of spectacular vegetation, often themselves covered with a skein of lichens and grass among which lay wild roses and violets.

Viewing a country on foot or from a carriage may seem impossibly slow to us today, but Allston's and Cooper's countrymen did get around, even then. "In the course of four or five hours I traversed almost the whole of Rome and got a glimpse of everything — the Forum, the Colosseum (stupendissimo!), the Pantheon, the Capitol, St. Peter's, the Column of Trajan, the Castel of St. Angelo — all the piazzas and the ruins and monuments." It could have been anybody's first day in Rome, but this one belonged to Henry James, who probably saw as much in his hired carriage as

In the nineteenth century, children of noble Italian families were tutored rather than being sent to school. Here, a private tutor and his charges pose against the backdrop of the Roman Forum, which had not yet been fully excavated. Houses and a church — long since razed — are clustered at the foot of the Palatine Hill, on the far right.

ARCHIVIO FOTOGRAFICO COMUNALE, ROME

tourists do today in those huge American Express buses with doughnut tires and aquarium windows.

The inconvenience of travel in the days of horsedrawn vehicles did mean, however, that people had to plan their journeys with great care, and the Americans who came to Italy in the nineteenth century were invariably well briefed. Since a European journey took anywhere from three months to a year, they prepared themselves for it by reading all the available travel literature, and some of it was very good. My own personal favorite is Marianna Starke, an Englishwoman whose 1830s guidebook was popular in New England before works by native writers supplanted it. What a police reporter this woman would have made! She does everything for you — packs your bags, makes up lists of things you mustn't forget to take along, tells you what to tip the old guide (the one with a wart on his nose) when you go see Leonardo's *Last Supper*. She tells you where and how you can cash a letter of credit to an Italian banker when you run out of money and what documents you need at every border. (Remember, Italy was divided into eight states at the beginning of the nineteenth century, and you needed a different document for each one.)

Just to raise the curtain slightly on one of her packing lists, she would first have you take on your Italian journey "leather sheets made of sheep-skin or doe-skin." Then, naturally, "pillows" and "blankets," as well as "calico sheets" and "pillow cases." So much for the bedding. A traveler must be ready to dismount and eat by the wayside, however, when the carriage axle breaks, so you must not forget a set of silverware and such cutlery as "a carving knife and fork," also "a pocket knife" as well as "table cloths and napkins." A "small lantern" is always useful; and, indeed, the gentlemen would hardly be comfortable without "pen knives, pens, razors, straps, and hones." Sensibly, she suggests packing "doubled soled shoes and boots which are particularly needful to resist the chill of brick and marble floors." One would need a moving van by this time, not a carriage. And it's only the beginning. Tell the maid not to forget "the silver teapot, tea, and sugar cannister."

She was writing principally for an English audience, since the upper classes of the British Isles had been rolling back and forth across the Continent on their Grand Tours for over a century. They knew how to move about in comfort. Before the age of steam, there was even a sail-powered ferryboat that left daily from the Thames River docks for Calais — a ferryboat because one brought aboard one's carriage and team of horses. Englishmen generally preferred taking their own vehicle on the Grand Tour, and with all that silverware and bedding, it's not hard to see why. One of the great sights of Europe then was to watch a really handsome Englishman's carriage with a team of six horses pulling into the piazza in front of the Hotel Bellavista, with the grooms jumping down to open the doors and porters running out of the hotel, the townspeople leaning out of their windows and balconies to see if another Lord Byron had come back. (He had traveled with three carriages, one of them a library on wheels.)

By midcentury, Americans had their own guidebooks. The one everybody seems to have preferred was Stanley Hillard's *Six Months in Italy,* published by Ticknor, Reid, and Fields in Boston, which came in two conveniently pocket-sized volumes. Hillard was less of a crass materialist and list-maker than the wonderful Marianna. He emphasized the moral and intellectual benefits of going to Italy. Hillard's readers had money and an itch to go and see what the old Continent looked like. But they needed a bit of convincing, particularly in those pre-1870 years when one still had to cross the Atlantic in a sailing vessel, perhaps to face pirates in the Mediterranean.

Hillard gave his audience a little nudge. "Whoever travels habitually has certainly seen Italy," he begins, perhaps putting them on the defensive at once. (Not a habitual traveler? Never seen Italy?) "No other country," he continues smoothly, "gathers together so many attractions, or seduces the foreigner with so many diverse charms. Not to feel attracted towards Italy, not to feel gratitude at having visited her, not to remember her with the most vivid interest — means to be indifferent to everything which has lived before our time. No soil has produced so many great men; none has left so abundant a heritage to the contemporary spirit; none has passed through so many changes; none offers so many attractions."

Hillard's circus-barker technique was eminently successful. More than Mrs. Starke or any of the earlier travel writers, he packaged Italy for the understandably hesitant and somewhat timorous Americans who had never ventured outside the eastern portion of their own continent. Armed with his blueprint for a safe and successful journey, they chartered a passage across the Atlantic, packed their bags, made their wills, and set off on the great adventure of an Italian tour, which they believed would inscribe something on their hearts and minds forever.

CHAPTER TWO

he carriage has deposited you at quayside, where the old salts from Bedford sneer a little at the greenness of your pallor. The wind has whipped up some surly, frothing whitecaps even in the harbor, and you think of three weeks out on that treacherous surface. Friends and relatives have bid you good-bye tearfully, knowing they might never see you again. A certain faintheartedness possesses you. Something vital that you forgot to pack and must go back for? A sudden seizure right there at quayside before the amused eyes of that nautical gallery? No, you couldn't let yourself — and yet . . . But now your luggage is being carried aboard on the shoulders of apparently unworried seamen, and — oh Lord — the captain is coming down the gangplank to welcome you personally and take you aboard. "Captain, any bad storms building up out there?" The question sticks in your throat, and after murmuring some polite civilities, you and your dread precede him up the gangplank. You are a prisoner now of the brig *Mary Stebbins,* and she will not release you (you hope) 'ere Leghorn.

So it must have been. For an American to sail to Italy meant rounding a quarter of the globe. It was abysmally dangerous. Ships simply vanished in storms or were left dismasted and drifting, with the heartless monotony of water swishing in the holds. Oil lamps shattered and set vessels ablaze. When the sculptor Hiram Powers and his wife sailed for Italy the first time in 1837, they survived both a shipwreck and a shipboard fire. Not until the 1880s did steam-driven liners begin to replace sail in the Atlantic, though sailing vessels with auxiliary paddlewheels had appeared as early as 1818. The technical problem to be overcome was that early steamers were not big enough to carry sufficient coal for a power-driven transatlantic crossing, and so sail lingered on and produced the era of the majestic clipper. Even clipper ships, big as they were, got into awful trouble. A real gale in the Atlantic could raise waves eighty-five feet high. During one crossing, Samuel Morse made the following succinct notation: "Calm in a terrible sea."

Even when the sea remained unterrible, crossing the ocean in a sailing ship was in itself a kinetic physical adventure. Unlike the stable platform of a steam-driven ship, which rests on a perpendicular axis, the sailing ship heels over to one side when it runs at an angle to the wind, just as a sailboat does, so that a passenger going from the East Coast of the United States to the Mediterranean spent thirty to forty days in a sloping world. When a good, fresh wind was blowing, the helmsman would normally put the ship at the shortest possible angle to the wind (close-handed) and sail that tack for several hours; then the ship would come about, with the sailors out on the deck to pull the sails around a new angle. The decks that had been tilting to starboard would swing over and tilt to port, and the ship would be off on its new course. There were constant variables to the journey. The wind was always dying out, freshening, changing direction, so that a ship might have to come about several times in a single hour. When it really blew, whistling through the rigging and straining canvas and spars, its force could put the ship over thirty or forty degrees on one side. Even with the upper sails rolled up (reefed), the waves surged up on deck, and if a heavy sea were running, anyone topside ran the risk of being washed overboard.

Belowdecks was no pleasure in a storm. The oil lamp overhead swayed back and forth, rattling on its chain; timbers on every side creaked as if the ship were about to break up; the hull seemed to slide over the edge of each mountainous wave and hang sickeningly for a moment before it thwacked the hollow slope of the trough and plunged downward again.

Yet some transatlantic travelers came to thrive on the dangers, to delight in the incomparable harmony of wind, sail, rope, timber, sky, and spacious sea changing their colors and shadow patterns under drifting clouds. Cooper, who had cut his teeth on sailing ships, left loving recollections of Atlantic crossings aboard luxurious yachtlike vessels, of neoclassic cabins with marble columns and stainwood paneling and fine carpets, sofas — even a piano. There was, in such travel, a sense of individualism: One was not a sardine in row 17, seat E.

James Russell Lowell, in 1851, sailed for Italy with a goat to provide his family with fresh milk. He wrote to his father toward the end of the voyage (when Sardinia was already in sight), "I wish you would tell Aunt Gardner how very useful the goat has been to us. We got out of our preserved milk and should have had none for our tea but for the goat." A distinctly urbane sailor Lowell must have been; and his letter is worth quoting since it so well describes the experience of a good crossing.

> We have been thirteen days in the Mediterranean, & unless the wind should change we may sail about for seven or eight more days before we reach Malta. We had a very good run from land to land (e.g., Boston to Gibraltar), making the light at Cape St. Vincent on the night of the seventeenth day out. I stayed upon deck until we could see the light — the Cape we did not see at all, nor any land till next morning. Then we saw the coast of Spain very dim & blue — only the outline of a mountain & some high land here and there.
>
> The day before we made land we had tolerably good specimen of a gale of wind, enough, at any rate, to get up so much sea that we were in danger of having our lee-quarter boat washed away, the keel of which hangs above the level of the poop-deck. As it was, we lost the covering of one of our portholes which was knocked out by the water which was washing about on the lower deck. I was the only one of the party at table that day & there was an amount of vivacity among the dishes as I never saw before. I took my soup by the process of absorption, the whole of it having suddenly leapt out of my plate into my lap.

He tells in the same letter how his little girl Mabel became a regular salt.

> She assists regularly in "bouting ship," as she calls it, standing at the wheel with admirable gravity. The Captain always takes the wheel & issues the orders when the ship is put about & as this ceremony had taken place pretty regularly every four hours for the last eight days, Mabel had acquired all the requisite phrases and at intervals during the day, a shrill voice may be heard crying

out, "Bout Ship!" "Mainsail ha-u-l!" "Jacks & Sheets!" "Let go & ha-u-l!," the whole prefaced by an exceedingly emphatic "Ha-a-a-ard a lee!" There is no part of the vessel except the hold & the rigging which she has not repeatedly inspected. With all the sailors she is on intimate terms & employes them at odd hours in the manufacture of various articles of furniture.

The Lowells sailed all the way to Italy, but most Americans had other business in Europe that they usually took care of first — visits to relatives in England, leisurely fortnights in the hotels of London and Paris, and, often, a tour of the principal German cities. To move about on the Continent, travelers first armed themselves with passports and letters of credit made out to banks in the principal cities they would visit.

They then turned over a good portion of their ready cash to an agent, known as *voiturin* in French or *vetturino* in Italian — literally, the "carriage man" — whose task it was to assemble a group of passengers (which might consist of a single family or unrelated individuals), plot the journey, provide or hire the diligence or coachman, reckon the places where horses could be changed, and write ahead to hotels and inns so that beds would be available at sundown when the day's progress came to an end. Unlike a modern travel agent, when all was ready, the *vetturino* swung himself up on the box next to the coachman and went along for the entire journey. He was the captain of the little caravel on wheels, responsible for the safety of his passengers, for seeing that meals were adequate and well cooked, and for sundry other details from translating the wishes of his charges into the language of the country to bribing customs inspectors at border crossings (which in Italy came with annoying frequency).

Usually, one paid the *vetturino* a lump sum at the beginning of the journey, which might take anywhere from a couple of days to several months. Once the all-inclusive price had been settled upon, a contract was drawn up and signed in the presence of a notary. Thereafter, one was very much in the *vetturino*'s hands, and he usually became the one foreigner travelers knew best. Sometimes he was an honest fellow, a boon companion and fatherly guide, and the parting at journey's end was a cause for tears. More often it was good riddance. As one weary tourist complained in 1854, "A word upon this *vetturino* system 'ere I leave it — I hope for ever. It is a perfect nuisance from beginning to end. From the moment you set off with one of these rascals, till the hour you arrive at your journey's end, it is plague, squabble, insolence and torment."

When the youthful Goethe started on his two-year Italian journey in 1786, he found carriages so rudimentary — unsprung two-wheeled carts with a cabin over them — that he jumped out and started walking. By the early 1800s, things had improved to the point that most carriages, or diligences, were similar to the Wells Fargo stagecoaches of Wild West fame — leather upholstery, seats for four with space for open-air passengers on the roof, and leaf or leather-strap suspension to take the spine-aching jolts out of all but the worst roads. Some carriages were even luxurious, such as the one described by an anonymous diarist that rose and sank on its springs "like a swan on a wave," with double cushions for comfort, a chessboard, backgammon tables, and "pockets stuffed with new publications, maps, and guides *ad infinitum.*"

Their luggage strapped to the roof, a good breakfast inside them (one hopes), our Yankee tourists settled themselves into their diligence and, with a *crack-crack-crack* of the whip and a great deal of swearing on the part of the driver, four horses were induced to set their boxlike world in motion. By our standards it was slow motion. Carriages averaged about three miles per hour, and in uphill country like the rugged Apennines their speed was even slower; passengers were usually requested to get out and walk so the horses could manage the grade. At the steepest points, oxen had to be hired from nearby farmers and hitched to the team as auxiliary power. The Bostonian Elizabeth Sedgwich witnessed a pitiful scene when one of those hired oxen shuddered, sank to its knees, rolled over in its traces, and expired. Since these beasts represented a good deal of capital to a peasant as well as being considered part of the family, the owner came bounding over the fields with a stricken look on his face, calling the dead ox by name, stooping over it, lifting its eyelid, and then declaiming his grief. "Oh God, dead, dead!" He stooped, lifting the eyelid again. "Dead, really dead!"

A collapsing ox or horse was one of the minor hazards of the road. Wheels and axles broke, thunderstorms washed out roads and bridges; sometimes the driver lost control of the team — and in mountain country that could be fatal. But the hazards everyone most dreaded were piracy and banditry. Just as we air travelers fear skyjackings, an American crossing Italy in a carriage would cast nervous looks out the window when they passed through thick, dark woods or any place that was suitable for ambushes.

The writers of gothic romances, particularly in England, had spread the idea that Italy was pulsing with banditti (a bit like the Mafia mania today), and the first reports from Americans visiting Italy were anything but reassuring. Washington Irving was aboard a brig bound from Leghorn to Messina in 1804 when it was intercepted off the island of Elba by a "pickeroon," as this particular pirate craft was called. The pickeroon's cannon sent an iron ball sailing between mainmast and foremast, and the brig hove to, boarded by a gang of cutthroats that Irving said later "would have shamed Falstaff's ragged regiment in their habliments, while their countenance displayed the strongest lines of villany and rapacity. They carried rusty cutlasses in their hands, and pistols and stilettos were stuck in their belts and waistbands." He emerged from the scrape unharmed but shaken. That night, he wrote, "the assassin-like figures of the ruffians were continually before me, and two or three times I started out of my bed with the horrid idea that their stilettos were raised against my bosom."

When he traveled across southern Italy Edward Everett, another of the earliest Americans in Italy and, like Irving, in his early twenties, did not actually encounter pirates or bandits but found the precautions against them disconcerting. In Naples, before the diligence set off at midnight, mass was held, as Everett put it, "for the bodies and souls of the travellers, that we might pass the more safely through the hands of robbers, or if not, then pass well thro' purgatory." Later, their single carriage was escorted through the thickly wooded Calabrian hills by a company of four mounted officers and twenty-four soldiers on foot — a veritable small army. Everett passed the time talking to his traveling companion, an Englishman who had been one of the peace commissioners sent to America after the revolution and who angered the young patriot by describing how George Washington had gotten drunk on wine at a party. "Which, with due submission to the ancient commissionaire," noted Everett indignantly, "I believe to be a lie." One might loathe one's traveling companions, but the monotony of moving along at a snail's pace day after day, the soreness of it, the sheer tedium, made even an argument welcome.

There was one piece of topography, however, where the train and the paved road have resulted in a net loss for the tourist — the crossing of the Alps, which was spectacular by carriage. The great patron of transalpine travel in the 1800s was none other than Bonaparte. Needing a good military road on which to shuttle his armies back and forth from France to Italy, he set thousands of men to work in 1801. Four years and 175,000 pounds of gunpowder later, they had blasted out a paved road twenty-five feet wide, with towering walls against landslides, fifty bridges over Alpine torrents, and six tunnels (or grottos, as they were then called). This eighth wonder of the world was the Simplon Pass, and it allowed a traveler to go from the Rhone Valley in Switzerland to northern Italy in a single breathtaking day.

The diligence set out at dawn from Brig, Switzerland, ascending through a gloomy forest of firs to the first and then the second refuge (small inns set along the road to shelter humans and animals in case of sudden storms). Through the course of the morning, passengers rode or walked beside the carriage up the innumerable turnings of this majestic road while in the distance the milky, shimmering crown of Mont-Blanc and the lesser Alps rose into view. Up, up they went, undisturbed except for the horn and clatter of a carriage roaring down on them from the other direction. Then it was past, and the slow but spectacular ascent continued, through forests, past waterfalls cascading downward in trajectories of hundreds of feet. At one or two P.M., after crossing through the gloomy 150-foot-long Glacier Grotto, the travelers reached the summit and the hospice staffed by the monks of the Grand St. Bernard order. Here — at 3,216 feet above sea level — they rested and ate while the weary horses munched their feed.

Then it was time to leave so they could reach Domodossola on the Italian side before nightfall. In 1869 Henry James made one of the last Simplon crossings before the railroad retired the carriages forever. He recalled nostalgically the heart-catching, downward-flying plunge into Italy, with coachman and team artfully keeping the momentum in check until, toward sunset, the first steeples and grape arbors began to appear; "the pink and yellow houses shimmered in the gentle gloom, and Italy began to whisper in broken syllables that she was at hand." ⋆

⋆ There were some twenty roads crossing the Alps into northern Italy. From Geneva, travelers sometimes went through the state of Savoy, up across Mount Cenis, and came down at Susa, west of Turin. From central Switzerland, one sometimes took the Splugen Pass, which was the usual route from Germany, as the Brenner was from Austria. Yet of all these roads, the Simplon was the most widely traveled.

The first thing that struck Americans as they rolled southward past the Lago Maggiore, with its magnificent Borromeo palace and free-roaming peacocks, was a pervasive softness in the air, a profusion of colors replacing the dark green of Switzerland, and the light that eighteenth-century artists like Claude had turned into an international legend. Fortunately, the legend was true; there was something extraordinarily rich, richly composed, and gentle in the Italian scene, and it seemed to come from God himself in the sky or, a man of the Enlightenment might have quibbled, from the old pagan deity of the Mediterranean sun. What Irving called "the serenity of the sky, the transparent purity of the atmosphere, and that nameless charm which hangs about an Italian landscape" would be described in similar terms over and over in the first letters home.

After the light and the beauty of the landscape, the second thing the American was likely to notice was the dirt, the noise, the sheer irrepressible vitality, confusion, and color that surrounded the carriage the moment it rolled through the streets of a town. The first Italians a tourist had any dealings with — apart from the *vetturino* and customs guards — were the beggars. The cities swarmed with them. When Benjamin West, the Quaker painter, was driven to the Vatican Picture Gallery his first week in Rome, so many beggars besieged the carriage — holding out their gaunt hands, screeching *"muoio di fame"* ("I'm dying of hunger") and other desperate imprecations — that the young American fainted. Things had improved but slightly by the time Emerson visited Rome; he hardly dared take a walk because of the army of beggars that followed him about. He complained bitterly in letters that the beggars would spring up around one even in the most tranquil ruins, spoiling Italy's "arcadian atmosphere."

Inns and hotels could be poor. Often, hotels were converted palazzi, and in winter they were icy. In small towns and villages, travelers were lodged in stalls. Since it was the *vetturino* who booked the sleeping accommodations along the route, his charges could do little but grumble. During a trip through Sicily in 1856, James Russell Lowell complained of having endured "such inns as it never entered into the heart of man to conceive; so nasty, so fleay, and all that." The most frequent causes for complaint were dirt and vermin, followed by noise in the courtyard, lack of heat, damp sheets, and a final nasty surprise when the bill was presented.

Tourists were cheated then, as now; and, as always, the out-of-the-way places were best and the people more apt to be honest.

The poet Bayard Taylor, who roamed all over Italy on foot in the early nineteenth century with a companion, recalled that in little country inns where the common people lodged, "we were always treated with great courtesy and *simpatia*. The inn-keeper would light a fire when we came in dripping wet from a thunderstorm, and place chairs for us right in front of the hearth, in the highest place in the room. There we would sit resembling the giants Og and Magog since we were invariably surrounded by all the children of the household, staring upward in amazement at our elevated hugeness. The inn-keeper and his wife would invite us to share their modest dinner, and it was amusing to hear their friendly, even joyous exclamations when they learned that we'd come from so far away."

On the whole, the distinction between countryside and town was even greater than it is today. For one thing, the countryside was abandoned at night. City people who find urban streets menacing under lamplight usually have no experience with the darkness and sense of isolation that descend upon the countryside after sundown even today; and once the isolation was even more marked because of the absence of artificial illumination. At sunset, man and beast moved off the fields and the carriages off the roads, all making for a gathered settlement where they could fend off cold and loneliness with the comfort of a fire or, if it were summer, the reassuring presence of one's kin, one's dogs. Wolves prowled the woods, and in the high passes the cold moonlight shone down on crosses nailed to trees that indicated where travelers, often pilgrims bound for the Eternal City, had been robbed and murdered. There were long stretches of countryside, particularly in the more mountainous country of central Italy, that could be lonely and frightening even by day. Only occasionally did the passengers spot any sign of life — a shepherd driving his bleating flock around the diligence, barefoot children running through a stony field holding out their hands, a cluster of huts on a slope with smoke trickling from a chimney. Banks of fog often rolled in during the colder months and blotted out everything for hours at a time, leaving the carriage marooned in a chill silence. Or snow fell. One New Englander confessed that "from Bologna to Florence I had the sharpest taste of winter that I have ever known, an experience for which we are hardly prepared in Italy. The snow was in many places five feet deep upon a level. The carriage, drawn by four supplementary oxen, reeled and plunged like a ship upon a stormy sea."

It was with a sigh of relief, therefore, that travelers coming down from the north put the central Apennines behind them and emerged into the Arno Valley. Florence was in sight at last! There's Giotto's tower. There's Brunelleschi's dome. And there, in the distance, specks of red roof tiles and mustard-colored stucco among dark, wicklike cypresses — the hillside of Fiesole beyond the city.

Americans tended to like Florence very much. "Dear, compact, bird's eye, cheap, quiet, mind-your-own-business, beautiful Florence," mooned sculptor Greenough during one of his infrequent absences, "now does my heart yearn for you!" To Stanley Hillard, there was no other place "which I would sooner select for a residence were I required to choose among European cities," and he praised "its clean, quiet streets, its lovely environs, its incomparable Cascine, its treasures of art, so near at hand and so accessible, its ample libraries, its agreeable society, and — pardon the bathos — its cheapness." I suspect New Englanders also liked it because it had, and has, a northern air compared to that of Rome, Naples, even Genoa. Its colors are pale yellow, sand, gray, gray-blue. The streets are cleaner than those in other Italian cities. Perhaps the city still reflects its long and proud independence, which the Florentines had sought to maintain against all odds.

After the end of the Republic in 1530, during the destruction of the Renaissance in the bloody Italian Wars, the city had been annexed to the Holy Roman Empire. Charles V, however, restored the Medici to power by nominating Alessandro de' Medici as Signore della Repubblica Fiorentina. The Medicis governed Florence until 1718. After a short-lived Spanish interlude, it passed into Austrian hands in 1739.

At the time Hillard and Cooper were there, the Austrians were more of a presence than an influence. At Doney's Cafe (the original one in Italy), these Americans would encounter Austrian officers in their splendid white uniforms having caffe latte in the morning. The city was ruled from Palazzo Pitti by an Austrian archduke, who in that era was the big, slow-moving Leopold II, sovereign of the grand duchy of Tuscany. The Florentines referred to him privately as *il granciuco* (the grand fool) and seem to have regarded him with arch Tuscan snobbery.

The *granciuco* gave frequent and lavish balls, to which all the foreigners went. According to Trollope, "the guests used to behave abominably" at these functions, and we have his description: "The English would seize the plates of *bonbons* and empty the contents into their coat pockets. The ladies would do the same with their pocket handkerchiefs. But the Duke's liege subjects carried on their depredation on a far bolder scale. I have seen large portions of fish, sauce and all, packed up in a newspaper and deposited in a pocket. I have seen fowls and ham share the same fate without any newspaper at all." Though neither he nor Marianna Starke mentions it, in my research I have come across a splendid suit of tails made for just such occasions, which was undoubtedly employed with good effect at many of the *granciuco*'s buffet suppers. This suit had rubber-lined compartments, comprising not only the outer pockets but inside ones as well. Moreover, the tails were also hollow and lined with rubber. The wearer would first stuff one of the tails with fish (by sliding them in), then fill the other with pieces of chicken, slices of roast beef, and other meat courses. The inner pockets were reserved for olives, hors d'oeuvres, pieces of cheese, cakes, and so forth. And, finally, the outer pocket could be filled with sweets and even wine. What it felt like to walk home in such dress can only be imagined, but I am reasonably satisfied that such a garment existed and was used in Florence in the nineteenth century at such occasions. Whether it was designed by an Englishman, an Italian, a German, or a Yankee is hard to say.

All these nationalities proliferated in Florence, not only as tourists but in resident colonies. These were on the whole stylish people, not indigent artists. A young journalist from the *New York Mirror,* Nathaniel Willis, described Florence in the mid-nineteenth century as "a mixture of all nations, of whom one third may be Florentine, one third English, and the remaining part equally divided between Russians, Germans, French, Poles, and Americans." This international café society could be observed nearly every afternoon at the Cascine, a gladelike park along the right bank of the Arno below the city. It was where people went riding in the afternoon, causing regular traffic jams of carriages filled with handsome women and their children and British nannies. For fifty dollars a month one

ALINARI

On foot and on horse, and in stylish carriages, affluent Florentines and their thousands of foreign visitors would turn out every afternoon to gossip and exchange glances in the Cascine, a park along the Arno River that was once considered one of the most elegant promenades in Europe.

could rent a carriage, two fast-stepping horses, a coachman and a footman dressed in the livery of one's choice, and grease for the wheels, so that many foreigners did join the afternoon drive along the Cascine. Sadly, the area has degenerated into a rendezvous for neckers in little Fiats and is now only slightly less dangerous after dark than New York's Central Park.

From Florence, it was only a three- or four-day trip by diligence to Rome (depending on weather and the availability of fresh horses). There were two ways to go, either by the Via Cassia, which went through Siena, or by the Via Flaminia, which hugged the side of the Apennines and took the traveler through Perugia, Assisi, and Spoleto. In these smaller towns of Tuscany and Umbria, Allston wrote, one could live comfortably for two thousand five hundred dollars a year — and by "comfortably" he presumably meant in a large house with servants and the other amenities. Yet few Americans stopped for very long in these still-enchanting hill towns. They were eager to get to Rome, rejoicing when the last foothills of the Apennines sank into the brooding and suggestive plain of the Roman campagna.

As a cardinal once observed, it was God's will that the campagna not be as beautiful as the Tuscan countryside because the jewel of Rome burned even more brightly in a plain setting. Yet it was not all that homely. The silt-colored Tiber wound through it; there were marble ruins scattered about in thickening clusters as one approached the city, these sarcophagi and vine-wreathed columns being the only herald of the approaching city until the carriage reached the hillside beyond the Due Pini (now a fashionable suburb of Rome), where the Cassia and Flaminia once again joined and became simply the Via Flaminia. On that hillside is the point where the coachman would reign in his horses and cry out, *"Ecco Roma!"*

It was a famous cry — like "All aboard" in the Pullman car days — except that it marked the end of the journey. The passengers would alight and see, in the distance, the walls and skyline of Rome stretched out on the horizon, from the Piazza del Popolo on the left to the incomparable cupola of St. Peter's on the right, a marble-colored, walled city with less than a tenth of the inhabitants it has today. *"Ecco Roma."*

The hillside plunged down to the banks of the Tiber, and there, in the Piazza di Ponte Milvio, people stood on their first really historic Roman ground. One can go and stand in the same piazza now. It's a fruit and vegetable market in the mornings, and there's always traffic rumbling through, but on October 23, A.D. 312, on that same hillside Constantine fought the battle of the Milvian Bridge against the forces of Maxentius, who was defending the city. In the course of his march on Rome, Constantine had seen — or dreamed — a fiery cross in the sky, and word of that vision spreading among his illiterate soldiers had so revived their morale that Constantine ordered them to paint their shields with a P cut in half by an X, the Greek abbreviation for Christ. Under the cross of the vision, fiery letters had appeared: IN HOC SIGNO VINCES.

As they stood in the Piazza di Ponte Milvio, our nineteenth-century Americans would turn back toward the hillside where they had first gazed on Rome and imagine Constantine's army, with its painted shields and the fiery letters in the sky, rushing down on Maxentius's pagan Roman soldiers, the Christians hacking through them and taking the bridge (which exists and functions today). It was an "onward Christian soldiers" scene before the hymn had been written. After they had stood on the historic ground for a few minutes, the travelers got back into their carriage, which rumbled across the arched Milvian Bridge for the last quarter-mile ride down the Via Flaminia to the Porta del Popolo (the gate of the people), which was a working gate then, Rome's border with the outside world.

To get through the gate, one had to show a passport and allow one's luggage (and sometimes one's person) to be searched. It was no pleasure because the police agents were part of the Holy Inquisition, and the very word sent shivers up Protestant spines. But usually the customs police just poked their hands into one's suitcases, and that was it. One would emerge from the rooms where the inspecting was done (on the right of the gate looking into the piazza; today they serve as barracks for the carabinieri). *Ecco Roma!* There it really was.

CHAPTER THREE

Throughout most of the nineteenth century, the now-famous Via Veneto was little more than a muddy lane running along the lower border of the Villa Ludovisi. This property belonged to one of the aristocratic families of Rome, and it has always been described as beautiful — gardens with oleander and ilex groves, moss-covered fountains, gravel-banked drives, and Roman statues. Only a fragment of the property survives today, and it is one of Rome's strangest monuments. Take the Via Campania, which runs along the Aurelian Wall next to the Hotel Flora, and after a hundred yards you'll find to your left a big but graceful Roman head, at least ten times life size. Streaked by the rain and by pollution, it stands imbedded in a baroque, scalloped shell within the Aurelian Wall. The head with its sightless eyes seems to have no purpose. It faces the ground-floor entrance of an expensive (and excellent) restaurant, the Girarrosto, the Costa Rican Embassy to the Holy See, a tailor's, a frame maker's, and a travel agency. The head is there because it once decorated the far end of the main walking path of the Ludovisi gardens. Today the gardens are gone, and buildings lie closely packed over those vanished oleander beds.

The tourists entering Rome in the nineteenth century did not go to the Via Veneto, therefore, but headed straight from the Piazza del Popolo to the Piazza di Spagna, which was usually so densely packed with the carriages of British tourists that the area was nicknamed *"il ghetto degli Inglesi,"* the English ghetto. Yet the Spaniards, lords of the peninsula in the sixteenth and seventeenth centuries, had prior claims. They had established their embassy in the Palazzo di Spagna, facing the piazza, and had given it their name.

The Piazza di Spagna and its surrounding streets are one of the least changed of Rome's neighborhoods. The yellow and orange stucco church of the Trinità dei Monti, with its twin bell towers, still dominates the stupendous flight of travertine steps for which the piazza is famed. Designed in the early eighteenth century by the baroque architect Francesco de Sanctis from funds bequeathed by a French ambassador, the steps have three flights of stairs and three landings to express the concept of the trinity, but rarely has a religious motive inspired such fancy. The steps lie against the hillside like a palazzo that has gently collapsed and been laid bare, and it was up and down those graceful blocks of travertine that a foreign tourist in the nineteenth century was liable to take his first walk inside Rome accompanied by porters and suitcases. The big hotels — the Hassler, the Excelsior, and so on — had not yet been built, and one usually found accommodations in a pensione off the steps, like the Casa Rinaldi.

By the 1820s, the Piazza di Spagna was a tourists' nook such as may not exist anywhere in the world today. One could hire English-speaking servants by the day. Many trattorie in the area, such as Dalbano, at 10 Piazza di Spagna, sent out complete dinners at a reasonable price and also supplied tourists (who had not heeded Marianna Starke's instructions) with plates, glasses, silverware, and table linen. If one wanted to eat in the pensione, one's servant could go to the street market in Via della Croce, where game was plentiful — wild boar, venison, woodcocks, turkeys, pigeons, wild geese, wild and tame ducks, partridges, and hare — as well as fruit, vegetables, fish, and every imported Italian delicacy from the dried salmon of Tivoli to sweet melons from Perugia. For foreign foods and Italian and French wines, one went to Lome's, but the great treat was to eat out at the wonderful trattorie and restaurants tucked away in the courtyards of nearby buildings, like Lepre's in the Via Condotti.

Today the Via Condotti is Rome's most fashionable shopping street — a slightly worn Mediterranean Bond Street, where Gucci, Bulgari, Valentino, Battistoni, and the other superstores of fashion are. The Condotti runs straight down from Piazza di Spagna to the Corso (Rome's major street, the continuation of the Via Flaminia), and it has had a long history and undergone many changes. Origi-

ARCHIVIO FOTOGRAFICO COMUNALE, ROME

The Tiber appeared as in this photograph for centuries, with its natural banks and fishermen's boats. The little port of Ripetta, near the bottom of Via Condotti, is clearly visible. After a disastrous flood in December 1870, progress-minded Italian authorities decided to build high stone banks along the Tiber and all but buried it out of sight.

nally the site of an aqueduct of the Virgin Waters (*condotti* means "conduit"), by the nineteenth century it was celebrated for Lepre's and the Cafe' Greco, which faced each other across the street like the twin arms of a magnet. At noon and every evening, the magnet drew flocks of rowdy, boisterous men with velvet jackets, flowing Van Dyck cravats, and berets. There were hundreds of foreign artists studying in Rome. They lived in the Villa Medici — a hundred yards from the church of the Trinità dei Monti — where Napoleon had established the French Academy; they lived in the Via Gregoriana and the Via Sistina, the aspiring unknowns beside such famed artists as the neoclassic sculptor Thorwaldsen (he was a Dane, and he used to quip, "I was born on March 8, 1797" — the day he had entered Rome). In the nineteenth century the tourists lived cheek to jowl with these resident artists, whose headquarters was also the Piazza di Spagna. One saw them in the morning and in the evening at Bouchard, where foreign papers and books were sold, or at nearby trattorie like the Tre Ladroni, the Falcone, the excellent Polidore on the Corso. Above all, however, one saw them at Lepre's and the Cafe' Greco.

"I dined on 19 cents at Lepre's," Mark Twain noted with understandable satisfaction in 1857. Indeed, Lepre's was an artists' hangout because its prices were low. The author of *Rome as Seen by a New Yorker,* William Gillespie, wrote in 1854 that "the Lepre is the most extensive Trattoria in Rome, and each one of its numerous rooms is usually occupied almost exclusively by visitors of some one nation and is named accordingly." There was a British Room, a French Room, a German Room, and even a Russian Room, where an ancient Italian waiter who had survived Napoleon's retreat from Moscow hobbled back and forth complaining in broken Russian of the chill in his bones to the great amusement of his customers.

Those old trattorie have vanished, unfortunately, along with their prices. (The Reverend Fisk once gave a three-course dinner party for six and spent two dollars, including tips!) Only two real landmarks from the old days remain in the area of the Piazza di Spagna. "Directly opposite to the Lepre," wrote Gillespie, "is the Cafe' Greco, the general rendezvous of the artists of all nations." The Greco (founded by a Greek, hence its name) still maintains its opulent nineteenth-century air of warm polished woods and cool marble, and one can sit at the same tables frequented once if not all

The favorite haunt of foreign artists in Rome during the nineteenth century was the Cafe' Greco, near the Spanish Steps, which still looks much the same today. Among its patrons were Goethe, Mendelssohn, Stendhal, Baudelaire, Wagner, the Russian writer Gogol, and the American novelist James Fenimore Cooper.

at the same time by Goethe, Thorwaldsen, Gogol, Schopenhauer, Mendelssohn, Berlioz, Stendhal, Taine, Baudelaire, Liszt, Wagner, and dozens of other artists. The Greco was already celebrated when the American painter James E. Freeman wrote in 1837: "One day [the painter John] Vanderlyn met me at the Greco and said, 'Thirty years ago I was on this very spot, and pointing to two different seats, observed, 'there sat Allston opposite me; that was Turner's corner, here on my left sat Fenimore Cooper; and here, I was told, Sir Joshua Reynolds, and West. . . .' " The other old tourist landmark is the Inghilterra (or England), the oldest of Rome's first-class hotels and still one of the best. Henry James stayed there, and it was from its door that the young novelist set forth on his first morning in the city. He had barely gone fifty yards when he came on an extraordinary sight,

I hurried out heedless of breakfast, and open-mouthed only for visions, which promptitude was promptly rewarded, on the adjacent edge of Via Condotti, by the brightest and strangest of all, the vista of the street suddenly cleared by mounted, galloping, hand-waving guards, and then, while everyone uncovered and women dropped on their knees jerking down their children, the great rumbling, black-horses coach of the Pope, so capacious that the august personage within — a hand of automatic benediction, a large, handsome, pale old face, a pair of celebrated eyes which one took, on trust, for sinister — could show from it as enshrined in the dim depth of a chapel.

Before 1870, the popes did not reside in the Vatican but in the Quirinal Palace, which Gregory XIII had begun in 1574 as a summer residence at one of the coolest, highest sites in Rome, atop the Quirinal Hill. When a pope died and a new one had to be chosen at the Papal Conclave (now held in the Sistine Chapel at the Vatican), the cardinals were sealed into the Quirinal's *manica lunga,* or "long sleeve," one of the longest wings of any palace in the world. After 1870, the Quirinal passed first into royal hands as the residence of the king of Italy and then, after World War II, became the presidential palace; but before 1870 the popes still lived there most of the time, and to get to St. Peter's they crossed the city by carriage — the sight James had come upon.

Rome was full of such sights. The living spectacle was so strangely interleaved with the supposedly dead pagan past that an American could, at first glance, only grasp one detail after another of what was really a crowded chamber of time, ageless and aged, seasoned, lived in, inhabited almost past reckoning. Rome was as Catholic as the cross erected in the Coliseum to remember the bloody, sacred martyrdom of the early Christians, as pagan as the wild revelry of Carnevale that followed the Lenten week. Washington Irving best described the sense of confusion that Rome imposed. "To describe the emotions of the mind and the crowd of ideas that arise on entering this 'mistress of the world' is impossible," he wrote. "All is confusion and agitation. The eye moves rapidly from side to side, eager to grasp every object, but continually diverted by some new scene; all is wonder."

How to grasp it all? The most natural way was to call at once on other Americans who had settled in the city and elicit their guidance. Almost everyone — save the most penniless and obscure artist — arrived in Rome with a list of friends of friends. Getting in touch with them, however, was a little more involved. In those phoneless and considerably more formal days, a ritual was observed. At a decent hour of the morning or afternoon (preferably the latter), you drove in your hired carriage to the home of the people you wanted to contact. Then you sent the footman upstairs with a calling card, on the back of which you scribbled: "My Aunt Debby asked me to look you up in Rome." Carriages had a coachman *and* a footman for just this purpose. Soon he would return bearing a return message that read: "Come right up" or "We're expecting you at five o'clock Wednesday for tea." If the latter, your carriage drove on to the next address.

The chief target of these assaults was the Crawford family, as much for the romantic aura surrounding them as for their guidance to Rome's sights. Theirs was one of the love stories of the nineteenth century. Take a beautiful young American heiress, Louisa Ward. She really was an heiress, for her uncle was Samuel Ward, one of the richest men on Wall Street. And she really was a beauty. When she went to Boston at age seventeen, Hillard wrote to Longfellow to say: "The lovely Louisa is here. I have seen her only once at Mrs. Ticknor's and was charmed by her sunny smiles, her dazzling teeth, her gentle voice and thoroughbred manner." With the young bloods of Boston and New York already chasing after her, she was put on a vessel to Italy as part of a bridal party that included her sister Julia, who had married Samuel Gridley Howe, and Mary Peabody, who had married Horace Mann.

In Rome, Louisa met a struggling young sculptor, Thomas Crawford. He was dashing, slender, manly, and had piercing dark eyes, but the only thing he had to recommend him was that Thorwaldsen, the great Dane, had taken him under his wing and regarded him as a promising artist. It was love at first sight, the greatest of all thunderbolts. Back in New York, Louisa was gently dissuaded. Her Uncle Samuel, upset, murmured dark words about Roman fortune hunters. Louisa wavered and lost heart; there were so many other matches. But Crawford put together his meager earnings and sailed back across the Atlantic to press his suit. Uncle Samuel met him and reconsidered. Nice clean-cut young man after all, this sculptor. Not the fortune hunter he had feared. Louisa married Crawford and they returned to Rome, where they set up house on the Corso. Crawford built a studio within the Baths of

Diocletian, certainly the most impressively situated studio in the world, and there he received dozens of Americans. "To visit the studio of a young artist," Hillard counseled in his pocket guide, "is one of the approved methods of disposing of an idle afternoon in Rome." Usually the Crawfords were happy to see American visitors since they were a source of commissions for statuary.

If one did not have an introduction to the Crawfords, one could look to other Americans settled in Rome. One could call on George Washington Greene, the first American-born United States consul in the city. Or Alice Mason, the slender and attractive — if brusque — former wife of Senator Charles Sumner. They had parted after an unhappy marriage, and she now lived in a big apartment on the Via della Croce with a vigorous, athletic woman, Alice Bartlett, who eventually married a Texan. Most of these people were Bostonians, but not all. Crawford was a New Yorker. The Haseltines represented Philadelphia society. There was usually a Middleton around, and they were from South Carolina.

All of these residents were accustomed to showing people the sights or, if they were busy, they would recommend where to start. By then you'd have taken your first stroll around the city and discovered that the Romans were every bit as interesting to look at as any monuments or picture gallery. In contrast to the more sedate Florentines they were a spectacle.

"All things are easy and careless in the out-of-doors-life of the common people," wrote the sculptor William Story.

> They sing at the top of their lungs as they sit on their doorsteps at their work and often shout from house to house across the street in long conversation, and sometimes even read letters from upper windows to their friends below in the street. All the windows are wide open and there is at least one head and one pair of shoulders leaning out of every house.
>
> . . . Towards twilight the girls put on their better dresses, and comb their glossy raven hair, heaping it up in great solid braids and hanging two long golden earrings. They come forth conquering and to conquer. You see them marching along in a broad platoon of five or six, all their brows as straight as if they had been ruled, and their great dark eyes flashing out under them, ready in a moment for a laugh or a frown.

In the evening the streets smelled of wood smoke and the lamps would be lit. In the piazzas, vendors sold fruit drinks made with water from the fountains while children threw out fingers in one of the world's oldest betting games and their older brothers and sisters held hands. You loved looking at this outdoor theater, but you couldn't very well write home and say that all you had seen in three days were singing tradesmen, platoons of marching girls, and lovers in the piazza under the moonlight. This glorious and rowdy proletarian vitality was a side show, an added bargain to the grandeur that you had traveled these thousands of miles to see, and so the next morning, after a breakfast of hot chocolate and croissants in your pensione (maybe with a couple of boiled eggs), you got into your rented carriage with the footman holding the door — *Buon giorno!* — and as the Piazza di Spagna wheeled about in a 180-degree circle, the horses broke into a trot and you were off.

One of the easily grasped things about Rome was that the city divided itself pretty evenly into two parts. The western side, including St. Peter's and the famous piazzas, was mostly baroque, and everywhere you could see graceful, rounded marble cupolas with bluish rain streaks rising among the brick red tiles and balconies of the rooftops.

The Rome of the Caesars lay to the east and south, past the Quirinal Palace and down the hill into the Piazza Venezia. The Palazzo Venezia would rise on your right, dusky and rather forbidding. The earliest Renaissance palace in Rome, it had been built by the Venetians in 1468 as their embassy to the Papal State (and its balcony would become notorious in a later age as Mussolini's pulpit). When the horses had clip-clopped past it, baroque Rome made a last attempt to hold your eye. Across from the Palazzo Venezia, the twin churches of Santa Maria di Loreto and Santissimo Nome di Maria cried for attention, but already they were past, and the carriage rolled slowly up to the Campidoglio, the Capitol, where Michelangelo's stupendous buildings lie like a marble frame around the bronze Roman statue of Marcus Aurelius. Here you descended; a few footsteps farther and the Forum came into view.

It was, in the early nineteenth century, pocked with excavations and still half-buried in the earth of intervening centuries, which covered the ruins at some points by as much as fifty feet. Romans called it, with much casualness, the *campo vaccino* — the cow field — where herds of sheep, oxen, and buffaloes were watered in fountains shaded by towering oak trees. Amateur archaeologists like the Duchess of Devonshire had only just begun digging up the

ARCHIVIO FOTOGRAFICO COMUNALE, ROME

Tourists to the Coliseum in 1860 felt a spine-tingling thrill as they imagined the bloodthirsty Roman crowds, the lavish games, the gladiators' clashing swords, and the heroic Christians offered up to lions that were caged in underground pens (then still unexcavated.)

Though wealthy amateur archaeologists like the Duchess of Devonshire employed gangs of prisoners from Rome's jails to dig in the Roman Forum as early as 1815, systematic excavation did not get under way until late in the nineteenth century. Until then, Romans lived in houses surrounding the Forum, and housewives casually strung their laundry between its marble columns.

Forum, using gangs of pick-and-shovel laborers hired out from the city prison.

A pastoral somnolence, a fantastic peace, lay over that majestic wreck. Before the incomparable backdrop of the Coliseum, the tourists with their copies of Tacitus and Cicero intruded on the everyday life of a half-rural, out-of-the-way neighborhood. Houses (now razed) lined the long quadrangle of the Forum on both sides, so that ordinary Romans traversed the undulating, grassy bed of ruins with shopping baskets while their children chased each other in loud, screaming games over the *campo,* fighting a losing battle for playing space with the archaeologists' ever-extending trenches.

To many American tourists, those jumbled blocks of marble and half-buried arches were the voice of judgment, the new Jericho. As she viewed the Forum, Harriet Beecher Stowe could not but rejoice that "the reign of disgusting, inconceivable brutality and cruelty is over." To such eyes, the *campo* was a battlefield and the Cross victorious. Others, less pious and perhaps more refined intellectually, found in this monumental Rome the consummation of their classical studies. "The incredulous may laugh," wrote George Washington Greene, "but Cicero, Horace, and Livy no where seem so eloquent and touching as amid the scenes which they have hallowed."

Beyond the Forum and the Coliseum was the Via Appia, whose mile on mile of bumpy pavement flanked by tombs, umbrella pines, and cypresses brought a shiver of recognition. "The Appian Way is here yet," wrote Mark Twain, "and looking much as it did, perhaps, when the triumphal procession of the emperors moved over it in other days bringing fettered princes from the confines of the earth. We cannot see the long array of chariots and mail-clad men laden with the spoils of conquest, but we can imagine the pageant, after a fashion." And imagine it they did when the carriage turned and brought them homeward in the late afternoon and the city rose out of the horizon in dark, moody shapes under a cold blood-colored sky. Then they could almost hear, louder than the clip-clopping of the horses or the squeaking of wheel and spring, the jangling of the chain as a thousand slaves' feet shuffled forward and, far up ahead at the front of the column, the arrogant cry of trumpets and the cheers of the Roman mob.

The Rome nearer at hand — the western side of the city — was less evocative but rich enough in architecture and art for the most insatiable student. "Of the 360 churches in Rome," wrote Freeman, "there is not one which does not contain some picture, statue, mosaic, or monumental structure either of positive excellence or historic interest." Even if one were to visit a church each day, it would take a year to go through all of them. You compromised and went to the most important ones, like Santa Maria Maggiore (St. Mary Major), where the Yankee eye gazed sharply not only at the frescoes but at the embalmed remains of Pius V in a glass case. Normally, you would plan a day of sightseeing around the two or three places you wanted to visit, and the choice was enormous.

You might make a date to meet your friends at eleven A.M. at the Porta Pinciana (at the top of today's Via Veneto), and ask the pensione to have a stable boy meet you there with horses saddled for your group. Having horses waiting outside the city gates was a normal indulgence and everyone did it — much as we'd rent a car today. Then you might ride out to see some Roman tombs along the Via Flaminia or the Nomentana and in the afternoon visit a church like the Gesù in downtown Rome. Or you might take a carriage out of the city in the morning, pass through St. Sebastian's Gate (still standing), visit one of the catacombs east of Rome, having a picnic lunch along the Via Appia, then come back into the city and be dropped off at Palazzo Farnese near the Tiber. Though these majestic palazzi, like the Farnese, were lived in, they also contained such valuable collections of paintings and statues that their aristocratic owners kept one wing, floor, or corridor, open to the public as a private museum. These were the "galleries" of Rome, where art students from all over Europe, Russia, and America would spend hours before their easels copying the Old Masters to learn the secrets of the craft.

As you entered one of the galleries, you would find a catalogue of the artworks in the form of a cardboard programme, as it was called, lying on a marble-topped table or sideboard, and many Americans, including Sophia Hawthorne, made extensive notes about each collection. Hawthorne at first accompanied his wife on these outings, but then he began to grumble that his arches were going flat from treading marble floors. So while she persevered and took her notes, he stayed home and began writing *The Marble Faun,* in which he made use of their joint research.

A very special sightseeing treat, which children liked, too, since it involved staying up late, was to go to the Vatican museum at

ARCHIVIO FOTOGRAFICO COMUNALE, ROME

Tourists in Rome in the nineteenth century would rent horses or carriages at the main gates of the city, much as people rent cars today, and ride out to a picnic spot like this one by the Aqueduct of Claudius southeast of the city. The stiffness of the pose is due to the long exposure time required by the photographer.

nine P.M. for a torchlight promenade through the sculpture galleries. Only fifteen people could be admitted on a given evening, so one usually had to sign up far in advance. The group was met by Swiss Guards and a bemedaled marshal and escorted toward the sculpture galleries by soldiers. There they met up with a guide who carried a sort of beacon at the end of a long stick. The beacon was made of closely bunched wax candles behind a shade, and as the guide led the amazed group down the thousand-foot-long corridors lined with marble gods and emperors, the statues seemed to leap and writhe when the bright, flickering light struck them and threw their shadows against the walls. "For two hours we walked through halls, salons and courts filled with statuary," William Gillespie wrote, "almost realizing the Arabian fable of the city whose inhabitants had all been changed to stone."

In one way or another, the Vatican influenced every American's view of Rome. It was the effective seat of government of the Papal State. Its religious functions were probably the most impressively staged in the world, even for the nonbeliever. And everyone wanted to see the Pope, either in a special audience, or a *bacio dell'anello* (kissing the ring), or in a small religious function, such as the special masses held in the Sistine Chapel, where one could see Michelangelo and Pius IX all at once.

St. Peter's impressed everyone by its majestic size, but beyond that, everyone's reaction to the Vatican and to the Catholic religion was different. For American Catholics, naturally, the journey to Rome was a pilgrimage, and the first awed moments in St. Peter's, the first glimpse of the Pope's kindly face, the timber of his voice, often became one of the emotional high points of their lives. The majority of Americans in Italy during the nineteenth century were Protestants, however, and they approached St. Peter's much in the spirit of an American visiting the Kremlin today.

So much was physically striking about the Catholic faith; it jumped at one's senses in dozens of ways. Priests were so often described by Americans as "villainous looking" that either the clergy must have been in a low state or the swarthiness of these ill-paid clerics, their unpressed (and sometimes uncleaned) robes, and the fact that they sometimes begged for alms made Protestant noses wrinkle. The contrasting splendor of the cardinals — many of whom were nobles — further offended American Protestants.

Also, the ceremonies at St. Peter's and the general flamboyance of the Roman church seemed positively pagan to New Englanders accustomed to quiet, severe worship in a prim wooden church. The papal court *was* rather exotic in those times, a thing so well known I don't expect any Catholic to take offense. The Pope was borne into St. Peter's on his gestatory chair, flanked by two heralds who carried spectacular ostrich-feather fans on long poles. The fans bracketed the Pope's figure decoratively as he was carried along. (Paul IV abolished the fans as part of the council reforms.) Surrounding the Pope was a procession that included gorgeously robed cardinals and bishops and a half-dozen Swiss Guards. In those days they wore not only the Michelangelo-designed striped dress uniform but, over it, gleaming armor like medieval knights. The armor came down to the waist like a jacket and was often beautifully worked by a silversmith. These Swiss Guards carried pikes or halberts. Officers of the Noble Guard (Roman aristocrats) wore a splendid Elizabethan-style uniform (called *costume spagnolesco*) with a round, crinolated white collar, a black velvet jacket, doublets, trunk breeches, and long swords that made a terrific clatter each time they knelt.

The worshipers were hardly less colorful, particularly for more exclusive ceremonies like Ash Wednesday mass in the Sistine Chapel, to which one was only admitted with a ticket. In order to get in at all people came at one P.M. for a mass that began at six. Even so, the crush was so great that a party of American women were once knocked to the ground. Some people brought folding camp stools, knowing that the seats would run out, and servants fought their way in and out with baskets of sandwiches and muffins. (Rome's better hotels even set up a catering service to and from the Vatican on such days.) On these occasions, the women in the Sistine Chapel were dressed to the teeth in sweeping gowns, furs, and jewels.

Americans contrasted this splendor with the poverty of most citizens in the Papal State, their ignorance and their lack of opportunity. It took only five minutes to walk from the Sistine Chapel, filled with nobles and bejeweled women, into the working-class neighborhood of Trastevere, where hungry, half-naked children crouched in doorways or held out their hands imploringly. These contrasts still exist in Rome, but they are nowhere as great as they were then.

When American Protestants judged the Vatican or the Catholic faith, therefore, they did it very much in terms of the Papal State. Julia Ward Howe expressed what many of her contemporaries felt in her book *From the Oak to the Olive*. "Vain is to plead the democratic allowances of the Catholic Church," she wrote. "The equality of man before God here is purely abstract and disembodied. . . . The distinctions between one set of human beings and another are held to be absolute, and the inferiority of opportunity, carefully preserved and exaggerated, is regarded as intrinsic not accidental."

I could cite a dozen such reactions. Papal Rome was really very different from what a New Englander, or even an American from the South, would consider natural. All modern states, including the American Republic, had been created by a mercantile middle class in search of progress, efficiency, justice. Those values virtually did not exist in Rome because it was not a modern state. The Pope ruled it; landed aristocrats had the power of oligarchs. It was a feudal system, updated a bit but not too much. Time, for example, was still reckoned according to the old system, and the day began at one quarter hour after sunset, when the bronze bell at St. Peter's rang out the Angelus. Thus, if you said, "I'll meet you at one o'clock," you meant roughly, "I'll meet you at one hour after sunset" — which of course falls at different times daily. It was fine for a society in which efficiency had no importance and no one needed to be punctual. No wonder Martin Luther and the other productive, order-loving Germans and Swiss rumbled and grumbled over Rome and finally broke away.

CHAPTER FOUR

fter you had been in your pensione for a week or two and taken a side trip to Tivoli, it was time to make some solid decisions for the next few months. You had formed friendships in Rome. You were enjoying it. There was so much to see. Why not stay on until early spring and then move up to Florence and plan to be on Lac Leman or in Baden-Baden for the summer? The first step was to rent a place in Rome, since the pensione would soon grow tiresome and it was impossible to entertain properly there.

So you called Mrs. Sumner, or Mrs. Crawford, or Mrs. Story; and one of them knew of an apartment, quite a big one, in one of the palazzi. Could you go and see it the next day at noon, and meet the principe's *amministratore* who would show it to you and discuss terms? Mrs. Crawford was free then, and she knew some people in the palazzo, so she'd take you. Her carriage would be at the foot of the Spanish Steps at eleven-thirty. It was the brougham, and the men were in green livery with white piping. Don't be late. She has another engagement at twelve-thirty.

You were punctual. Mrs. Crawford was wearing a charming white crinoline dress with hoops and a rather daring new whatever-it-was. You chatted about the Storys, and before you knew it the carriage had pulled up before a huge entrance flanked by marble lions and Mrs. Crawford was saying, "Don't pay the first price he asks. It's always best to bargain in Italy, even with an *amministratore*. The British always do, and to the Italians we're just *inglesi*. Also, let's see if the windows of the bedrooms have a southern ex-

42

posure. That's rather important here." Then, lifting her parasol: "There, I think that's the apartment up on the third floor in that corner." You stepped back to see it and saw what might become your windows among a hundred others. "This palazzo is just for one family?" you would ask, still a little confused.

Mrs. Crawford's son, who became a best-selling writer of romances, replied to that question when he wrote *Sant'Ilario,* one of the best and most authoritative novels about Rome before 1870. It has a silly plot, like most of his books, but the feel of Italian life is absolutely sound and accurate. Here is his description of the palazzo of the Montevarchi, one of the noble families in the book:

> The palace was a huge square building facing upon two streets on front and behind, and opening inwards upon two courtyards. Upon the lower floor were stables, coach-houses, kitchens, and offices innumerable. Above these there was built a half story, called a mezzanino — in French, entresol — containing the quarters of the unmarried sons of the house, of the household chaplain, and of two or three tutors employed in the education of the Montevarchi grandchildren. Next above, came the "piano nobile," or state apartments, comprising the rooms of the prince and princess, the dining rooms, and a vast suite of reception rooms, each of which opened into the next in such a manner that only the last was not necessarily a passage. In the huge hall was the dais and canopy with the family arms embroidered in colors once gaudy but now agreeably faded to a softer tone. Above this floor was another, occupied by the married sons, their wives and children; and high over all, above the cornices of the palace, were the endless servants' quarters and the roomy garrets. At a rough estimate the establishment comprised over a hundred persons, all living under the absolute and despotic authority of the head of the house, don Lorario Montevarchi, Principe Montevarchi, and the sole possessor of forty or fifty other titles.

Your illusions about life in a palace might not survive the main staircase, which was noble in its proportions but dirty and overworked. In the course of a day hundreds of people walked up and down it — and not only walked. It was common for stouter cardinals and other important prelates to go up and down the staircases of these big palazzi on muleback; indeed, the stairs had a gentle, sloping grade precisely for that reason. By the middle of the nineteenth century, moreover, many nobles rented out sections of their

palazzi not merely to visiting foreigners but to artisans and tradesmen who set up their shops in the *mezzanino,* the floor just above
the ground floor. That made the traffic on the main staircase heavy
at times.

But you went on past that traffic, and on the third floor the ad-
ministrator showed you a vast, freezing apartment with frescoed
walls (somewhat peeling). There were twelve reception rooms,
rather shabbily furnished (oh, look at the frayed upholstery on the
chairs; who's been living here); they were each open to one another,
without doors, and you didn't know what to do with them, but the
actual living quarters — a huge salon, a tiny one, a dining room,
five bedrooms, and a single bathroom (alas) looked cosy enough.
The kitchen had a wood stove, though you were informed that
cooking could also be managed over either of two brass charcoal
braziers that could also be used to heat the rooms. You would have
to be careful of the fumes, though. You couldn't fall asleep and
leave the braziers lit all night, or the carbon monoxide fumes could
kill you if the windows were closed. And the price? A hundred and
twenty-five dollars a year? It wasn't unreasonable for all this space,
but how would you ever heat it!

Heating was always a problem despite braziers and fireplaces,
particularly for New Englanders, who were used to cold outdoors
but a warm house. The Hawthornes were miserable during their
first two months in Rome because they were shivering with cold.
Nor was the problem really resolved until after World War II. On
her first visit to Rome in the 1920s, Alexandra Flowerton, a New
York girl who later married an Italian, remembers going to visit an
apartment being let on the Corso d'Italia by the daughters of Baron
Wrangel, a White Russian general who had escaped to Italy. Baron
Wrangel's daughters were charming but the place was freezing, and
when the prospective tenant asked why the heat wasn't turned on
they pointed to the windows and smiled, crying, "That's our heat.
The sun." And that was in 1925! With temperatures that often sank
below 40 degrees in January and February, few Americans found
solar heating adequate, though Rome was in fact sunny in winter
compared to northern cities.

It might be weeks before the new tenant caught sight of the principe or the marchese whose palazzo it was. Or the marchese might
be very visible, very pleasant, and invite the new American(s) for
dinner or for tea right away. I fall back on family history now. My

Russian grandfather Alexander Amfitheatrof lived in the Palazzo Massimo when he arrived in Rome in 1914. Prince Massimo could trace his lineage back to the Roman family of the Maximi in the first century B.C. and was considered a very high prince indeed, but people avoided him because he was said to have the evil eye. If they absolutely had to speak to him, Romans would put their hands behind their backs and make the sign of the horns by extending the second and fifth fingers — a shield of sorts against the unlucky nobleman's terrible powers. My grandfather, being Russian, wasn't much concerned about the evil eye and struck up a friendship with the prince simply by not avoiding him and not making horns with his fingers. Thus he was regularly invited to the prince's apartment, where they discussed Russian literature and Roman politics.

Until the watershed year of 1870, the Roman nobles were still very powerful. The Pope was nominally the feudal lord of Rome and as such the head of the Roman aristocracy. Every year at the Feast of the Epiphany, the Roman princes would present the Pope with a token tribute, generally either a silver object, like a bowl, or ten pounds of wax. (The wax was used to make candles.)

The princes, in turn, possessed the crushing economic and political power of true oligarchs. They were the Rockefellers and Harrimans of post-Renaissance Rome, and they had gotten to the top by being tougher and shrewder than their neighbors. Apart from that of Prince Massimo, the other great families were not terribly old. They had emerged, usually, when a man in a squat suit of armor came out of the woods leading an army a little bit stronger than someone else's. The warrior's son became a merchant or a banker and hired others to do his fighting; then one of the merchant's sons might become a cardinal or, even better, a Pope. Any Roman can go down the roster of popes after 1500 and pick out the aristocratic names at a glance because they're the names of famous palazzi in the city — Alessandro Farnese (Paul III), Ugo Boncompagni (Gregory XIII), Ippolito Aldobrandini (Clement VIII), Camillo Borghese (Paul V), Alessandro Ludovisi (Gregory XV), Maffeo Barberini (Urbano VIII), G. B. Pamphili (Innocent X), Fabio Chigi (Alexander VII), Giulio Rospigliosi (Clement IX), Emilio Altieri (Clement X), Benedetto Odescalchi (Innocent XI), Antonio Pignatelli (Innocent XII), and Lorenzo Corsini (Clement XIII).*

---

*There were also several Medici popes and others who did not build palazzi in Rome.

Often these families were of non-Roman origin. The Barberini were Florentines, the Chigis came from Siena, the Rospigliosis from Pistoia, the Odescalchi family from Como. Once established in the Vatican hierarchy, however, these families became powers in the Papal State. They appropriated enormous tracts of land both inside and outside the city. The Borghese family, for example, still owned eighty-four acres of land in or around Rome at the start of the nineteenth century, including what is now Villa Borghese. The country estates amassed by these families were even vaster. Because it was harder to control the countryside, however, the Roman families allied themselves with local feudal lords, who in turn maintained order — often with great harshness. Until 1870, for example, the Duke of Bracciano could still put any of his subjects to death without a public trial. It was a power he presumably did not use, but it was written into his deed over the lake of Bracciano and the surrounding countryside. Bracciano is a half-hour's drive from Rome.

Because they were so powerful, the aristocratic families inevitably had an influence over the lives of even temporary residents of Rome (or Florence). For one thing, these families set the social calendar. It may seem curious that Americans went to Rome early in the winter and stayed through the spring. Granted, it was a relatively sunny city, but it was not the Bahamas. Why didn't people go there in summer the way they do today, or at least in the fall or late spring, when the weather was nicer? There were two reasons. The minor one was that Rome was considered unhealthy in the summer because the surrounding countryside was malarial. The major reason, however, is that the social season did not begin until the end of November, when the nobles came back to the city from their castles and estates in the country.

Prince Guglielmo "Bill" Rospigliosi, today a tall, erect, silver-haired gentleman, graciously helped me understand the social calendar of those times. Bill is the grandson of a Rospigliosi who married a Haseltine from Philadelphia, and being himself perfectly bilingual, he became one of the best-known foreign correspondents in Rome in the years before and after World War II. "In the beginning of September," Bill explained, "the aristocratic families would leave their palazzi in Rome, or Florence, since it worked the same way there, and go out to their country estates for the hunting season and for the fall seeding. Many of them actually administered their lands quite competently, whatever may be said now about the idle aristocracy."

The nobles then returned to the city in early December, and that was when the social season really started. Receptions and balls began before Epiphany and went on (with a break during Lent) until Carnival in March, when the nobility returned to the country for spring seeding. Then they came back to Rome in July and remained in the city through July and August "on the theory," Bill explained, "that the big stone palazzi were cooler than anywhere else. It's exactly the opposite of what people do now in the summer, but of course they didn't go to the seashore then." Then the nobles would return to the land early in September for hunting and seeding, and another cycle was complete — it had worked that way for centuries.

This aristocratic migration greatly influenced the influx of well-connected foreign visitors, who came to Rome for the winter season precisely because it *was* a social season, when the great palazzi were torchlit at night until three or four in the morning and thousands of dancers in fanciful and rich costumes whirled on the ballroom floors beneath ceilings frescoed with angels and crystal chandeliers, when the Corso was thickest with carriages and the gossip and romance freest.

Once an American family had settled in, therefore, after those first trial weeks, the ladies would be anxious for an introduction to the Farnese or the Rospigliosi, the Doria or the Barberini, in order to be invited to the balls and out of sheer social prestige. If the American family was well connected with the American colony in Rome, such introductions were not difficult to come by. When I was researching this question of why Americans seemed to gravitate like iron filings toward the aristocratic families in Italy, Harry Brewster in Florence gave me a reason so simple and down to earth I'd overlooked it entirely. Harry is the grandson of the philosopher Henry Brewster, who lived in Bellosguardo, and the Brewsters are the descendants of the Elder William Brewster, the religious leader of the *Mayflower*. Harry grew up in the Palazzo Antici-Mattei in Rome, and he knew that world (as he knows the Tuscan world) very well. "The children of the aristocrats nearly all had British or Scottish nannies," he told me. Of course that was a reason. The aristocrats spoke English! Well before it became a vogue to marry American girls, Italian aristocrats had been meeting, courting, and marrying English girls who came to Italy with their families on the Grand Tour. Once they became pregnant, these English principesse at once sent for their old nannies, and by the 1840s it had become the proper thing among the nobles to have a British nannie for one's children even if both parents were Italian. How easy it is to overlook the obvious. The nobles spoke English whereas most middle-class Italians didn't, or if they spoke it they spoke it haltingly and with a funny accent.

After you'd been introduced into Roman society, the first invitations to Epiphany balls would begin to arrive. The Italians didn't celebrate Christmas as they do today. The Feast of Epiphany on January 6 took its place (it was actually more correct historically since it celebrates the day when the Three Kings brought their gifts to the infant Jesus). On January 5, children would put their shoes outside the door, hoping the Three Kings would leave something for them. All during the week of the Nativity that preceded Epiphany, the crib was prepared, and every house had a crèche showing the Nativity scene. Bagpiping shepherds from the Abruzzi would go up and down the streets blowing their tremulous, nasal tunes and singing hymns. It was a festive holiday time. For a fortnight before, seamstresses were busy making ball costumes, and it was impossible to make a last-minute appointment at the dressmaker's. At Epiphany the streets were thronged with carriages all evening bearing guests back and forth from one palazzo to another.

The scrubbed marble steps shone, torches blazed, footmen in splendid uniforms stood at each landing, and all was polished to make a dazzling impression. One of the first Americans to publish a report on a princely ball was William Gillespie, who attended a huge party at Palazzo Torlonia. Unlike most aristocrats, Torlonia practiced a profession — he was a banker — and each year he invited to his palazzo all the foreigners who did business with his establishment. Gillespie wrote:

> Your invitation sent a fortnight in advance tells you that the prince and princess beg the Signore to do them the honor of coming to pass the evening in their palace at eight o'clock. On the appointed evening you enter your carriage at *ten o'clock,* and half mile before reaching the palace you find a file of carriages extending from it that distance. After a long trial of patience, you are driven into the palace court and set down at the foot of the grand marble staircase, covered for the occasion with scarlet

cloth. The first antechamber is crowded with the servants of the guests, holding their master's cloaks. Beyond these are other rooms, through which your name is echoed by the announcing servants, generally undergoing many strange transformations, and at last you enter the grand salon, where you are received by your host and hostess.

A numerous suite of magnificent rooms is now open to you, some lined with paintings, others devoted to chess and cards, and even supplied with newspapers. . . . But the music will soon attract you to the ballroom which is the focus of the crowd.

The wonder is that Gillespie could remember all those details, since he seems to have spent the evening gazing at the Roman women, whom he reported to be the most beautiful in the world: "Their complexions have a cloudless purity like the inner petal of the magnolia; their dreamy eyes reveal dizzying wells of passion in the depths of their intense darkness, and their magnificently developed forms unite the charms of Venus with the dignity of Juno." Not all Americans were as impressed with these goddesses or with the balls themselves. Samuel Gridley Howe went to one in 1843 with his Julia Ward and groused afterward that it had been a "vulgar, tawdry, stupid affair with such a crowd that I could scarcely breathe."

The young girls enjoyed themselves, though (and, at times, so did their mothers). The dancing would last until dawn, and among the young it was chic to make one's entrance at midnight or even later. The girls were always escorted by their mothers or aunts, but a late arrival had its advantages on that score, too. Mary King, the daughter of a president of Columbia College, grew up in Rome and recalled that "we used to arrive at the balls about 12:30 or 1 just so as to have one waltz before the cotillion which was usually the best of the evening, as all the serious people had gone, and the mammas were at supper fortifying themselves for the long hours before them, so the ballroom was comparatively empty and one could get a good turn." It was in the early morning that the American girl whirling in the arms of a young principe, or conte or marchese, might allow him to call on her later in the week or go riding with him in the campagna if her mother consented. Couldn't he organize a riding party with a few other American or English girls along? Did he know her friend Annabelle French? There she was, dancing with . . . The prince looked in the direction indicated and saw a radiant, smiling girl. People met and fell in love as they always have, and each meeting seemed to the two people terribly strange and special whether they had met in a ballroom or in the street.

It was not easy to enter an aristocratic Roman family in the early part of the nineteenth century, when the nobles still had their property and power. It's not simply that they were snobbish, which they were, and generally preferred their sons to marry aristocratic girls and not republican Americans. The cultural barriers were much stronger than they are today. There were real differences in outlook and customs, starting with the crucial one of the woman's role in the family. Decisions were almost always made for her, and she would have to bend them gradually by force of will. People forget how authoritarian fathers were then, and the princes were particularly so. There's a scene in Crawford's *Sant'Ilario* where old Montevarchi calls in his middle daughter, Flavia, to tell her she's going to be married.

> "Flavia," said her father, addressing her in solemn tones, "you are to be married, my dear child. I have sent for you at once, because there was no time to be lost, seeing that the wedding must take place before the beginning of Advent. The news will probably give you pleasure, but I trust you will reflect on the solemnity of such engagements and lay aside —"
>
> "Would you mind telling me the name of my husband?" inquired Flavia, interrupting the paternal lecture.

This was fiction, but barely. A woman, particularly a young woman, and *particularly* a daughter-in-law, was expected to submit to the authority of the head of the house and even more frequently to that of the older woman. I was talking about this one day with Marchesa Origo, the daughter of a New Yorker, Bayard Cutting, whose beautiful autobiography is the best thing that has been written about growing up into Florentine and Tuscan society in the twentieth century. She was speaking of a time after the patriarchal rule had begun to decline, yet she told me, "I learned the gentle art of keeping my mouth shut. A great many English and American wives did." She did not infer, however, that these marriages were necessarily failures. Often, they worked very well. "There seems to be something in the mixture of American women and Italian men that goes off well temperamentally," she said that day. "There's a sexual force in Italian men that finds its counterpart in the extraordinary drive many American women have.''

If the marriage was not happy, or the girl could not adapt to her station in the palazzo, she would sail home again or begin a stubborn, sly, vicious kind of rebellion that easily led to adultery or at least to a public display of disdain for her husband. That, too, was a traditional role for upper-class women in Rome, probably because they were so repressed. Bored, also. They had a great deal of time on their hands, and they would often pass the afternoon driving up and down the Corso in their carriages, then being driven from the Piazza del Popolo up to the Pincio, where they would circle a few times and come back to the Corso, perhaps dropping off cards at one or two addresses. They would look at each other's clothes as the carriages passed and look at young men who rode by to look at them. Rome was not a very big city then. It had about two hundred thousand inhabitants in the 1840s, less than a tenth of its present population, so that when a young man rode past your carriage four or five times or threw a bunch of violets into it at the Carnevale (when everyone threw nosegays and sugar plums into each other's carriages), it wasn't very hard to find out who he was and it wasn't at all hard to encourage him because there was little opprobrium attached to it. New Englanders were perpetually shocked by the freedom with which Roman women appeared in public with their *cicisbei* (a strange Venetian dialect word meaning "pretty boy"). The *cicisbeo* was not necessarily a boy. He might be a married man, but at any rate he was a married woman's constant escort without having the honor of being her husband. "There seems to be no kind of shame attached to the dissoluteness of manners," Longfellow wrote to his brother in 1828. "Whenever I go to the principal street of the city at the hour for promenade, I see a lady of the highest tone, who has a rich young banker as her *cicisbeo,* driving in her carriage, with her daughter, her husband and her lover!"

The woman in the carriage was a symbol, also, of all that was so perplexing to Americans. How could Italy be so morally polluted and yet have produced art of such spirituality? Despite a vigorous resurgence of values in Florence during the early Renaissance, things had not been so very different during those "great centuries," the fourteenth and fifteenth, from what they were three centuries later. The Borgia Pope Alexander VI, who had commissioned some of the finest frescoes in the Vatican, had kept a mistress, and everybody knew it. The spirit of the Borgias seemed to correspond, moreover, to the pagan iconography of Catholic art and its underlying sensuality, which had helped to condemn the Catholic Church, in puritan minds, as the "Scarlet Woman" and "the Whore of Babylon."

One explanation offered by some Americans was that Italy needed a Protestant reformation to cleanse itself, even if some of the pagan beauty of Italian art might be consigned to the bonfires of a future Savonarola. "I prefer a place where the men and women are better, though the statues and paintings might be worse," Theodore Fay, the New York author and editor, had written after traveling through Italy, and probably the majority of Americans agreed in principle. Yet very few of them sought out the Italians who wanted to change things and overthrow the old order.

The patriots who would follow Mazzini and Garibaldi under the banner of a free, united Italy were closer to the Americans in mentality and aspirations. They came mostly from the middle class, from the more progressive north, and were bitterly anticlerical. They would have hung the Pope, given half a chance, and they dreamed of bringing to Italy something of the cleansing fire of the Protestant revolt in northern Europe two centuries earlier. Many of these patriots were Freemasons. Unfortunately, there was very little contact between the Americans in Italy and these reformers, despite a great cannonading of admiration from a distance. In 1848, for example, when the followers of Mazzini and Garibaldi got up a real head of steam, there were huge demonstrations on their behalf in New York and other cities, with crowds of fifty thousand people cheering wildly and petitions of encouragement from Congress. Yet once they set foot in Italy, the Americans who had come to Rome or Florence for the winter preferred to mix almost exclusively with the aristocracy.

There were various reasons for this, and Harry Brewster has suggested a good one — the aristocrats spoke English. Everyone I've talked to about that period, people who would have some special knowledge of it, also reported, however, that Americans were awestruck at the idea of mingling with blueblooded people, not having an aristocracy of their own. (Most newspapermen will tell you this is true, that Americans will read almost anything about royal families and aristocrats.) Also, the Italian middle class was quite provincial. Only a few professional men and fewer women ventured into the wider society of Europe. The interests of the stay-at-homes were centered on their city and their social circle and its gossip — a boring conversational diet to someone from the outside. It hasn't altogether changed even today. Gore Vidal concluded after living in Italy for over a decade that "the Italians tend to be rather formal, and totally absorbed in themselves and their families." The aristocrats were often as narrow but more fun. They entertained often and had British friends. All of these factors served to entice American republican legs up noble staircases.

That being so, however, the Americans were stuck with their dilemma. While they felt the social order was shameful, they sought out and befriended a ruling class that with few exceptions wanted nothing more than to see itself perpetuated. Most Americans took Italy for what it was. One cannot fault them. It was not their country, and they had no real right to get involved in its internal struggles. The system, however corrupt, was not inimical to them. They had come for the ruins, the charm of Italy, and its art, and it might well have seemed in that slower age that none of these attractions would ever be affected by political events. The artists had more trouble sorting out Italian realities, however, and for them the problem was more complex.

The rich Catholic iconography of the art at first seemed accessible to the American painters and sculptors who sailed to Italy early in the nineteenth century. They would copy it, intending to improve on it and paint, as it were, a better Madonna. It was very much in the American spirit to think that way. But the very close-wovenness of the iconography, so many threads of so many colors, made it more difficult to unravel than it had seemed at first. The pictures in the galleries could be copied, certainly, but they were all little pieces of a vast mosaic of art that had flourished for centuries in an Italian social context, in a hierarchic vertical culture fed by ancient streams and conflicts, and how could one paint a better Madonna or a better religious picture of Renaissance inspiration unless one understood the thinking that had gone into the Italian ones?

Allston was the first casualty. Washington Allston! The man whom his contemporaries considered a genius, the greatest artistic talent of his generation. His was the saddest of all Italian love stories. Under the spell of the Old Masters, he had returned to Boston from Europe in 1818, proposing to execute a vast religious canvas — twelve feet high and seventeen feet long — called *Belshazzar's Feast,* based on the Old Testament legend of the prophet Daniel. Sponsors raised the unheard-of sum of ten thousand dollars to back his effort, and Allston set to work. He finished it quickly enough, but then showed it to Gilbert Stuart, who saw certain flaws in the perspective. Allston saw them, too. The canvas was not worthy of the Old Masters! Allston began to repaint. He did little else for the next eight years. When his old studio barn was claimed by the landlord, he pleaded with the moving men to walk in backward so they would not see the canvas. By then the huge painting was a freak-show monstrosity, with figures done over and over again until some of them had become giants and others dwarfs. He had just finished repainting the figure of the king in July 1843 when he collapsed and died — liberated at last from what his brother-in-law, the novelist Richard Henry Dana, called "that terrible vision, the nightmare, the incubus, the tormentor of his life; his unfinished picture."

The story of Allston's pupil Samuel Finley Breese Morse has a bittersweet ending instead, for after all the man invented the telegraph and became as rich and famous in his old age as anyone could wish to be. Morse is a great favorite of mine in this book, despite his sometimes narrow Calvinism that made him run for the office of mayor of New York, on the Know-Nothing ticket. He was the Gary Cooper of American art, rugged and principled. As a promising young artist, he had vowed innocently that "my ambition is to belong to those who shall revive the splendor of the fifteenth century," and he believed that by going to the Continent to study, he and other Yankee lads would return home with a glorious gift to their countrymen. It was a generous dream, and it failed him early.

Back home, nothing came easy. To make money, he painted portraits in his native New England and in the South, but the doors that seemed to open before him slammed shut again and he was forced to trudge to the next town, leaving his young wife in New Haven with his parents because the couple could not afford their own home. When she died prematurely, he was on the road. He suffered for his genius. Even after he had painted *Congress Hall,* the marvelous interior portrait of the old Congress in Washington, D.C., with all the members in attendance, nobody came to see it when it was launched on a traveling exhibit. Fellow artists knew how good Morse was. They elected him president of their professional society in New York, but by then he was turning in frustration to other things, including the study of electricity, which had fascinated him as a student at Yale.

In 1829, Morse got some money together and decided to give the muse a last chance. He sailed to Rome and immediately found himself in a congenial atmosphere, admired and productive. For a few months his spirits soared while he went on marvelous walking trips with fellow artists and painted arcadian landscapes in little outlying towns like Subiaco, where the docile shepherds were happy to spend an afternoon posing for "an artist" and comely local girls (Subiaco is Gina Lollobrigida's birthplace) appeared with pitchers of cool water and baskets of fruit. It was bliss, yet the shrewd Yankee in Morse rejected the temptation to stay on. He knew that Italian iconography would always be foreign to him. It belonged to another culture and religion. He loathed the Papal State and all it stood for. The most he could hope to do in Italy was to become a second-rate painter of romantic scenes, and he would not settle for that. He left Rome, bound for home, in 1832.

A spectacular lightning storm in Venice, which Morse witnessed while huddled under the arcades of St. Mark's Square, rekindled his barely dormant interest in electricity. Never was a storm more providential. During the voyage home aboard the brig *Sully,* Morse brought his ideas together and jotted down what the world would soon call the Morse code along with sketches of the first workable telegraph. He would hardly have achieved all this if his mind had not been seeking something to replace the art that had so ravaged his dreams. "I did not abandon art," he would say, "she abandoned me"; but actually, like most fateful decisions, it had been a two-way street.

In his luggage when he disembarked from the *Sully* were the sketches for the telegraph and one of the masterpieces of American art, *The Salon of the Louvre,* which he had painted in Paris on the way home, with James Fenimore Cooper looking on and offering friendly encouragement.

Cooper had not delved very deep when writing about Italy, merely using it for its color. Hawthorne instead tried to get behind the iconography and work out a formula that would explain Rome in particular and Italy in general. He had not really planned this difficult undertaking. The Hawthorne family arrived in Rome in the

winter of 1858, at the end of Nathaniel's term as U.S. consul in
Liverpool. He and his wife, Sophia Peabody, wanted to tour
Europe before returning home, and they made a beeline for the
Eternal City, expecting sunshine and blue Mediterranean skies. Instead they found a rainy, gloomy winter, and in the icy dampness
of their rooms on the Via di Porta Pinciana (just off the Via Veneto), Hawthorne cursed "the languor of Rome, its weary pave-
ments, its little life, pressed down by a weight of death." Everything seemed to go wrong. Their little girl, Una, lay in bed
chattering with fever in the unheated apartment and nearly died of
pneumonia. The nurse was followed around by an Italian lothario
who lurked in doorways and behind trees and only succeeded in
frightening her.

With the return of the sun in late February, the family's spirits revived. They took walks on the Pincio and in the green woodland of
the Villa Borghese and toured the galleries, where Sophia Peabody
diligently took notes on her reactions to hundreds of busts, statues,
paintings, and tapestries. The fifty-four-year-old Hawthorne began
to feel a kind of melancholy, ambivalent, middle-aged-man's passion for the city, which led him to conclude that "Rome certainly
does draw into itself my heart, as I think even London, or even
little Concord, or old sleepy Salem, never did and never will." On
the other hand, once he'd left Rome, he decided that he never
wanted to see the city, its bottomless well of history, and its
"wicked filth" again.

He was much happier in Florence, settling into a vast, forty-
room villa in Bellosguardo whose tall windows overlooked the
Arno and the Florence skyline. There he began to organize his notes
for a new novel, which he called *The Marble Faun* after its Italian
protagonist, a faunlike, half-mythological, half-human nobleman
who was intended to combine the pagan and the Christian in one
person. The allegory was labored. It was based on a superficial understanding of Italian society, and though the novel would be full
of wonderful observations, its characters were jerked along like
marionettes. The failure of *The Marble Faun* had a great deal to do
with Hawthorne's premature death five years later.

Though these failures were warning signs, the romantics persevered nonetheless. Often they were disappointed with their years
in Italy and returned home empty-handed — but not always. Now
and then the dreamer and the dream came together like a person

stepping into a perfectly formed cutout. I will tell, in the next chapter, the story of two such people. One was a woman who found a freedom and an emotional completeness that her heart had craved. The other was a man pursuing an inner voice. Both were marvelous romantics, and their stories are worth telling for themselves. Together, they also sum up a subtly ambivalent American view of Italy, an impatience for political reform mingled with a deep-rooted, nostalgic desire that it not change at all.

CHAPTER FIVE

curious Roman in the year 1848 might have spotted them walking along the Corso, or in the Piazza di Spagna, and assumed that the thin, well-dressed man in his thirties, with the rakish suggestion of the artist in his floppy tie and well-trimmed beard, and the shapely, not quite pretty woman beside him were husband and wife. In fact, they were only friends and at first only tenuously so. In Rome they were immediately identifiable by their looks as *stranieri* and usually taken as English, though half of Boston society would have known their identities at a glance. Indeed, in the eyes of Boston both were misfits, which perhaps, among other motives, is why they were in Rome at all. The man was William Wetmore Story, and the woman, Margaret Fuller.

William Wetmore Story was the son of one of the first men of Massachusetts, the Supreme Court justice Joseph Story. And when this great man had passed away and the citizens of the commonwealth decided to honor his memory with a marble bust, his son, also a lawyer, already the author of fat, authoritative tomes on the law, volunteered to undertake the sculpting of the bust himself. His was a strange offer. He would accept the commission in order to go to Italy and learn how to be an artist.

The committee must have had a moment of giddiness. It was true that the young lawyer had puttered around for years with modeling clay, but there was a considerable difference between being an amateur and being a professional. Suppose he returned with a mangled block of marble, like a child's snowman, and said, self-pleased, "Gentlemen, my late father." What would they do then, send someone else? But since he was their friend and obviously gifted, they entrusted him with the task, and in 1846, Story and his dark-haired, plump, pretty wife, Emelyn, sailed for Rome.

Neither of them knew whether he would emerge at the end of a year or a year and a half as a sculptor. It was a chance he had taken, an attempt to break out and let something develop in himself that the law had smothered. Could it be done? Could he, by chipping away eight or ten hours a day, become a sculptor and finish a bust? Certainly, the Crawfords must have sometimes giggled in their bed, and the Greenoughs, up in Florence, hearing about it on the grapevine. So old Writs and Torts was going to be a sculptor, eh?

The snickers upset Story, but otherwise he was having a wonderful time. This was life! He tipped his hat to the flower girl on the corner and the doorkeeper, and he whistled as he unlocked his studio while they gazed admiringly at this tall, debonair *inglese* who wore a rakish Van Dyck beard and mustache and always had a smile for the *bambini*. What a signore this one was! Story hammered and chipped, stepped back and squinted, and when Margaret Fuller dropped by late in the afternoon, he would talk self-consciously, and she would take notes for an article she proposed to write about him. Once or twice he took Margaret home for dinner, and she and Emelyn reminisced about Boston and gossiped about Rome.

The atmosphere at those first meetings was not relaxed. Emelyn did not much like Margaret, who was in Italy with other Bostonians, the Springs, as a roving correspondent for Horace Greeley's *Tribune*. A rather brusque, plain though full-bodied New England spinster, this lady journalist had always struck Emelyn as pretentious. When other girls had giggled over boys and chatted about clothes, Margaret had sat at Emerson's feet discussing philosophy with him. She had edited *The Dial* and written a feminist book, *Women in the Nineteenth Century,* and held rather precious "conversations" for a gaggle of Boston maidens that included Horace Greeley's future wife as well as Hawthorne's. Sophia Peabody had even written her a sonnet that closed with the couplet:

> *Behold, I reverent stand before Thy shrine*
> *In recognition of Thy words divine.*

The whole thing smacked a bit of lesbianism, and Emelyn Story, who was snobbish and socially ambitious, did not like odd, unattached people. Yet within a few weeks she was telling Margaret, "How have I misjudged you," in testimony to a burgeoning friendship.

Thrown together in Rome, the two women had discovered common ground in both William Story's and Margaret's paternity. The fathers in both cases had been brilliant, driving men in public life (Margaret's a congressman and senator). Story had adapted by trying to become a copy of the older man until the effort collapsed with Justice Story's death, and the son sought escape in Italy and in art. Margaret's rebellion had been blunter. She seems to have entered into a grim competition to stand taller than her father on his own ground, becoming in the process an intellectually daunting and perpetually frozen virgin. "Tis an evil lot," she had once written despondently, "to have a man's ambition and a woman's heart."

Emelyn, at last perceiving the connection, warmed to her, but as soon as Margaret's tragic proclivity to spinsterhood had been established, she dropped out of sight, only to reemerge weeks later changed and softened. "I am not the same person," she confided mysteriously to the Storys, "but in many respects another." Then it was time for Margaret to leave Rome with the Springs, bound for northern Europe on the homeward leg to Boston. The Storys bid her good-bye fondly and were still mystified when Margaret returned unexpectedly after less than a month.

Then the secret came out. She brought him to tea one afternoon, a slender, dark-haired, quiet young man almost ten years younger than herself. He was the Marchese Angelo Ossoli della Torre, the younger son of a once-powerful feudal family that still possessed a palazzo in Rome and a huge fortress in the Sabine country. The marchese seemed to the excited Storys shy and vulnerable, with large black eyes fringed with heavy lashes, a large nose, and a full mouth all set on a small, oval face. Yet his effect on Margaret was obvious. She had blossomed, becoming, at moments, strikingly sensuous, her eyes radiant and her flaxen hair, which had once been lusterless, glowing like the dark blond hair so typical of upper-class Roman women.

The Storys, wishing to be helpful and cordial, were uncertain what to make of this surprising marchese, and he seemed disconcerted. Their open, boisterous friendship at first meeting confused him. Why on earth did they keep asking him about paintings, about statues at the Vatican gallery, or about this or that palazzo? Yes, of course, he knew about them in a general sense. Like every Italian, he had grown up surrounded by beautiful palazzi, fountains, paintings, and statues. They were part of the universe, like the very air or moonlight. But he did not read books about them, and, in fact, he rarely picked up a book of any sort. Why read about life when it was present, in reality, before one's eyes, overpoweringly full and immediate? The things he had studied were not art or history but the arts of a nobleman: how to sit on a horse, skill with a rapier, etiquette, stylish dress. Story, after some cheerful attempts to draw out the young man, lapsed into a perplexed silence interspersed with polite smiles while Margaret blushed and glanced at her Ossoli anxiously. Afterward, she asked him to be patient with these foreign friends, but he did not seem to mind. He was so gentle, the gentlest and sweetest of lovers, the ideal lover for such a liberated and almost middle-aged woman — the opposite, one may guess, of her authoritarian and Puritan father.

They had met, these unlikely lovers, at St. Peter's in the dusk of an April day, when Margaret had become separated from the Springs. The hushed, darkening cathedral had been emptying, with no sign of her companions, when the young Italian had approached Margaret across the marble floor, politely respectful, asking her in a sweet, melodic voice if he could assist her. Was he trying to pick her up? He explained at once that he was on duty in the cathedral and that one of his responsibilities was to help visitors who were lost. Gratefully, she accepted his offer to escort her outside and see her into a carriage, and, when St. Peter's Square proved to be deserted, she allowed him to walk her home. As they strolled across the Tiber toward Piazza Venezia, Margaret's questions began to draw him out.

He was a marchese, yes, but his sympathies lay with Mazzini. He believed — the only one of his family — in a free, united Italian republic without clerical domination. When Margaret told him that she had recently talked with Mazzini in London, he stared at her wonderingly. This American woman was unlike anyone he had ever met. Even during those first minutes he would glance at her to find her gazing at him deeply, probingly, but without any coquettishness, as no Roman woman would have done, and she asked question after question, bluntly, directly, about his ideas, his family, his hopes for Italy. When they parted beneath her lodging on the Corso, he asked shyly if he might call on her.

Two days later Ossoli returned as he had promised, offering to show her the sights of Rome in the six weeks that remained before she was due to resume her European tour with the Springs. Together they toured the city, and one can imagine those two figures, the dark-haired, erect marchese with his frockcoat and cane, Margaret resting her hand on his arm as they stood in the grassy Forum among the archaeologists' trenches and the shepherds watering their animals. One can feel the pressure of that hand mounting on that arm as the days ran out and the words becoming fewer, interspersed with anxious silences as Margaret prepared to leave Rome.

"Dear youth," she wrote to him with a boldness and directness that remain breathtaking after more than a century, when language has become physical, "you are the only one in Rome in whom I recognize my kin. I want to know and to love you and have you love me." And, "Soon I must leave here. Do not let me go without giving me some of your life in exchange for some of mine."

Was he stunned by the sexuality of those sentences? One can only guess. His reply was staggering and wholly unexpected by his correspondent: He proposed marriage. In confusion, in tears, Margaret fled north with the Springs. "I loved him, and felt very unhappy to leave him, but the connection seemed so every way unfit," she wrote later to her sister Ellen. Yet in the carriage that bore her to Florence and across the Apennines into the Veneto, the great decision matured in her heart. In Venice, she informed the Springs that she would not continue into Germany with them, leaving the reason vague. Alone, she toured northern Italy — Vicenza, Verona, Mantova, Milan — drafting articles for the *Tribune,* recording her meetings, surreptitious and dangerous, with the young, middle-class revolutionaries who yearned, like their disciple Mazzini, to drive the Austrians back across the Alps and to liberate Italy. Early in September, after a feverish illness in Florence, she reentered the Eternal City, rushing into Angelo's arms, to that consummation of flesh she had so long desired and withheld.

Her decision had been difficult in more than one sense. She had only four hundred dollars with her, and Ossoli, despite his title and handsome clothes, was virtually penniless since his older brother had full control of the family purse. Margaret, having been disappointed in her hopes for an inheritance and knowing that she could expect no help from her widowed mother, who was herself hard pressed, wrote to Horace Greeley and asked for a large advance. When he assented, though not without a rumble of displeasure, she began working harder than ever on her dispatches, which Greeley, recouping his investment, ran on the front page. They were mostly political pieces. With the intuition of a born reporter, she felt that the situation was unstable, ripe for a violent change. Ossoli fed her information. He himself was eager for revolution. He had enlisted in the newly formed Roman militia, the Civil Guard, and a proud Margaret, along with the Storys, went to watch her lover and his companions practicing close drill. The Storys sympathized and helped the struggling couple with little loans whenever they could manage it. Emelyn was more than ever admiring of Margaret's character, writing that her friend was "possessed of so broad a charity that she could cover with its mantle the faults and defects of all about her." The Storys, in fact, went around Rome telling their friends how Margaret had given her last fifty dollars to an unsuccessful American artist who was broke.

The spring of 1848 was thick with premonition. A half-century of restoration and peace was crumbling. First, the long-abused subjects of the Neapolitan state revolted in remote and backward Sicily, forcing the hapless Bourbon monarch, King Ferdinand I — nicknamed Re Bomba (King Bomb) by his subjects because of his frequent use of artillery against them — to grant a constitution. Then the northern revolt began. In Paris, the tocsin sounded, and huge barricades went up in the streets while King Louis Philippe, the "citizen king," fled. Then Berlin revolted, then Milan — where the people, in five days of furious street fighting against the Austrian cavalry, the legendary "five days of Milan," drove Radetsky's forces from the city and, temporarily, from all Lombardy. The news of Milan's resurrection was received in Rome, Margaret reported, with indescribable rapture. Men were seen dancing; women, weeping with joy. "I have seen the Austrian arms dragged through the streets of Rome and burned in the Piazza del Popolo," she wrote.

To Greeley, therefore, her letter in the spring of 1848 came like a blow to the solar plexus. Its gist was that she was quitting. Greeley raged, Greeley swore, Greeley howled and took her letter home to his wife, who urged moderation. Barely restraining his temper, but underlining madly, the editor wrote his errant correspondent on November 14, 1848: "The sum you asked me to advance was more than I had anticipated, and it came rather hard on me — but the truth is I always *am* bothered about money. Then, just as I had forgotten *that,* along came your notification that *you would write no more* — and *that* annoyed me."

Greeley went on to chide her for breaking off "just as Italy and Europe were in the throes of a great Revolution." Poor Greeley; one can imagine how annoyed he was. The events in Europe were breaking news, and his star reporter had temperamentally resigned. But Greeley could not know the real reason for Margaret's abrupt decision: she was pregnant. All that winter she had been fighting off nausea, too sick most of the time to even go outdoors. The strain on her thirty-seven-year-old body can only have been increased by the psychological stress of her being unmarried. Though the faithful Ossoli declared himself willing to marry her, he apparently had to wait for a special dispensation from the Catholic Church because of her Protestant affiliation. The former New England bluestocking and transcendentalist editor, the spiritual den mother to the most elevated young ladies of Boston, was an unlikely *ragazza madre* (the Italian term for an unwed mother, meaning literally "girl-mother"). And Margaret, mortified and fearful lest someone discover her condition, exiled herself to a remote eagle's nest in the Apennines, at l'Aquila — hence her letter to Greeley that she would "write no more."

In July she moved to Terni, a rural town on the Via Flaminia fifty miles north of Rome, where it was easier for Ossoli to visit her. And on the fifth of September, 1848, after a difficult labor, a son was born. Because of the dual religions of his unmarried parents, baptism was delayed, but eventually the child was christened Angelo Eugenio Filippo Ossoli. To Margaret, he was Nino.

She was not, however, a doting mother. After barely a month, she left the baby in the care of a wet nurse, a kind, though ignorant and dirty, peasant woman, and made her reappearance in Rome. Most other Americans had been away for the summer months, and Margaret hoped that her own absence would be accepted as normal. Besides, the political situation had become so precarious that it overshadowed everything else in people's minds. It took Margaret only a few hours of rapid-fire questions with the Storys to catch up.

First of all, the Pope's able prime minister, Count Pellegrino Rossi, had been knifed to death on the steps of the chamber of deputies under the untroubled gaze of dozens of armed sentries. The

Roman mob then besieged the Pope's palace. Margaret, who had made up with Greeley and received a two-dollar raise (from eight to ten dollars per article), was there to report it: "Today all the troops and the people united and went to the Quirinal [palace] to demand a change of measures. They found the Swiss Guard drawn out, and the Pope dared not show himself. They attempted to force the door to his palace, to enter his presence, and the [Swiss] guard fired."

The Romans called out their own counterforce, the National Guard, in which Ossoli was serving, and soon the Quirinal Palace was ringed by hostile cannon. In northern Europe the flames of revolution were subsiding, suffocated by loyal generals serving their monarchs. Yet they were now bursting forth in Rome. The Roman Guard gained the upper hand, and the great heroes of Italian liberation, Garibaldi and Mazzini, were summoned to the Eternal City to lead a revolutionary Roman Republic.

Margaret was delighted. She had never concealed her republican sympathies, and, sending off exuberant dispatches to the *Tribune* one after the other, she wrote that "Italy is being educated for the future, her leaders are learning that the time is past for trust in princes and precedents." One evening there was a soft rap on her door. Opening it, she saw the lean, dark, grave visage of Mazzini, looking, she gushed in a womanly confession to her readers, "more divine than ever after his strange new sufferings."

The divine revolutionary, once she had seated him on her sofa, explained solemnly that the Roman Republic faced a perilous future. Pius IX had exercised all the latent power of a Roman pontiff. In an abrupt, simple, and supine gesture, he had slipped out of the Quirinal Palace one night, in the carriage of the Bavarian ambassador, in the guise — so it was rumored — of a coachman. The carriage rumbled past the Coliseum and disappeared down the old Appian Way. From their capital at Naples, the Bourbons had at once offered the Holy Father sanctuary at the Fortress of Gaeta, only seventy miles south of Rome but within Neapolitan territory. Now the Pope was broadcasting appeals to every government in Europe as well as to every Catholic in the world.

From all the points of the compass, armies had begun to converge on the insurgent capital — Re Bomba's Neapolitans marching up to Frascati in the hills east of the capital, Spanish marines landing near Gaeta, Austrian armies preparing to drive southward to Rome once they had snuffed out the last embers of rebellion in northern Italy. But it was France that won the race, landing an expeditionary force of fifteen thousand troops at Civitavecchia under the command of General Charles Oudinot, who told his men that the people of Rome "consider us liberators." Besides, he added, "the Italians never fight."

On April 29, the French columns set off for Rome, marching through the warm, half-deserted countryside as the British had marched at Concord, in rectangular boxes, in elegant uniforms, with their snowy white gloves holding the stocks of their rifles. Inside the walls of Rome an eerie calm prevailed; no one has described it better than Story: "All the streets deserted, gloomy, and morose, as before some terrible thunderstorm. The women all fled to the houses . . . the shops all shut, with here and there a door half-open revealing the form of a soldier peering out."

Confidently Oudinot marched his columns straight for the Porta Cavalleggeri just behind the Vatican, but as they drew close, musketfire began pouring down from the massive old walls. Through the canes and bushes that covered the slopes behind the Janiculum Hill came a wild rush of young Italians, charging with bayonets and drawn swords. They were the bloods of Garibaldi's legion, some in red shirts, some in plumed hats, and they hurled themselves on the immaculate professionals, "clawing at us," lamented one French officer, "like dervishes." The stunned Frenchmen tried to stem these fierce attacks, gave ground, and finally retreated pell-mell into the countryside. By nightfall, General Oudinot's army was back in Civitavecchia.

Rome enjoyed a lull of peace, but it was deceptive. The republic's leaders wrangled about the French threat, Garibaldi proposing a quick thrust to drive the invading force into the sea while Mazzini, whose view prevailed, argued adamantly for diplomatic negotiations with the special French envoy, Ferdinand de Lesseps — the future builder of the Suez Canal. On the third of June, Oudinot, having built up his forces to thirty-five thousand men, returned to the walls and the siege of Rome began. Many Americans had already left. The remaining few huddled together in the Casa Dies, the house of a painter on Via Gregoriana. A few took part in the defense of Rome, like the sculptor Thomas Crawford, who enrolled in the guard and fought on the walls alongside the Garibaldini. Through her friend Princess Belgioioso, Margaret was ap-

ARCHIVIO FOTOGRAFICO COMUNALE, ROME

A young and hugely popular Pope when he was elected to the throne of Peter in 1846, at the age of fifty-four, Pius IX (Giovanni Maria Mastai-Ferretti) could not fulfill the political expectations he had aroused among Italians eager for their country's unification. His fate instead was to reign for thirty-two years as the last temporal ruler of the Papal State.

ARCHIVIO FOTOGRAFICO COMUNALE, ROME

One of the earliest war photographs ever taken, this historic print shows French siege cannons facing Rome's Janiculum Hill in 1849. A French expeditionary force under General Oudinot had been sent to retake the city from republican followers of Garibaldi and Italy's other great apostle of nationalism, Giuseppe Mazzini.

pointed one of the directors of the Fate Bene Fratelli Hospital on the Tiber Island, where the wounded defenders were brought on bloodstained litters. Already acting as probably the first woman war correspondent in the history of U.S. journalism, she was seeing at first hand the terrible aftermath of battle: the pain, the screams of men whose legs or arms were being amputated, hearing the death rattle and the whispered prayer, the cry of "Mamma!" in moments of agony. "I have, for the first time, seen what wounded men suffer," she wrote somberly to her readers.

The renewed French attack brought the ambulance carts rumbling down the Janiculum and across Trastevere to the island. As each shattered body was carried into the hospital, Margaret wondered with dread suspense if the victim was her own Ossoli, now serving on the most exposed stretch of wall directly facing the French siege works. A scribbled note from him brought the un-

Another 1849 photograph shows a sentry atop the French siege works. Because of the long exposure times, only stationary figures could be photographed.

settling if realistic advice: "I beg you not to overtire yourself, and to take care of your health so that at least you can take good care of Angelino — so that if I die he will at least have you." Margaret, anxious that she herself might not survive the siege, had concluded that she must confide the secret of little Nino to someone, some fellow American, someone she could trust. It was to Emelyn that she turned. In her diary Emelyn wrote:

> I well remember how exhausted and weary she was, how pale and agitated she returned to us [*from the hospital*]. After one such day, she called me to her bedside and said that I must consent, for her sake, to keep the secret she was about to confide. Then she told me of her marriage.

The two women talked until late into the night by the light of an oil lamp. Taking the younger woman's hand, Margaret begged

Emelyn to bring Nino to her mother in Massachusetts if both she and Ossoli should be killed. Hesitantly, Emelyn assented. It was a heavy responsibility — and then she confided in Margaret. She and William had had enough. The siege had sapped their nerves. They had asked Lewis Cass, Jr., the American minister, to arrange a safe conduct for them out of Rome. They would go north, to spend the next few months in Florence, until the fate of Rome should be decided. Margaret understood, though it was a bitter surprise. Later, in the darkness, she wept helplessly, knowing that the roads to Florence passed through, or near, Rieti, where she had abandoned her baby to the care of the wet nurse. She had only to ask Emelyn to be allowed to join them in the carriage. Not to do so seemed unnatural, almost inhuman. In her dreams she could hear the baby coughing, crying to her. She would wake from these nightmares drenched in sweat, her forehead burning. "I often seemed to hear him calling me amid the roar of the cannons," she wrote, "and he seemed to be crying."

She did not leave with the Storys. Rome was her battle. Her man was at the ramparts. She had her responsibilities at the hospital — and her new book. Margaret was writing the history of the Roman Republic, and she would see it through its final hour.

Rome fell in July 1849. A city had set itself against the established powers of Europe, and the wonder was that it had held out, alone and unassisted, for four months. The republic had been defeated, but for its foes, and the Pope first among them, it was a Pyrrhic victory. Among a new generation of Italians, the heroic defense of Rome would become a legend so real, so stirring, that it would finally make the liberation and union of Italy inevitable. Garibaldi would rise like the Phoenix from the defeat of Rome to lead his *mille* into Sicily exactly ten years later, in 1859. All that, however, was in the future. French soldiers were occupying the city, seizing and arresting republicans. Margaret and Ossoli went into hiding. He had survived, unscathed, where hundreds had fallen. But now the French would be searching for him, and Margaret entreated the decent, loyal Cass to aid them. False papers were secured for the young nobleman, and the two lovers, huddled in a rented carriage, passed the French roadblocks and reached Rieti.

A shock awaited Margaret. Nino was close to death, starved and covered with sores. The wet nurse, her milk exhausted, had grown tired of caring for the castaway child of this eccentric foreign woman who, moreover, had simply vanished. The baby had been abandoned to die. Torn by guilt, Margaret nursed him back to health. "I have been on the brink of losing my little boy," she wrote. "All I have undergone seemed little to what I felt seeing him unable to smile or to lift his little wasted hand. Now by incessant care I have brought him back (who knows indeed if that be a deed of love?) into this difficult world."

The "incessant care" was not enough to wipe away her reproach; increasingly, she longed to withdraw, to rest, to find safety. Increasingly, she thought of taking her husband and baby son home to America, to Massachusetts. "Coward and footsore, gladly would I creep into some green recess, apart from so much meddling and so much knowing, where I might see a few not unfriendly faces." A few days later the Ossolis were in a carriage bound for Florence, the first leg in their journey to America. This time Margaret, who had vowed never to be separated from her baby again, cradled Nino in her arms. "In him," she wrote, "I find satisfaction for the first time to the deep wants of my heart."

Florence was back under Austrian control, and there, too, the Ossolis had trouble with the police. They were under surveillance, and only the intervention of Cass and Greenough — plus Ossoli's American passport — kept them from being arrested. Margaret faced another type of inquisition before the *grandes dames* of the city's Anglo-American community. Elizabeth Barrett Browning, who became a warm friend of Margaret's but who knew her only as a journalist, wrote with delicate malice that "Miss Fuller has taken us by surprise at Florence, retiring from the Roman world with a husband and a child above a year old. Nobody had even suspected a word of this underplot, and her American friends stood mute in astonishment." From Florence, the gossip raced through central and northern Italy and across the Alps. William Story, hearing it in Venice, was deeply offended that Margaret had not trusted him enough to inform him. He soon forgave her, but in the villas up in Fiesole and Bellosguardo, overlooking Florence, the scandal was an endless source of satisfaction. And Ossoli, so obviously slow-witted, a stud . . . Oh, it was delicious.

In a small village church somewhere in Tuscany, on a date that remains a secret, Margaret and Angelo were at last legally married. The couple probably drank a glass of Chianti afterward with the rustic, half-illiterate priest — so different a padre from those Greek-

quoting, encyclopedic Calvinist pastors of Cambridge and Charles-
town. How strange and various is life to the adventuring spirit!

On the twelfth of March, 1850, Pius IX reentered Rome from his
enforced exile. Having endured a siege and hardships, many
Romans who had originally supported the republic felt a sense of
reassurance at the Pontiff's return. Also, Rome without a Pope had
seemed to them deeply unnatural. Fear for the future and nostalgia
for the past combined to make Pio Nono's return a festive occasion.
Throughout the city torches burned, crowds cheered, and bands
and orchestras played. With a salute — fittingly — of three
hundred cannons, the French soldiery received the papal benediction in St. Peter's Square. For Angelo, the Pope's return seemed to
settle his fate. It might be years before he could return to Rome;
nowhere in Italy would he be truly safe. The obvious solution was
to emigrate. Margaret, moreover, had finished writing her *History
of the Roman Republic,* and she needed to find a publisher as well as
to mend her personal relations with Horace Greeley, who had been
scandalized by tales of her "free love" in Italy.

On the seventeenth of May, 1850, at Leghorn, under a shining
blue sky, the Ossolis boarded the *Elizabeth,* a three-masted American merchantman under the command of Captain Seth Hasty, a
rugged, frank Yankee shipper from Maine whose wife shared with
him the perils of the sea. The *Elizabeth* was practically new; she carried, on this crossing, a cargo of old paintings, almonds, olive oil,
silk, 150 tons of Carrara marble, and Hiram Powers's statue of John
C. Calhoun. Margaret approached the voyage with voices of fore-
boding. "This time," she wrote, "I feel a trembling solicitude on
account of my child, and am doubtful, harassed, almost ill." The
voyage, in fact, began tragically. On the eighth day out, Captain
Hasty broke out in a fiery rash, his throat so constricted that he
could barely swallow. At Gibraltar he died, and the ship was de-
tained in quarantine for a week.

When it sailed into the Atlantic, an inexperienced first mate,
Henry Bangs, was in command. Two days out, Nino broke into a
feverish, burning rash. But the baby recovered, to the joy of all on
board. The trade winds blew gently, and the vessel sailed calmly
toward New York Harbor. On the last night of the voyage and
within sight of the American coast, the wind freshened and turned
to gale force. Bangs close-reefed the sails and remained on course
for New York, but off Fire Island, at four in the morning, in a

thundering sea, the *Elizabeth* drove hard into a sandbar. As breakers pounded the hull, the Powers statue of Calhoun — which Margaret had once admired in the artist's studio — broke loose and punched through the hull. Margaret, in her white nightgown, came on deck with Nino in her arms. Ossoli stood beside her, calm and resigned as he had been at the siege of Rome, the opposite of the usual caricature of the gesticulating, overexcited Italian. In the darkness, spray swept over them like driving snow. The *Elizabeth*'s boats were swamped. Attempts were made to swim ashore on loose planks; Mrs. Hasty succeeded, reaching the land unconscious but alive while others drowned in the breakers. A wave took Ossoli and he disappeared. Margaret handed her Nino to the steward and was herself washed overboard. Her body and that of Marquis Ossoli were never found. The steward was washed ashore, drowned, with the still-warm but lifeless little body of Nino in his arms. The pages of Margaret's *History of the Roman Republic* were lost in the Atlantic.

The news of Margaret's death devastated the Storys, as it did others who had known and befriended her. Wrote Elizabeth Barrett: "It shook me to the very roots of my heart." All felt that Margaret had been destined to suffer because of her extraordinary gifts.

The Storys, having spent the summer in the British Isles, were in Scotland when they learned of the tragedy. "Came home to find letters and the saddest of all news of Margaret and her child and her husband," Emelyn wrote. "How deeply I felt it, how sad I was made, I cannot here say; but pale was the sky, dull the face of nature when I thought of the friend I had lost." For Emelyn, Margaret's death seemed to cap all the depressing memories of those last months in Rome — the fear, the bombardments, the valiant lost cause. "My mind last night was so filled with thoughts and memories of Margaret Ossoli," she confided to her diary, "that I found no refreshment even in sleep. The vision of her as I saw her last on the steps of our house, and the memory of those troubled days in Rome kept coming back to me, and I felt so deep a sorrow that I could neither look before nor behind."

The Storys were at that moment cutting themselves loose from the tragic Roman months of revolution to return to Boston with their children and belongings. Italy was behind them now, its arcadian charm rent and smudged. William's plaster casts and marble blocks followed them when they sailed from Liverpool — with what apprehensions of the Atlantic one can only imagine. But they reached Boston safely, and briskly set about their former business. William had learned to sculpt well enough to execute the bust of his father, and now he must return to the law. In his absence, he found that, if anything, he had gained in stature among his peers, and at once, with characteristic energy, he set to work writing his *Contracts,* which he finished in record time (by 1874, the work was in its fifth edition). As the days went by, however, William's attention began to flag. He gazed out of the window at the snowy, smoky outline of the Boston rooftops and pined for the sight of those abandoned ruins and ocher walls. Like a tight collar, Boston slowly strangled his spirit and made him long for the liberty that Italy, and Rome in particular, seemed to represent for him.

One winter passed, and the discussions began between husband and wife. They decided, finally, that they were Bostonians at heart and that their true life lay there, in their native ground. But it was not time for a permanent reentry. They would try another Italian interlude, with William prepared to make another furious effort to become a professional sculptor. Rome might be papal again, but they would overlook the politics and speak their minds with compatible spirits like the Crawfords and Lewis Cass, Jr. In the summer of 1851, therefore, they sailed back to their beloved Italy. Story realized that it was a controversial decision, that his fellow Boston lawyers and jurists, who had looked to him to follow in the footsteps of the great Justice Story, would consider him more radical than ever — "Wild Bill" — so be it!

The crossing was again uneventful, but as the exiles approached the walls of Rome, Emelyn felt some apprehension. They had, after all, been outspoken supporters of the republic. But William's passport contained, after his name, the honorific "Esquire," and since the last two letters of that word, *re,* mean "king" in Italian, the Storys were startled to see the customs police bowing deeply and bawling out, "His Majesty, the King of the Esqui." Grandly, their carriage rolled into Piazza del Popolo.

A Story embellishment? Possibly, but it fits them. They moved smoothly, almost effortlessly, through charm of character, and money, and perhaps destiny, past the usual barriers of life. Rome, suffering a harsh restoration, received them like old friends, and by the following summer they were inhabiting Villa Ceni in the picturesque town of Castelgandolfo (the traditional site of the Pope's summer residence in the Alban Hills outside Rome). Story described it in this letter to James Russell Lowell: "a magnificent salon, sixty-three feet long and twenty-five feet high, with a billiard table at which I spend quite a third of my time playing with Cass." And he added, with his usual poise: "Tell Page [William Page, the painter] he must come here next winter. No place is like Rome; I have seen them all and I know it."

Before the Storys left this spacious villa to return to the city, William wrote a letter to Lowell that perfectly conveys the flavor of the enchantment of Italy for Americans like the Storys, who could afford to observe it, to choose what they liked and discard what they did not:

> Such a summer as we have had I never passed and never believed in before. Sea and Mountain breezes all the time, thundershowers varying with light and shade in the Campagna, donkeyrides and rambles numberless — a long, lazy, luxurious *far niente* of a summer, such as you would have thoroughly enjoyed. Just now the Pope is here and all is *festa*. Every day he makes a new excursion with all his *cortege,* and every town he visits has a rumpus to receive him. . . . When he rides, in his great gilt coach with his four black giants of stallions, what kneeling to his benediction as he enters the square, while tapestried hangings wave from the upper windows of the castello and boys cling to the grating of the tower! And the band bursts into a clash of music, and the organ inside the church, which is strewn with flowers and box, and lighted with pyramids of candles, groans and thunders softly. I never tire of these doings.

Clearly, the Storys had made their ideological peace with the restoration. They drank in the sensuous magic of Italy on its ancient plane of pagan color and emotion. Two months later, they were settled snugly and happily in a beautiful apartment at 93 Piazza di Spagna. "Every day that we live here," Story confided, "I love Italy better and life in America seems less and less satisfactory." And again: "There are a great number of Americans here this winter, but I have kept out of American society, having exchanged it for Italian, which I find agreeable." During that thoroughly agreeable winter of 1852–1853, he worked on several neo-Grecian pieces and an idealized Pan, molding, as well, a bust of his friend Lowell. Days of strenuous work in the studio were interspersed with others when the whole family would climb into their carriage in the morning and be driven to view ruins, monuments, galleries, and churches, or be wheeled out of the city walls into the countryside, taking a picnic basket with them, Story sketching while Emelyn played with the children. Emelyn's diary contains this glowing entry:

> To walk with William and Frank [Heath] around the Praetorian Camp — after having had the usual difficulty in determining where to go. Thence to a grassy hillside, whence W. made a sketch of old Rome as seen through an ivied arch; and afterwards to St. John Lateran, where we walked about the church and went into the vault under the Corsini chapel. Coming home by the Coliseum we met the Crawfords. Oh, golden day!

Fated to become rivals, the Storys and the Crawfords instead became friends. By the late spring, William was sharing an apartment with his fellow sculptor, both of them temporary bachelors while their wives and children were in the countryside. In July, William went by carriage to Florence, and then — an additional day's drive — to Bagni di Lucca, which had been the favorite summer place of the English for decades. Today, one can drive there from Lucca in about half an hour. The two-lane road, lined with majestic oaks, winds its way up a rustic valley, and one can easily imagine the carriages once rolling up that same bough-shaded road that has not been widened in two centuries. As its name implies, Bagni di Lucca was a hot mineral bath spa; above the pretty town, a dark, thick growth of chestnut trees lined the slopes. "Every evening we drive along the richly-wooded banks of the wild, roaring Lima [river]," William wrote,

> or else beside the rushing Serchio, where Shelley used to push his little boat to the Devil's Bridge. I have never lived an idler life. While the wind blows through the windows coolly, we sit and read and fall asleep over our books — and feel intensely virtuous when we achieve a letter. Of society there is none we care to meet but the Brownings, who are living here. With them we have constant and delightful intercourse, interchanging long evenings together two or three times a week and driving and walking whenever we can meet.

The golden days of that summer were followed, however, by weeks of tragedy in Rome, as both the Story children became critically ill with "Roman fever" (malaria?). In November their six-year-old boy died. His sister, Edith, survived, though the fever returned in gale force several times, and several times the little girl was, as Mrs. Browning wrote from Rome, "all but given up by the physicians." The boy's death, the near-death of his sister, sent huge cracks through the Storys' enchanting arcadian Italy. Of all human events, death most vividly and jarringly marks the passing of time. And shattered, too, was Story's self-confidence in his ability as a sculptor. Emelyn probably had less inclination to give him the rich emotional assurance that his insecurity demanded. Story brooded among his plaster casts and marble blocks. How many years had he been in Italy? Three? . . . four? My God, it was seven! Seven years . . . nearly a decade, and, let's see, Bill, what have you produced in all that time? What! Only a statue of your father and a few stylized fauns. Won't do, Bill, won't do.

Sadly, he helped Emelyn close up the apartment in the Piazza di Spagna. They drifted up to France, spending the winter of 1854–1855, their "last" European winter, in Paris in the company of Lord Lytton, de Tocqueville, and James Russell Lowell. But once back in Boston, William again pined for Rome. "He might live as an anxious, even as a misguided artist," Henry James wrote of him, "but he could not, apparently, live as anything more orthodox."

He worked at the law, adding another four hundred pages to his *Contracts*. It made him no happier. He wrote desperately to Lowell, who was still in Europe, of his beloved Italy: "My taste is spoilt for everything else — foolishly enough. Shall I ever be as happy as I was then? Ah, heaven, we can never repeat. Ardently as I desire to return, I *fear*. Things are so changed, *I* am so changed."

On July 2, 1856, the Storys were aboard the early Cunarder *America,* bound for Italy "for good." Richard Henry Dana, no longer "before the mast," was a fellow passenger and a fellow Italophile to reassure William and Emelyn of the wisdom of their decision. Others in Boston had clearly thought them crazy or decadent — including William's mother. If they were going to be stigmatized as eccentrics, nevertheless, the Storys would do it in style. On this definitive return to Rome they rented their definitive home, almost a palazzo in itself — an entire floor of the enormous Barberini Palace. The great travertine house had been built by Pope Urban VIII by cannibalizing the stones of the Coliseum, leading to that noted quip: Quod non fecerunt barbari, fecerunt Barberini (What the barbarians did not do, the Barberini did). Not only did the Storys move into an apartment as vast as the deck of an ocean liner, but the landlord, possessing more rooms than he knew what to do with, also threw in "upper rooms above the apartment," which William described as "some twenty at least, of every kind and shape, going oddly about, up little stairs, through curious holes, into strange lumber rooms, and then suddenly opening into large and admirable chambers." All this architectural excitement, Story added, for $250 a year — less than the rent they were getting for their prim little house in Boston.

In this marvelous labyrinth of a palazzo, the windows of which overlooked the sandy brown, slate gray, yellow travertine panorama of Rome, the Storys became the city's premier society couple among Americans. They had only to reach out to fulfill that social destiny that had always been indicated for them. "A dinner of forty-three persons in the studio above," William noted casually. Everyone who came to Rome came to see them. Their children did not merely read the tales of Hans Christian Andersen but heard them from the writer's lips when he was a house guest. The parties were legendary, combining as they did the brahmin of Roman society and the brahmin-bohemian of their artistic milieu. "Great gaiety and many costumes," William noted in his diary after a party organized by his son Waldo and Crawford's son Marion (the future writer) to celebrate the end of Carnival. "Marion as the Mephistopheles and I as Cimabue. . . . Lady D. and her daughters came . . . we had the whole English legation and several of the French."

For a few more years their social firmament was dominated by the orbits of those close and loyal friends, those peripatetic and cultured spirits who moved back and forth across the Atlantic, fading from Rome to reappear after a season — bundles of letters having been exchanged in the interim. The affection of those encounters and reencounters still leaps out at the reader from their letters and diaries. "You need not to be told how entirely we owe you the delightful summer we have spent at Siena," Browning writes to Emelyn in 1859. In the same year William received the following from Charles Sumner, convalescing from a near-fatal bludgeoning at the hands of South Carolina's P. S. Brooks on the Senate floor.

An abolitionist, Sumner had nearly paid for his convictions with his life: "Rome now, as when I first saw it, touches me more than any other place. Then I have been so happy with you. Perhaps it will be long before we meet again; but I cannot forget these latter delicious days."

In 1860 Mrs. Browning died. She had lived just long enough to receive the news of Garibaldi's invasion of Sicily, the beginning of the liberation and unification of her beloved Italy. Browning retired to England, and Story wrote to Charles Eliot Norton: "You cannot imagine how I shall miss him. For three years now we have been always together, never a day has passed (with the exception of two months' separation in the spring and autumn when he went to Florence) that we have not met."

Though Browning would return to Italy and to the Storys' loving company, in some mysterious way the death of his frail, slender, semi-invalid wife, Elizabeth Barrett, unraveled the knot, and those marvelous friendships loosened and drifted apart. The decade of the 1860s changed the social landscape both of Italy, where a new nation came into being, and of America, where a nation came apart. With the start of the Civil War in 1861, few Americans traveled to Europe except on official business. The Storys followed the fortune of the Union from Palazzo Barberini — from afar — and this absence more than anything else made remote their ties with the American homeland.

It is pleasant to be able to report that Story won his unlikely gamble to become a ranking sculptor. Busts of government officials and bodies of goddesses proliferated in his studio like a fabulous coral growth, all of smooth, gleaming white marble. It was what the age admired, and the 1862 Exhibition in London saw him suddenly hailed as a great talent and his *Sybil* and *Cleopatra* surrounded by crowds. Ebulliently, Story wrote to Norton: "I hope I have established myself on a new footing as an artist. I am going back to Rome full of good intentions and strong for work." Having started later than Greenough, Powers, and Crawford, and lacking their years of academic training, he had managed to rise to their same technical level. There was no lack of commissions now, orders that came not only from his circle of Boston friends and admirers but, at last, from the commonwealth and from Washington — the public monument being the mark of final recognition for a sculptor. In 1881, his bronze statue of Colonel William Prescott was set up on

RALPH CRANE

Rome's little Protestant Cemetery became the final resting place for dozens of foreign artists, including the poet Keats, American novelist Richard Henry Dana, and sculptor William Wetmore Story.

Bunker Hill. Three years later, his fine monument to Chief Justice Marshall, "erected by the Bar and Congress of the United States," was unveiled in Washington, D.C.

The final, mature years were approaching. Among the circle of friends who had shared that extraordinary appetite for Italy at mid-century, for the old Italy, the pre-united, pastoral Italy of the corrupt Papal State and the Bourbons of Naples, the nostalgic tone grew more and more marked. "How I wish you were here again as in the olden times, and that we again could wander about the streets of the city and through the mountain towns," Story wrote to Norton. And, a bit later, more plaintively: "Has the wild love of travel gone out of your blood as it has of mine? Are you growing respectable, solemn, professional and dignified?"

Before the eighties ended, the old group was dissolved forever with the death of Browning at Venice in 1889 and, a year and a half later, that of "Uncle James" Russell Lowell. For the Storys, too, the span was ending. They walked more stiffly through those great, high-ceilinged rooms at the Palazzo Barberini, rooms that were increasingly silent. Of the Story children, the eldest, Edith, had married a distinguished Florentine, who had a position at court. The others were busy, interesting young people, the middle son, Julian, serving his apprenticeship as an artist. On October 31, 1893, the mother and father festively celebrated their golden wedding anniversary at Edith's summer home in the Tuscan hills. Not a year later, Emelyn Story was dead.

"She was my life, my joy, my stay and help in all things," wrote William to an old friend. "What is left seems to me but a blank of silence, a dead wall, which when I cry out — and I *do* cry out — only echoes back my own voice. I cry out, where is she? And no answer comes."

On the fifth of October, 1895, William Story died. He and his Emelyn lie buried in the Protestant Cemetery in Rome, near Keats, near Richard Henry Dana.

CHAPTER SIX

any Americans were conscious of the rising tide of nationalism in Italy, and, like Margaret Fuller, sympathized openly with it. Italians, in turn, usually regarded Americans as a pathfinding people from a nation not so much revolutionary as morally alive. When Harriet Beecher Stowe visited Rome in the 1850s, a jeweler whose shop she entered recognized her as the author of *Uncle Tom's Cabin*. Handing her a beautifully wrought black onyx statuette of an Egyptian slave, he said, "Madam, we know what you have been to the poor slave. We ourselves are poor slaves yet in Italy. You feel for us. Will you keep this gem as a slight recognition for what you have done?"

William Dean Howells, appointed U.S. Consul to Venice during the Civil War for having written a pleasing campaign biography of Abraham Lincoln, heard the city's common people muttering rebelliously when they were out of earshot of Austrian officers or their police spies. Gondoliers, rowing him across the Grand Canal, confided to the young American their love of liberty and asked about Jefferson and Lincoln. All the gondoliers, Howells wrote, "awaited Garibaldi as in a second coming."

Following the defeat of the Roman Republic in 1849, the red-bearded revolutionary had made his way to New York aboard the English packet ship *Waterloo*. After a grand welcome from his many American admirers, Garibaldi faded into a modest existence on Staten Island where he joined the local volunteer fire brigade and a Masonic lodge. For a while he worked on the docks, carting barrels of tallow. Though he took out first papers and would often claim, toward the end of his life, to be an American citizen, he did not remain in the United States long enough to become one. He soon returned to the sea and to his earliest calling as a sailor, finding a command at Lima, Peru, and crossing the Pacific.

He sailed his merchantman, the *Carmen,* to Hong Kong and Canton, then down to Australia and back to America, biding his time. In 1860, Piedmont's moves on the European checkerboard gave him his chance. Loading a thousand men (including a few Americans) onto side-wheelers off Genoa, Garibaldi invaded Sicily. His admirers in the U.S. had raised a hundred thousand dollars in support of this enterprise, which was received with wild enthusiasm in New York and other American cities. The youthful Henry Adams, meeting Garibaldi in newly liberated Palermo, thought him "the very essence and genius of revolution."

A Philadelphia sea captain, William Dahlgren, even bought three vessels in Marseilles which he baptized the *Washington,* the *Oregon,* and the *Franklin,* using them to ferry supplies to the red-shirted invaders as they crushed the last Bourbon garrisons in Sicily and crossed the Strait of Messina onto the tip of the Italian boot. (For these services Dahlgren would be made an admiral in the new Italian navy.) As Garibaldi's scruffy irregulars drove north to liberate Naples, they met the blue-uniformed troops of Piedmont's King Victor Emmanuel, who had at last broken the Austrian stranglehold on northern Italy. Though Garibaldi was a guerrilla leader, he was willing to help the short, stout Victor Emmanuel, monarch of the independent northern Italian kingdom of Piedmont, to extend his rule over the entire peninsula. For the first time since the fall of the Roman Empire fourteen centuries earlier, Italy was being united under its own government. Tuscany adhered to the swiftly coalescing Italian state, and then Venice. The final prize, however, eluded the victors for a few years more. That prize was the Papal State, and the historic Italian capital, Rome.

(Overleaf) *In the final year of the Papal State, 1869, Pope Pius IX imparted a Sunday blessing to thousands of the faithful assembled with their carriages. Nowadays, the crowds in St. Peter's Square are so great that private vehicles are banned. The huge awning over the balcony of St. Peter's (the loggia of the benedictions) indicates a summer's day.*

Soldiers from the victorious Italian army posed self-consciously in front of Rome's shell-pocked Porta Pia, where the defeat of the papal garrison a few days earlier, on September 20, 1870, completed the unification of Italy. It commenced eleven years earlier with King Victor Emmanuel of Piedmont's military campaigns in the north and Garibaldi's invasion of Sicily.

In 1870, the crushing defeat of Napoleon III at Sedan in the brief Franco-Prussian War at last lifted the umbrella of French arms from the Eternal City which General Oudinot had established there. The colorfully uniformed Zouaves were withdrawn to defend "la patrie," and Rome lay open, inadequately defended by its own papal army. As the combined Italian forces breached the ancient Aurelian Wall at Porta Pia on September 20, the city's populace went half mad with exultation, and fear.

Pius IX — for it was still he on the throne of St. Peter's — left the Quirinal Palace for the final time, his enormous dark carriage rumbling over the cobblestones on what would truly be a historic ride. The Quirinal was abandoned and the doors sealed, so that King Victor Emmanuel's officers had to seek out a locksmith before they could get in. As Italian soldiers fanned through Rome, driving back the last dispirited papal troops toward the Tiber, American residents took care to fly the Stars and Stripes from their balconies as well as the new Italian "tricolore" to ward off revolutionary looters. A stray bullet passed through an upper window of the American consulate on Via Sistina, but U.S. citizens escaped any personal injury. When Consul David Maitland Armstrong and his small staff saw a white flag flying from the dome of St. Peter's they knew the battle was over.

The Pope, shaken and stricken by the loss of his temporal domains, barricaded himself in the Vatican and refused to recognize the new Kingdom of Italy. As Catholics the world over offered prayers for their Pontiff, depicted as a "prisoner of the Vatican," the new government began seizing church property all over Rome, ejecting nuns and priests, and turning the buildings into offices or barracks.

The threat of confiscation hung over the little North American College on Via dell'Umilta off Piazza Venezia, where some twenty American seminarians were enrolled. Romans had grown used to seeing these boys marching through the city two abreast as they went to their classes wearing a distinctive uniform of military cut which, except for the long black gown worn under the jacket, gave them the look of Civil War chaplains. The boys were woken at five-thirty every morning by the beadle's cry of "Benedicamus Domino," to which they replied as cheerfully as possible "Deo Gratias." Study and prayer continued all day until ten P.M. Despite this spartan regimen, the American seminarians were proud of their

Miss Angela Middleton, an American belle in Rome, was photographed before a painted backdrop, in 1878, with the French painter Albert Besnard (seated) and Count Primoli, a famous nineteenth-century photographer of Italian life. So many Middletons came to Rome during the nineteenth century that eventually several members of this wealthy South Carolina family intermarried with Italian aristocrats.

college and quickly established a high academic standard. In competitive exams, one American lad reported, "we beat the Propaganda all to pieces," "the Propaganda" being the missionary college "for the propagation of the Faith."

The American hierarchy went apoplectic when Italy's equivalent of the Supreme Court finally decided in 1884 to seize the American College, stripping it from the Sacred Congregation of Propaganda in whose name it was held. By then, American bishops had invested a quarter of a million dollars in the seminary and they were furious at the idea of being kicked out. Bishop Michael Corrigan of New York, an early alumnus, called on President Chester Arthur and won his support. Cables went out to the American ambassador in Rome, William Waldorf Astor, who called on the Foreign Minister to make remonstrances. Astor's intercession was successful, and the Italian government ruled that the North American College was American property and exempt from seizure. The American seminarians continued to be marched around the city in double columns for years, and at the turn of the century they took to playing baseball at Villa Borghese, with a copy of Spalding's rules in the rector's hands.

Though foreign governments quickly recognized Rome as the new capital of the Kingdom of Italy, Roman society continued to feel the shock of 1870 for years afterward. Led by Prince Massimo, the "black" nobles who had held high positions at the Papal Court went into a kind of mourning for the vanished past. Shutting their palaces, they gave no more balls or supper parties and kept much to themselves. One great American matriarch of the age, Louisa Ward's daughter Mrs. Winthrop Chanler, who had converted to Catholicism, held social gatherings for these "blacks" at her splendidly ornate rooms in the Palazzo Odescalchi (designed by Bernini). The Abbé Liszt was a habitual guest and composed some of his celebrated pieces on Mrs. Chanler's piano.

Another American, Francis Augustus McNutt, also entertained these despondent papal nobles in the Palazzo Doria Pamphili, in Piazza Navona, which he restored to its former splendor after evicting nineteen tenants. McNutt was probably the only American to have been a chamberlain in the pre-1870 Papal Court, and he and his wife gave two balls a year at which all good "blacks" from those bygone days were welcome. At these affairs, McNutt reported, "veritable princesses and forgotten dukes, ancien regime, who had not been seen at social gatherings for many years, emerged from the shadows of their closed palaces and lent the distinction of their antiquated *grandezza* to our salons."

McNutt was able to entertain in this lavish style — his wife's servants once poured four hundred cups of tea in a single afternoon while footmen in pale blue livery stood at the foot of the grand staircase — largely because he had married a Newport heiress whose money was available for the restoration and upkeep of the Doria Pamphili palace. In the later decades of the nineteenth century, the phenomenon of American wealth suddenly burst over the Italian social scene as it did over the rest of Europe. Previously, the image of Americans had been that of a rather frugal homespun folk, but across the Atlantic, where Italian, Irish, and Polish immigrants were welcome to man the forges and dig the coal, enormous fortunes were materializing. The national income of the United States actually trebled in the quarter century between 1875 and 1900, and it was a time when the rich could keep their money. The kind of Americans who traveled to Italy often had a great deal of money. It had been handed down intact by successful immigrants like Henry James's Irish grandfather, who landed in Boston penniless and left a fortune valued at three million dollars. Money, which vanished from the defeated Confederacy but which accrued in the banks of the victorious North. Money, which posed the question of how it should be spent.

Not surprisingly, it was a woman who personified American money in Italy at the close of the nineteenth century. Celebrated in Boston for her devil-may-care wit and her flirtations, Isabella Stewart Gardner was enough of a nouveau riche to discover the pleasure of possessing what had lain in aristocratic hands for generations, and yet clever enough to dissimulate the element of greed with a generous and intelligent hospitality to people such as Henry James and John Singer Sargent, who sometimes saw through her but cherished her friendship.

Small, shapely, formidably energetic, New York–born "Belle" Stewart was married to an amiable Boston real estate millionaire, Jack Gardner. (He was once characterized as "a pullman car coupled to a locomotive.") The Gardners began making periodic trips to the Continent in the 1880s, when travel was much safer and more comfortable than it had been a half century before. Large, luxurious steamships had replaced sailing vessels on the North Atlantic and increasingly, in Europe, the railroad train chuffing clouds of smoke and steam took over long-distance travel from the horse-drawn carriage. The age of the motorcar had not quite yet arrived, however, and when Mrs. Gardner alighted from a first-class train carriage in Paris, or Rome (where she was met by the Storys), her host would help her up into a fine landau or brougham drawn by a team that would clip-clop gracefully down the leafy avenues.

Usually the Gardners would sail to Southampton in the late spring, see expatriate American friends like James and Sargent in the English capital, and then cross the Channel to Paris. After social calls and fittings for Isabella at Worth's, the famous couturier, the Gardners would head southward across the Alps to Venice where their summer home was a palace on the Grand Canal owned by an expatriate Bostonian, Daniel Curtis.

In the course of an argument on a Boston streetcar, Curtis had punched a man in the nose. The man had turned out to be a judge, and after spending three months in jail Curtis had exiled himself more or less permanently to Venice where he rented and then bought the beautiful red Palazzo Barbaro close to the Academy Bridge where the Grand Canal makes a final sweeping s-curve before debouching into the lagoon at St. Mark's.

The Gardners spent two hundred British pounds to rent the Palazzo Barbaro for the summer, and what they got for their money would be difficult to come by today at any price. When their train reached Venice, the Curtises' three resident gondoliers, Batista, Tito, and Fernando, would be waiting for them with enthusiastic smiles and cries of welcome. The Gardners would be helped into one of the black gleaming gondolas, their luggage loaded into the other. Mrs. Gardner could sit back against the cushions, her delicate skin protected by a bonnet and veil, and, lifting the veil with a gloved hand, renew her aquaintance with one palace after another down the Grand Canal until the noble Renaissance shape of the Barbaro came into view from beneath the arches of the Academy Bridge. Waiting for her on the landing would be Arcangelo, the butler, and Fernando, the cook, with the various parlormaids. In Venice, as nowhere else, Mrs. Gardner lived like an aristocrat — "Donna Isabella."

Late-morning excursions on foot (St. Mark's was a short walk over the narrow and intimate Venetian lanes) would be followed by lunch, perhaps a nap with the shutters drawn against the midafternoon heat but with the reflected light of canal water still seeping up through them to play on the ceiling, then tea in the gondola as the Gardners were rowed to view a painting, or to some artist's studio. The Barbaro was usually full of houseguests during the summers when the Gardners were there, and at her candlelit suppers in the great *sala,* Isabella would bring together resident expatriates like the Newport widow Katherine De Kay Bronson, who had been Browning's companion during his final years, and the various artists and musicians passing through Venice.

In the course of these glorious Venetian summers, Mrs. Gardner began to acquire Italian paintings. She started slowly enough around 1880. Some years before, Harvard's Charles Eliot Norton had encouraged her to collect first editions of Dante and other Italian poets but the lady, with her shrewd business sense, saw that at that moment the real bargains were to be had not in books but in Old Masters.

Italian aristocrats were increasingly hard pressed to meet the bills the *amministratore* kept bringing into the study. The new government in Rome had passed new property taxes, and, worst of all, a law banning primogeniture. This meant that a princely estate and its land could no longer be inherited solely by the eldest son. Property now had to be divided between all the legitimate heirs, and the breaking-up of princely fortunes was inevitable. At the same time, wealthy Americans were urged to acquire the masterpieces of Europe almost as a civic duty.

At the opening ceremonies of New York's Metropolitan Museum in 1880, the principal speaker, Joseph C. Choate, reminded his affluent audience that "probably no age and no city has ever seen such gigantic fortunes accumulated out of nothing as have been piled up here during the past five years." He then offered, with well-tuned wit, a timely suggestion: "Think of it, ye millionaires of many markets, what glory may yet be yours, if only you listen to our advice and convert pork into porcelain, grain and produce into priceless pottery, the rude ores of commerce into sculptured marble." He finished his speech to thunderous applause, which echoed as nowhere else in the drafty halls of Italian palazzi whose owners sorely lacked those rude ores of commerce. A good many Italian aristocrats were disposed to sell the palace bit by bit in order to maintain, for one or two lifetimes longer, their traditional style and social prestige.

The Gardners bought eclectically at first, and some of their early purchases in Venice and elsewhere turned out not to be Old Masters but only poor relations of the Old Masters. Isabella, however, was a quick study, and at a Paris auction in 1892 she snapped up for a mere six thousand dollars one of the finest of Vermeer's paintings. Titled *The Concert,* it depicted a Dutch drawing room, bathed in Vermeer's lovely light, in which a young girl is singing while another accompanies her at the keyboard. Since only thirty-six Vermeer canvases are known to exist, this small, exquisite domestic scene is today worth well over a million dollars.

Two years after that coup, the Gardners invited to lunch at the Palazzo Barbaro an art scholar who would guide Isabella's purchases from then on. Young and strikingly attractive, Bernard Berenson had been a prize pupil of Charles Eliot Norton at Harvard, and the Gardners — sight unseen — had contributed to a special scholarship fund launched by Norton to enable the promising graduate to continue his studies in Europe. Born into a modest Lithuanian Jewish family, Berenson had been brought to America as a child but the old continent had remained in the roots of his consciousness. In the course of his long life, Italy became his true home, as it had for so many other artists and scholars.

In that year of 1894, Berenson renewed his tenuous acquaintance with Isabella Gardner by sending her a copy of his first book, *The Venetian Painters of the Renaissance,* with a gentlemanly note: "Your kindness to me at a critical moment is something I have never forgotten." The young man was then living with a lady of American Quaker descent, Mary Costelloe, who had relinquished her husband, and to some extent her children, to live at Berenson's side, but whatever Mrs. Gardner thought of this scandal it did not keep her from seizing the opportunity and engaging Berenson as her art buyer in Italy. In return for a commission, he was to purchase for her the finest Old Masters coming on the market. Though Jack Gardner (who may have been jealous of Berenson for other reasons) would suspect the agent of jacking up his commissions, Isabella had entered into a brilliant partnership with the man who was virtually to rewrite the history of Italian Renaissance art.

Through his ever-widening circle of contacts, Berenson was able to spot paintings almost at the moment their aristocratic owners decided to part with them. Often, Berenson also had the dual role of guaranteeing that the Old Master was genuine and correctly attributed. His services were worth whatever he charged, and soon letters were speeding to Mrs. Gardner at her Boston home offering her such masterpieces as Botticelli's *Virgin and Child.* The painting was owned by one of the most important of the "black" aristocrats in Rome, Prince Chigi, and his price was sixty-three thousand dollars. Though the painting was classified as a "national treasure," Berenson was able to smuggle it to Boston before the enraged Italian authorities could act. His sources in the art market made it possible for Berenson to cast a wide net, and each time one deal faltered (like the attempt to buy Gainsborough's *Blue Boy*) Berenson had another waiting in the wings. Soon after the Gainsborough affair, Berenson wrote excitedly to say that Titian's *Rape of Europa* was available for a hundred thousand dollars. He instructed Mrs. Gardner to cable YEUP (yes for Europa) if she wanted it and

NEUP if she didn't. She flashed back YEUP. In 1898, she also bought Rembrandt's stupendous *Storm at Sea* through Berenson, plus Rembrandt's earliest self-portrait for only fifteen thousand dollars.

These paintings, plus more than a dozen others which Berenson found for Mrs. Gardner, were enshrined in Fenway Court, the Venetian-style palazzo which the grande dame of Boston built for them. Today, the building and its treasures comprise the remarkable museum she bequeathed the citizens of Boston.

The trade in pictures, lucrative as it was, troubled Berenson deeply. He had wished to be a scholar, not a dealer, and in 1900 he began building his great art library in a spacious villa at Settignano, outside Florence, called I Tatti (probably because it had originally been inhabited by an Italian family named Tatti). Berenson rented the villa initially from its English owner, Lord Westbury, but with the earnings from his picture dealings he was soon able to buy it and an entire hillside as well, to ensure his privacy.

For Berenson, Florence was a logical choice. It could claim to be the international capital of art, not only because of its Renaissance palaces and museums but because the whole city — from the narrow and historic streets around the Palazzo Vecchio to the villas tucked away in the surrounding hills of Bellosguardo and Fiesole — was steeped in an air of aesthetic contemplation. There was virtually no industry in Florence; it was not an administrative center. It was a city where people lived amid culture. Small, tidy, and refined compared to Rome, Florence was also an easy city for Americans to settle into because the British had been there for generations. They had long since hung their Madonnas in the living room, and they spoke some Italian just as their servants had a smattering of the King's English. The hillsides around the city were sprinkled with English schools like Miss Sheldon's, and there were even five or six English-language newspapers in Florence at the turn of the century. Each of these papers sent a reporter around to the hotels (like the Boston, alongside the Arno) to check the register once a week and find out what families were in town. Well-introduced newcomers among the Anglo-Americans could get invited to Princess Poniatowski's midweek parties or the banker Fenzi's gala Saturday-night balls, where English and French were spoken by all.

At first, Americans were discreet interlopers in what amounted

Handsome and magnetic as a young man, Bernard Berenson so fascinated Mary Costelloe (daughter of a Quaker minister who had settled in England) that she left her barrister husband and risked the loss of her children to run away with the American art historian to Italy. She and B.B. — as Berenson's friends called him — were married in 1900.

Berenson's private secretary, Nicky Mariano, became his closest companion in Florence. Pretty in her youth — she was a World War I refugee — "she types my MSS," Berenson wrote of her; "she discusses my prose, she keeps house, runs affairs and charities, smooths down malcontents, receives troops of callers, arranges all social matters, walks with me, etc., etc., etc."

to a small Britannic colony. But it was not like Americans to be retiring and soon they were in the thick of the city's artistic and social
life. James Henry Wilde, who resigned his seat in Congress in 1843
to devote a few years to the study of Italian literature, added great
luster to the reputation of his countrymen by discovering in the
archives of the Palazzo Vecchio proof that a portrait of Dante lay
among the figures in a fresco decorating the chapel of the Bargello.
Francis Alexander, another American, became the city's foremost
art restorer. Every morning picture dealers would hang a mournful
row of battered canvases on a wall facing his study and talk and
argue volubly among themselves, until Alexander finally appeared
at the window with all the majesty of an Oriental potentate to see if
there was anything worthy of his attention. The city's urchins
thought him enormously rich because he carried silver coins in his
hat.

Years before Berenson arrived on the scene James Jackson Jarves
put together a stupendous collection of early Renaissance paintings,
in very trying personal conditions. An American eccentric who had
edited a newspaper in Hawaii in the 1840s, Jarves was bitterly opposed by his own family and hounded by financial woes, and yet
managed to amass a collection that the Yale Museum now reckons
as one of its most valuable possessions. Jarves also wrote many
books and articles about Tuscany in particular, and his *Italian Ram-
bles* is one of the best descriptions of life in those years.

Berenson, however, was able to drive his roots deeper than these
other American expatriates, and leave a lasting imprint in the very
selective memory of the Florentines. Though anti-Semites at all
social levels attacked him for years, his fame grew steadily among
people whose opinion counted, and it was typical of Florence that
no one looked askance on his liaison with Mary (before they married) or his other love affairs.

As in other times and places where the pursuit of art is placed
above commerce, in the scale of social values, and moneyed people
are able to withdraw in refined tranquility from the ordinary strug-
gle for survival — as in ancient Rome or twentieth-century Hollywood — nineteenth-century Florence witnessed a greater emphasis
on sexuality and a corresponding moral tolerance. A great many
unusual people, and unusual couples, lived in the villas at Fiesole
and Bellosguardo.

Berenson's companion was the daughter of a prominent Quaker

minister settled in London, whom the young art scholar had met at a dinner party when the handsome young woman was already the wife of a distinguished English barrister and the mother of two small children. Mary Costelloe came from a family that was artistically and intellectually inclined (her sister Alys was Bertrand Russell's first wife), and her fascination with Berenson was, at first, more or less accepted by her husband. When the affair continued, however, both in London and on the Continent, the couple parted, and he won custody of the children. Mary's money helped to support Berenson during his early, struggling years in Italy, before he became the well-compensated consultant to Mrs. Gardner. To Mary's considerable relief, he did the honorable thing and married her in 1900, when they settled at I Tatti.

Because there were so many interesting people with interesting stories in Florence, the villas at Bellosguardo were great listening posts for writers like Henry James. It was in one of them that he first heard the story of Claire Clairmont, the English beauty who had been Byron's mistress, and of the attempts of an English sea captain to get his hands on the precious manuscripts Byron had left her. When the old woman finally died, the captain rushed back to Florence only to find that her spinster niece had inherited them, and that her price for the papers was marriage. He fled from the house. James changed this tale only slightly, giving it an American heroine and setting it in Venice, when he turned it into his short novel *The Aspern Papers*.

As with any city that has a very strong character (one thinks of Paris, London, New York), Florence impinged itself on people's lives, and its indigenous stories tended to repeat themselves generation after generation. One common theme was that of the failed romantic. James wrote of the young American artist who came to Florence intending to paint the perfect Madonna, but then "the noiseless years had ebbed away and left him brooding in charmed inaction, forever preparing for a work forever deferred." Another theme, in life and fiction, was romantic and sexual betrayal. In our own post–World War II days, I know of a lovely American girl who came to Florence to study art and fell in love with a count who gave her a Ferrari. He also gave her a little bambino, and after the birth it transpired that he was not a count at all but a businessman from a town in the Adriatic with a wife and three children. He had

In the summer of 1913, shortly before World War I would put an end to the gracefully stylized world of their art, the novelist Henry James sat for this portrait by his old friend from Italian days, John Singer Sargent. Though some critics carped that the portrait made James look like a businessman, the author called it "a very fine thing indeed. Sargent at his very best and poor old H.J. not at his worst."

escaped into a dream life, and gone into debt to buy the Ferrari. I actually saw the Ferrari, with its beautiful pearl gray body by Pininfarina rusting under a fig tree. Henry James would have appreciated the story behind that Ferrari.

CHAPTER SEVEN

ust in the years, on the cusp of the nineteenth and twentieth centuries, when Isabella Stewart Gardner was assembling her priceless collection of Old Masters and Berenson was becoming famous for his studies in Renaissance art, the influence of classical and Renaissance Italy on American minds began to ebb. This change happened by degrees, and for complicated reasons that were more easily identified afterward.

At the time of the American Revolution and for a period following the idea of imitating the forms of ancient Greece and republican Rome held a very important place in the thinking of the men who had fought the War of Independence against King George III. To a certain extent, too, Americans were reacting to influences from the Continent, and particularly from France where the neo-classic style seemed befitting to the grand empire, so reminiscent of ancient Rome, of Napoleon Bonaparte. Yet Americans had another motivation for their veneration of classical models. For obvious reasons they felt an aversion to the English heritage of their fathers, and it seemed to many of them that the new republic in the New World should look for inspiration to the democracies of the ancient world and to the republican period of the early Renaissance, which found its apogee in Florence.

Thomas Jefferson taught himself Italian as a young man, reacting to those same inchoate sympathies. Later, as minister to France, when he was in love with the Italian-born painter Maria Cosway, he endured the discomfort of a muleback crossing of the Alps to

SMITHSONIAN INSTITUTION (NATIONAL COLLECTION OF FINE ARTS)

A too-slavish imitation of the prevailing neo-classic style led American sculptor Horatio Greenough to fashion this toga-clad statue of George Washington as a Roman senator. After Greenough shipped the huge statue to Washington, D.C., from his studio in Florence, it was exhibited at the Capitol amid general derision.

make a brief foray into northern Italy. Though Jefferson was unable to reach Florence or Rome, Italian influences stayed with him all his life and his celebrated house, Monticello, was modeled on an Italian Palladian villa.

All through the nineteenth century, the classical buildings of Greece and Rome exerted a strong fascination on American architects. Courthouses, state legislatures, railroad stations, and the dwellings of the wealthy were erected with the imposing pillared facades and pediments that characterized Greek and Roman temples. Yet there came a moment, late in the century, when Americans inevitably began to feel that the industrial revolution would lead to the creation of entirely new forms in their expanding urban landscape — when the phenomenon of "modern architecture" began to unwind from the sheets of still-inconceivable technological progress.

That broad perception of a wholly new age was still indistinct in the middle years of the century, when sculptors like Greenough, Crawford, and Story struggled in Italy to imitate the classical past and Charles Eliot Norton lectured to overflow audiences in Boston on the divine poet, Dante. Norton's Harvard students were not merely attending a poetry course, but a learned exposition of the values and political ideals that had allowed the city fathers of the early Renaissance states to create, by their inspired use of public and private money, the greatest flowering of architectural and artistic expression the world had ever known. If the Renaissance masters had built incomparable churches and other public edifices, and if those buildings had been so magnificently frescoed on the inside by painters from Giotto to Michelangelo, then there had to be choice involved. People in power had made the right decisions.

That question of choice intrigued Americans at midcentury because it was obvious to them that their own cities — which had been mere villages in the wilderness — were undergoing a rapid expansion. Money was available for noble edifices and their decoration by native artists. Would American choices be as inspired as those of the Renaissance city fathers? At a time when New York's Flatiron Building and the other prototype skyscrapers were still in the future, the Renaissance continued to shine like a guiding beacon toward those choices that would have to be right not only at the moment, but in the centuries to come.

Like every other deep-seated ideal, that of the Renaissance, and of

Italian classicism in general, had a powerful momentum. And so it happened that toward the end of the nineteenth century, just as the counterinfluence of the new technology was becoming apparent, the eminent American architect Stanford White kept a yacht anchored off Leghorn onto which workmen carried marble balustrades, fireplaces, and cornices. All these bits and pieces of stately Italian homes were destined for the neoclassic mansions of American millionaires who remained, in that eminently capitalist age, the taste-setters of the nation. And when J. Pierpont Morgan built his famous library on New York's East Thirty-sixth Street in 1905, the beautiful building was in Renaissance style.

With the establishment still enamored of this rather old-fashioned Italian influence, the notion that America should have a school of architecture and the arts in Rome continued to gain ground. Louis XIV, after all, had established the famous French Academy in the Villa Medici near the Spanish Steps, where a young artist who had won the coveted four-year scholarship known as the Prix de Rome was able, in James Russell Lowell's approving words, to take "the coinage of the past and remint it to suit his own purposes, giving to it his own image and superscription."

Why should America not have its own academy, perhaps situated on one of Rome's other hills, where architects could "remint" the temples of Rome and the palaces of Florence for statuesque public buildings in the expanding cities of the United States? The question was hotly discussed at the Chicago World's Fair in 1893, which the sculptor Augustus Saint-Gaudens called "the greatest meeting of artists since the 13th century." In that bullish spirit, he enthusiastically discussed plans for an American academy in Rome with architect Charles Follen McKim (Stanford White's partner), who would design some of the nation's finest turn-of-the-century buildings, such as the Boston Public Library and New York's University Club. McKim and Saint-Gaudens, inspired by the Renaissance, believed that in a public building the paintings and statues were not just decorative but were on an equal plane with the architecture, and that concept was the linchpin of the projected academy.

An American school of architecture was opened in November 1894 on the top floor of Rome's Palazzo Torlonia yet it was an unsatisfactory compromise, plagued by debt from the first day, and McKim became the agent responsible for something a great deal more solid and important. He was a fearfully busy man. He had

been asked to redesign the Capitol in Washington, D.C., and to re-
store the White House, among other major commissions, and it
was a testament to his energy that he continued, in spare moments,
to pursue the ideal of an American academy.

The problem was money and it was not resolved until McKim
was summoned by that most famous of American financiers, J.
Pierpont Morgan, to design the Morgan library and a house for
Morgan's daughter. A shy man, McKim raised the subject of the
American academy at various times, until finally Morgan, stung by
the spirit of competition, consented to match an endowment of
$130,000 pledged by another millionaire, Henry Walters, a railroad
man and art collector.

Early in the new century Morgan made one of his periodic trips
to Rome and concluded that the academy should be built on top of
the Janiculum hill, where an American expatriate, Mrs. Clara Jessup
Heyland, had offered her Villa Aurelia for $500,000 as part of the
grounds. Morgan judged the price too steep, yet he slyly took an
option on land adjoining the Villa Aurelia. After Mrs. Heyland died
and generously bequeathed her massive, salmon-colored villa to the
yet unbuilt academy, Morgan threw in the land he had secretly
purchased. Altogether Morgan advanced $365,000 to the project.
Other pledges of funds from Walters, William Vanderbilt, Henry
Frick, and Harvard ensured that the long-deferred plan would come
to fruition at last.

Though McKim had died in the meanwhile, his firm was se-
lected, fittingly, to design the academy. The building that material-
ized was large and handsome, of Florentine inspiration, with a
graceful central courtyard. At the time of its inauguration, on the
eve of World War I, there were only three schools of architecture in
the entire United States.

Morgan saw the nascent academy for the last time in 1913, when
the grounds were covered with scaffolding. Ill and lame — he
would die in Rome later that year — he climbed, with difficulty, to
an upper balcony of the Villa Aurelia to survey the construction.
Offering to buy even more land, he cried, "Spread it out! Spread it
out!" as if afraid that the old dream of American classicism in Rome
might falter at the last moment, on the very slopes of the Janiculum.

Morgan had built U.S. Steel and had come to dominate Wall
Street so totally that in the panic of 1907 the entire country held its

breath while Morgan consulted and decided in his East Side Renaissance Library. In his secretive heart, Morgan had always cherished for Rome a love typical of so many nineteenth-century Americans. He would arrive in the spring and check into the new Grand Hotel where the management reserved a corner suite for him. Huddled in the back of a hired carriage under a funnel-like top hat, Morgan spent hours wandering about the city, for its Promethean atmosphere moved him always as did the melancholy grandeur of its ruins where time could not obliterate the forms, the pretensions, of the original achievement.

Morgan was deeply impressed by the Vatican as well, where his friend Salvatore Cortesi, the Rome bureau chief of the Associated Press, took him to call on Pius X and the Secretary of State, Cardinal Merry del Val. Once, when the cardinal was delayed, he sent word to Morgan who was waiting in the Borgia apartment with its vaulted ceiling and frescoes by Pinturicchio. "I am perfectly happy here," Morgan told the emissary; "I only wish I could have a bed so that I could lie on my back and remain for hours looking at this ceiling."

A player of solitaire in moments of tension, Morgan would drop in on his American expatriate friends in Rome and spend hours at the card table, betting cautiously, sometimes losing on purpose to draw a squeal of delight from a pretty woman who had bested the king of Wall Street. He knew the Storys well, and their new American neighbor in the Palazzo Barberini, Princess Jane San Faustino.

Born Jane Campbell in Kentucky, not beautiful but witty and strong-minded, she had married Carlo Bourbon del Monte, who was the prince of San Faustino, rather later than the average for most brides. And perhaps in part because she was a woman rather than a girl, she quickly established herself as a power in Roman society. She was direct and unpompous, as most Americans are, and these qualities matched up well with the traditional naturalness of the Roman aristocrats, who then had little of the bourgeoise smoothness of nobles today. The aristocrats of Rome had spent much of their time, for centuries, on country estates, they frequently preferred to speak in Roman dialect, and their turn of speech was fundamentally earthy. It was not an aristocracy of exquisite, high-strung performances, like the court at Versailles.

Since she was not artificial and had character, Jane San Faustino fitted very well into Roman society. People sought her presence and in time she became a legend. Her parties were among the most lavish in Rome. One year she turned half of her enormous apartment into a Roman *osteria* (a typically Roman tavern) with clusters of grapes hanging from the ceiling. The titled young bloods and jeune filles pined for her invitations, especially to her Grand Ball in November which opened the Rome social season. Carriages, and later motorcars, would be lined up by the dozen outside the Palazzo Barberini, disgorging ambassadors with sashes, generals, admirals, aristocrats of historic name, Roman principesse, and a goodly number of American girls. All over Europe it was the era of the American girl and nowhere so much as in Italy.

Mary King Waddington, sister of General Rufus King, the U.S. minister to the Papal State just before and after the Civil War, who was brought up in Rome and married a future Prime Minister of France rather than an Italian aristocrat, recalled overhearing an Englishwoman at a tea party complaining sourly that "when I was young, people came to Rome to educate themselves and enjoy the pictures. Now one sees nothing but American girls racing on horseback over the Campagna with a troop of Roman princes at their heels."

The object of the chase was sometimes not so much the girl as her dowry of dollars, to pay the ever-mounting cost of maintaining a noble life-style. In James's *Golden Bowl* there is a hauntingly subtle description of the fictional Prince Amerigo in which the prince, who is marrying a wealthy American girl, Maggie Verver, is introduced to the reader as if he were the palazzo he is trying to save. His eyes are described as "the high windows of a Roman palace, of an historic front by one of the great old designers, thrown open on a feast day to the golden air."

Around the turn of the century one of the titled families of Florence was faced with selling off its valuable estates and vineyards. The only asset left, or so the story goes, was the old nobleman's handsome and amusing son. The other relatives got some mad money together and shipped him off to America with instructions to marry an heiress. Within a few months he returned, accompanied by a pretty and very wealthy bride. The vineyards, which today are worth millions of dollars, are still in the family.

For those "black" Roman aristocrats whose families had remained loyal to the defunct Papal Court, marriage to an American had a special significance and a value beyond that of money. "In

those days it was absolutely the thing to have an American wife,"
explained Prince Rospigliosi, himself the descendant of a marriage
between a Roman prince and a Philadelphia Haseltine. "Before
then, when Rome was still under the popes, the aristocratic families
were very closed. They only married one another. The idea of marrying an American was like a wave of liberation." Marrying is
always a great change in one's life. The idea of marrying an American girl was tremendously attractive to the younger generation after
1870, because it was a leap over the frustrating obstacles of a past
that was no longer alive in anything but form, and of a future for
which these young men were mostly unfitted. "It was a way for
them to make a new start in life," Prince Rospigliosi concluded.

By the end of the century, the obstinate attempt of the "black
families" to oppose reality was beginning to collapse anyway. The
children could not be expected to mourn the end of the Papal State
indefinitely, and they increasingly turned out for suppers and
dances alongside their peers among the "white" aristocrats — those
loyal to the new order who served at the court of King Victor Emmanuel and his successor, King Umberto.

One of the first times the "blacks" came back into society was at
the 1876 Carnival ball in the residence of George Wurtz, secretary
to the U.S. legation in Rome. Wurtz was considered an eccentric in
that he claimed to be the only American royalist, but he and his
plump wife gave splendid parties, and the next morning all Rome
heard that "blacks" and "whites" had been seen dancing together in
the ballroom of the Wurtzes' apartment in the Palazzo Antici-Mattei. I would like to know how many American girls were also
swirling around that dance floor, and what they thought of that
strange, archaic, yet poignant Roman feud. Did a "black" Romeo
find his "white" Juliet in the Wurtzes' ballroom, or was she a Boston debutante in town for the season?

The American girls who did marry Italian nobles, "black" or
"white," discovered that they had very few rights, particularly if
they were Protestants. A Catholic husband did not need a formal
divorce to leave his Protestant wife (and take her money), because
the union was not recognized by the Catholic Church. At that time,
even a Catholic bride had few rights in Italy. Her property was au-
tomatically administered by her husband. He also had final jurisdic-
tion over the children, where they should live and be educated. A
leading woman lawyer in Rome, Olga Pryor, remarked recently,

"Only after World War II were Italian women able to obtain the vote, equal rights in the job market, and — last of all — equal rights with their spouses over property and children."

Most of the marriages endured, however, and children were born of them. The children were half-American, yet they grew up in an Italian atmosphere, in the constant awareness of being aristocrats. Theirs was a lonely upbringing in many cases. When Berenson's secretary Nicky Mariano went to dinner once at the Villa Medici in Fiesole, where Lady Sybil Cuffe then lived, she asked why Lady Sybil's daughter Iris (the future Iris Origo) was having supper upstairs with the governess and not with them. "Iris never appears at the dinner table because she has not yet come out," Lady Sybil replied.

Henry Brewster, whose own father had grown up as an expatriate in Bellosguardo, remembers the loneliness of his childhood. "I was always with my Scottish nannie, or the servants, and was only occasionally presented to my parents as an object." He feels that his mother suffered over this separation, which was imposed by his father. "My father was a very nice man, but very conventional in his ideas, and he regarded it as the right thing that I should be with my nannie and not too much with my mother."

The nannie, of course, was an added foreign element in a child's life, with another nationality, another culture, and another set of memories and prejudices. It is not surprising that many of these children grew up with deep inner uncertainties. Often they remained deeply attached to a villa, a set of people, a city in Italy, because it rooted them.

Mrs. Winthrop Chanler, visiting New York, received an unusually blunt warning on this score from Henry James. Expatriation, he said, amounted to "shifting the burden of decision on the shoulders of the next generation." Troubled, she turned for advice to the artist John La Farge who had lived in Europe and particularly in Italy. "Dear Henry," was his reply, "he forgets how easy it has become to cross the ocean. The issue that so worries him has ceased to exist."

CHAPTER EIGHT

The years between 1900 and what would be called the Great War were the halcyon period for Americans in Italy. Industrial wastes, smokestacks, and the exhausts of noisy, darting little motorcars had hardly begun to intrude on the pastoral beauty of a landscape that had always been measured by the pace of the human footstep. Shepherds with their flocks and farmers' children driving great snowy oxen still dotted the countryside.

The great craze was not yet driving, it was bicycling. People gave up their horses for bicycles, and undertook journeys of hundreds of miles. There is a letter by an American banker named Bates who lived in Geneva and pedaled all the way to Sicily and back for his health, after his doctor advised him that it would be salutary. It was certainly a strenuous prescription. As any G.I. who fought in the Fifth Army can testify, except for rare stretches of fertile plain, Italy is one rough mountain range after another. Bates also had to pedal through the Alps at the beginning and end of the trip. He did it, though, and reported that when he came to the steep parts he would simply heave the bike up on his shoulder.

Walking remained a favorite form of locomotion. Henry B. Fuller, a Chicago businessman who worked in an office "where little business was done" and consequently had time to pursue a second career as a writer, wandered all through central Italy on foot or in dilapidated old diligences. His peregrinations produced a charming travel book, *The Chevalier of Pensieri-Vani,* which described the twilight of a classical time when gentlemen scholars could still roam through a storied countryside and find time for *pensieri vani* (idle thoughts). The smart men's club in Florence in those years was the Walking Party, which marched on Thursdays, as explained in a ditty composed by one of its British members:

> *I will not comment on the fact that Thursday was the day*
> *Selected by the members, on which to slip away;*
> *However you'll admit it's odd, it raises certain doubt,*
> *Since THURSDAY, you will recollect, is when the cook goes out!*

Slipping away on the servants' day off, some forty British former colonial officers, American gentlemen of leisure, and a few men of other nationalities would trudge up the hill to Fiesole to have lunch at the Aurora Hotel (which still exists and is reasonably priced and pleasant). Maggie Fergusun told me, "I can remember my mother and I having our meal alone on that day because daddy was at the Walking Party." She recalls that the club almost broke up in heated dispute when some of the members started riding the new Number 7 streetcar up to Fiesole. In clement weather, groups of Florentines would walk all the way to Bagni di Lucca, where Queen Victoria had come in the summers to take the waters.

The pace of life was still slow; people were easygoing and polite. On one of his return trips to Italy, William Dean Howells noted with admiration that "the Italians had not learned bad manners from the rest of us." He reveled in the courteous intimacy of the ordinary people, and wrote, after a few months in Florence, that "I would rather have had a perpetuity of the *cameriere*'s smile when he came up with our coffee in the morning than Donatello's San Giorgio, if either were purchasable; and the face of the old chambermaid, full of motherly affection, was better than the facade of Santa Maria Novella."

Italy was a country that you could take pretty much as you wanted. Back home relatives of Americans in Italy often wondered indignantly why in God's name Cousin Elizabeth or Uncle Ben chose to live in a musty land that seemed so operatic compared to the industrious and pioneering United States. Little did they realize, often, that the question contained the answer: some people did not want to display their patriotism, or be responsible for the company budget, or even be good neighbors, and were much happier tucked away in a villa in the hills of Tuscany, or Lake Como, where they made their own lives as they pleased (assuming they had some income). The civil authorities in Italy left them alone. Taxes were minimal. And if they were atheists, or homosexuals, or lesbians, unless they tangled flagrantly with Italian law, no one held them accountable for what, in other countries, would have been regarded as sinful peculiarities. There was no need for the unconventional to drop their eyes when they passed the chief of police on the sidewalk. Italy was an old and humanistic civilization. People were tolerant, and sympathetic.

There was a good-natured informality to life, beneath the late Victorian formality. When Buffalo Bill and his Congress of Rough Riders came to Rome, the Duke and Duchess Caetani invited the celebrated cowboys to lunch and then challenged them to a contest: the cowboys would have to keep their saddle on the hot-tempered Caetani ponies, raised in the Pontine marshes, while the Caetani grooms, or *butteri,* would try to tame the American bucking broncs. After lunch, everyone went outside the walls of Rome and the contest was held. Not surprisingly, the Americans won it.

The novelist Marion Crawford, who was Mrs. Chanler's half-brother and one of the celebrities of the time, could remember standing as a boy on the Aurelian wall, along with John Singer Sargent and other American boys, and bombarding with acorns the pigs that grazed outside the Porta del Popolo, when nearly all the land outside the walls was farmland. When Crawford reached manhood Rome was a European capital, and the former sleepy fields and meadows were covered with ditches and scaffolding. Via Veneto was laid out in the midst of a huge property scandal in the 1880s, involving bribes and a Belgian cardinal. Under the original post-1870 city plan, a piazza as large as Piazza Navona was to extend from the Porta Pinciana to where the American embassy stands, covering the whole upper part of the Via Veneto to the width of a block on either side, but real estate interests prevailed and it was never built. On the lower part of Via Veneto — up to World War I — there was a dairy, with cows, where one could buy fresh milk.

The Tiber, which for centuries had flowed between gentle green banks through the heart of Rome, was hidden from view like a shameful thing by engineers who argued that steep stone banks were needed to prevent flooding. In time automobiles began to appear among the horse-drawn carriages, their skinny hard-rubber tires rolling over horse droppings on the sandy, yet-unpaved road along the Tiber. Crawford derided the noisy flivvers as "sudden death carts" and swore that he would not buy one.

A brawny, handsome man, Marion Crawford was the son of Louisa Ward and the sculptor Thomas Crawford. He had grown up in Rome but had remained American, a true cosmopolitan spirit who found his first job as a cub reporter on the Allahabad Indian *Herald* (in Pradesh state). A successful novelist by the time he was twenty-seven, he courted his American bride in Constantinople, then settled with her in a magnificent villa on the Amalfi coast where every morning he diligently wrote five thousand words in a studio overlooking the sea, with Capri in the distance.

The Crawfords went to Rome, London, and home to New York and Boston almost every year. At a Brooklyn shipyard Crawford bought a seventy-foot schooner that had been driven aground in a storm and offered for scrap. He refitted the yacht and thereafter sailed it across the Atlantic.

A good many Americans who had known and loved the old, preindustrial Italy, Crawford among them, were uneasy at how the new nation was turning out. So much had been expected from the Risorgimento by its foreign admirers that some disenchantment was natural, but the Italian Kingdom appeared to many eyes as a rather tinny copy of the great European powers north of the Alps. The iridescent hopes that a united Italy would write a new page in world history were fast disappearing. Instead, Italy burgled Africa for its own little group of colonies, and grandiose ministries that hardly reflected the real state of affairs in the country arose inside Rome. As one foreigner observed sardonically, "Strange that Italy should have the largest finance ministry in the world, and the smallest finances."

As a fledgling colonial power, the Kingdom of Italy had to maintain a large army and navy, and it had to have iron and steel mills, machinery, hydroelectric power, and all the trappings of a modern industrial state. These things took money, and in a country with few natural resources for export, the government was forced to increase taxes sharply. Small landowners and peasants in the south who had been just able to get along in the slow, agrarian economy of the Bourbon kingdom, were now, in effect, put out of business, and agriculture languished.

"Improved agricultural methods are what Italy needs above all

ROLOFF BENY

One of Italy's finest writers in this century, the patrician Marchesa Iris Origo is the daughter of an American, William Bayard Cutting, Jr., and Lady Sybil Cuffe. After a sheltered childhood in Fiesole's Villa Medici, the Marchesa managed an agricultural estate near Siena with her husband and wrote her books. The Last Attachment, *on Byron;* Leopardi; *and the autobiographical* Images and Shadows *are the best known.*

Built for Cosimo de' Medici on the Hillside of Fiesole overlooking
Florence and the Arno valley, the magnificent Villa Medici was home to
Iris Cutting, the future Marchese Origo, during her school-age years. Her
mother, Lady Sybil Cuffe, bought the house from Lady Oxford in 1911,
at the close of an epoch when Florence was filled with foreign artists and
aristocrats of a dozen nationalities. (© *Eric Lessing, Magnum Photo*)

Like his contemporaries Washington Allston and Samuel F. B. Morse,
John Vanderlyn studied in Rome. His *Ariadne,* exhibited in 1812, became
the first famous nude in American art. The painting (*overleaf*) suggests that
Vanderlyn became familiar with the work of Giorgione and Titian.
(*Joseph & Sarah Harrison Collection, Pennsylvania Academy of Fine Arts*)

A more adventurous spirit than this languid nineteenth-century portrait suggests, Margaret Fuller — the daughter of a Massachusetts senator — arrived in Rome with an assignment to write dispatches for Horace Greeley's *Tribune*. The revolution of 1848 and the siege of Rome in 1849 transformed her into the world's first woman war correspondent. She also helped nurse the wounded at a hospital run by the pioneering Italian feminist Princess Belgioioso. (*Portrait of Margaret Fuller by Thomas Hicks courtesy of Constance Fuller Threinen*)

(*Opposite*): The late American heiress and art collector Peggy Guggenheim traveled the Grand Canal in her personal gondola. In 1949, after a stormy marriage to the artist Max Ernst, she bought the Palazzo Venier dei Leoni, which is known in Venice as the "unfinished palace" because it consists of only one floor surrounded by the city's largest private garden. Her great collection of twentieth-century art is on permanent display in the palazzo, which is now a museum administered by the Solomon R. Guggenheim Foundation. (*Christopher Cox*)

The American Academy's director in 1979, Michigan classicist John D'Arms, enjoyed lunch with the Fellows at a long outdoor table set in the academy's graceful courtyard. This summer scene typifies the relaxed and convivial atmosphere at the academy — the only privately funded U.S. overseas academy of the arts. (*Courtesy M. Vallinotto.*)

(*Opposite*): New York's Francis Cardinal Spellman (at lower right) sat pensively in St. Peter's with other cardinals during the Second Vatican Council. The use of Latin in complex theological debates placed the American participants at an initial disadvantage, though they later exerted great influence over vital issues like religious freedom. (*Hank Walker, Time-Life Photo Collection*)

This photograph of an anonymous couple, strolling along a fishermen's quay in the Italian Riviera town of Portofino, seems to sum up everything that left tourists so enraptured with Italy in the years of the postwar economic boom when the national spirit could not have been sunnier. (*Walter Sanders, Time-Life Photo Collection*)

else," Maud Howe wrote despondently. "She has the finest soil and climate in Europe. She could supply half the continent with fruit, [olive] oil, and wine if she had a little more common sense!"

By the end of the nineteenth century, instead, the country hemorrhaged people. A half-million Italians were forced to emigrate each year, most of them to the United States. To close the circle, one of the justifications for Italy's African colonies was that so many peasants were turning into emigrants. If they went to America, the Italian state lost them for good. If they went to the colonies, they remained Italian.

Emigration was the great safety valve in a poor and badly ruled country, but it did not prevent outbreaks of that most telling form of rebellion — terrorism. People who are shocked today over the Red Brigades usually forget that Italian anarchists were the terror of Europe just before World War I. In 1894, they murdered the French President, Sadi Carnot. Three years later they shot to death the Prime Minister of Spain, Antonio Canovas. The following year Luigi Luccheni, in a particularly revolting crime, stabbed to death the Empress Elizabeth of Austria in Geneva. In 1900, a young Italian immigrant returned to Italy from New Jersey and, at Monza, shot to death King Umberto in revenge for the suppression of strikes.

Italy's social tensions were largely invisible to the Americans who moved through their privileged orbits in Rome and Florence, and as yet there was little large-scale unrest in most parts of the peninsula. It took the First World War to bring these tensions to the surface. In 1914 the government did not immediately commit Italy to either side, but approached the Allies and the Austro-German Powers to see what conditions it could obtain. The thing was very coldly done. The Prime Minister, Antonio Salandra, later admitted that the majority of Italians were against intervention at the time he concluded the Treaty of London on April 26, 1915, pledging Italy to enter the war within one month.

Yet, on May 23, when war was actually declared against Austria, there was strong popular support for it. The Austrians had been regarded as the oppressors for over two centuries, and it seemed like a continuation of the Risorgimento to wrest away other Italian-speaking areas from the Austro-Hungarian Empire.

The problem was that to wrest away those territories along Italy's northeastern frontier, the Italians had to attack into the Friu-

ARCHIVIO FOTOGRAFICO COMUNALE, ROME

Via Condotti looked virtually the same in the 1880s as it does today, except for a profusion of awnings over the doors and windows of shops. The photograph was taken from the base of the Spanish Steps. The fountain in the foreground, called the "barcaccia" (or skiff), by Gian Lorenzo Bernini's father, Pietro, is much-beloved by tourists as a place to dip their feet on hot summer days.

lian Alps. Ernest Hemingway, who had come over as a nineteen-year-old volunteer ambulance driver, described in *A Farewell to Arms* the black humor among Italian soldiers as they attacked one mountain range at a cost of thousands of dead only to see, beyond it, an identical mountain range. It was a campaign plotted by bumbling statesmen and generals, and by 1917 morale was dangerously low and the troops were worn out.

The Austrians were in much the same condition, except that the withdrawal of Russia from the war following the Bolshevik revolution made dozens of Austrian and German units available for action on the Western Front. Before shifting these predominantly German troops to France, it was decided to hit Italy first with a sudden attack and try to knock her out of the war.

The attack was launched at night on October 24, 1917, at Caporetto — a mountain village now in Yugoslavian territory. It was spearheaded by German troops, and among the Germans was a young officer, Erwin Rommel. The Italian line buckled, and by the next day the retreat of the Italian armies had turned into a rout which carried the attackers practically to Venice.

Many more Americans fought in the Italian campaign after Caporetto. The violinist Alfred Spalding, Walter Wanger, the future Hollywood producer, and New York's Fiorello La Guardia were aviators stationed at the joint U.S.-Italian air base near Foggia, and flew missions in big Caproni bombers to help stabilize the front along the Piave River. By then, Hemingway was in Milan's Ospedale Maggiore, having been seriously wounded by an Austrian mortar shell and decorated for heroism. He would base his descriptions of Caporetto, in *A Farewell to Arms,* on his later eyewitness reporting in Asia Minor, when he was covering the Greco-Turkish war as a correspondent for the Toronto *Daily Star* and saw panic-stricken Greek refugees evacuating Smyrna (now Izmir).

Though Italian troops regained most of the territory lost in the Caporetto debacle, the great retreat there was a political event too. It exposed the shallowness of Italy's attempt to become a major power on the nineteenth-century imperial model, and the price people had paid for superficial or incompetent leadership. Revolt was in the air. Workers seized factories, and Italy seemed on the verge of revolution. Fascism arose, as a counterrevolution, and something more. It proposed that Italy could only become great by increasing its commitment to nationalism and resurrecting the long-dead

Wounded by an Austrian machine gun and mortar fragments in 1918, volunteer ambulance driver Ernest Hemingway recuperated at Milan's Ospedale Maggiore where his infatuation with an older nurse partially inspired his novel A Farewell to Arms. *Hemingway received two medals for his courage in carrying other wounded men to safety, including the second-highest Italian award for valor, the "Medaglia d'Argento."*

Roman past of Caesar and Augustus. The new Caesar — or so he wished to be regarded — marched on Rome in 1922, five years after Caporetto. The king acquiesced meekly. All over Europe, defeat on the battlefield had been fatal to royal houses. The Romanoffs were dead, the Habsburgs and Hohenzollerns in exile. The Italian royal family could count itself lucky, at first, to have been propped up by Benito Mussolini.

Hemingway returned to Italy as a roving correspondent for the *Star* when Mussolini had already marched on Rome. He was one of the Americans who was not taken in by the dictator, and it is worth remembering, now that Hemingway's writing is beginning to be dismissed, just how good a man he was. In terms of Italy, certainly, he was the heir to all the fine young Americans like Washington Irving, Cole, Morse, Margaret Fuller, and Thomas Crawford, who had come to Italy with a great curiosity to learn and an equally strong sense of values. In a piece that appeared in the *Star* in January 1923, Hemingway cut Il Duce down to size at a time when many Americans were enamored of him — "Mussolini, Europe's Prize Bluffer" it was called. Hemingway had gone to a press conference at Lausanne, where an international meeting was in progress. Mussolini was sitting at a desk, absorbed in a book, and Hemingway could imagine the leads being composed by his fellow correspondents: "When we entered the room, the black-shirted dictator didn't even raise his eyes from the book he was reading, so intense was his concentration." The *Star*'s correspondent sneaked around the desk on tiptoe and stood behind the famous dictator to see the book. "It was a French-English dictionary, and Mussolini was holding it upside down," Hemingway informed his readers.

In all respects, large or small, fascism came to represent a real break with the Italy of the past, though it was not always immediately apparent. "It's amazing when you think of it," Harry Brewster said to me one day in Florence, "how clearly the two great wars divided this century into such different eras." He was talking about his family, but it was also true in a general sense. We were walking toward a little trattoria in the working-class neighborhood below the Bellosguardo Hill, past narrow, two-story houses with mustard-colored walls. In the first fourteen years of the century, the fine carriages still rolled through that little street, and the residents of the neighborhood were artisans or maids and cooks for the people inside the carriages — Edith Wharton and Henry James among them — who used a lot of domestic help. But with World War I that kind of leisurely international society broke up. Florence lost perhaps half of its foreign residents.

Then came fascism. The walls of the little street down which we were walking were plastered with posters of Mussolini. People gave each other the Fascist salute and were no longer necessarily so polite to foreigners. In Milan the futurists said that the trouble with Italy was its reverence for the past. Art, culture, the villas of Tuscany, Edith Wharton, and the carriage were all to be thrown into the garbage can. What Italy needed, they said, was machinery and guns. Harry Brewster, who was seventeen when Mussolini came to power, didn't want to live under fascism, so he went to England, became an English citizen, and completed the return leg of that long journey begun by Elder William Brewster when the *Mayflower* sailed from England bound for Plymouth, Massachusetts.

The American attitude toward fascism was a many-sided thing, as it has been more recently in other countries. "Mussolini was not popular in Boston," Henry Cabot Lodge told me once, and surely he was not. Yet at a reception a few years ago in a country that was just emerging from the Fascist coil, the wife of the American ambassador remarked vigorously to several people in the receiving line, including myself: "These countries need to be ruled by a strongman, or they don't function — isn't it a shame?" I include this indiscretion because it so perfectly synthesizes what the general American feeling was toward Italy after Mussolini marched on Rome. God help us, we're still stuck with the old saw that finally the railroads ran on time, and no one bothers to add the corollary that a huge, twenty-year chunk was taken out of the nation's civil development, and that finally twenty thousand Americans had to sacrifice their young lives, and hopes, and whatever they could have become, to remove the evil.

Undoubtedly, in the twenties many Americans reacted to Mussolini with the Nordic bias so trenchantly expressed by the ambassador's wife. Chaos was going to end. Italy was going to work as northern countries did. It was going to goddamn well shape up. What illusions! The shaping up was mostly a Potemkin village, as World War II would prove so clearly, and the illusions fostered during those twenty years left the Italians fundamentally off balance as they entered the postwar years. Twenty years of a Fascist regime is a long time. The Great Depression hit America hard, but it did not kill Congress or a free press, and it did not last twenty years.

To Americans living in Italy, the problem of how to respond to fascism was naturally much more immediate and often painful. If you were married to an Italian and he enthusiastically put on his black shirt, what were you going to do? Many American expatriates, or those who had married Italians, were initially relieved by the march on Rome. The country had seemed on the verge of a Bolshevik revolution in 1920. Now the danger of that, or the illusion of the danger, had passed. The memory of rioting strikers faded as union leaders fled abroad or were clubbed into silence. On the tiny island of Ventotene, fifty miles northwest of Capri, you can still see the arid, sun-scorched prison buildings where the regime isolated its Socialist and Communist enemies. In contrast to other dictatorships, however, the Italian one was relatively benign. It didn't dent the Italian love of life, and in the regime's early years there was an enthusiasm among the Fascists for remaking and re-forming Italy, for doing great things, that most foreigners found appealing.

The American writers and artists, and the society people who were in Paris in the twenties, would come down to Italy often to visit the charming little towns on the Italian Riviera or the expatriate haunts of previous generations of Americans in Florence and Rome. The very rich went to Villa d'Este, the great hotel on Lake Como that was always awash with limousines, furs, jewels, and love affairs. It was the age of the Rudolph Valentino gigolo types, and the Villa d'Este, like other luxury hotels of this type, had professional escorts in evening jackets to trot the ladies around the dance floor. "Mothers and daughters were always falling in love with the same one, and there were terrible dramas," remembers a woman who was a young girl then. September was the season of the millionaires at Villa d'Este. Pierpont Morgan, Jr., would come from America, and sometimes an early Hollywood star like Mary Pickford as well.

The Venice Lido became famous in the early twenties, thanks in part to an American-style promotion campaign in which Elsa Maxwell was involved. This extraordinary fat woman made her living by arranging parties for governments, clubs, hotels, or simply for rich people, and she could pick up the phone and call the Aga Khan or the Rothschilds.

The Lido, which she launched in 1923 with spectacular parties, is a narrow strip of sand dividing the Venetian lagoon from the Adriatic Sea. Today it's out of fashion except for conventions and the film festival, but in those years it was exciting, elegant, and fun. You went out to the Lido at night from Venice, seated in the glass-enclosed cabin of a speedboat, with its leather seats and polished wood and brass, the dark water gliding by with contrails of spray, perhaps a beam of moonlight laid on the water, and at its edge the runny, magical city lights. Twenty minutes, and you were stepping onto the dock of the Casino, where people gambled and danced and drank until the early hours, when they returned by speedboat to the city.

In the late morning, you'd make the same trip back to the Lido and go to a private beach, very flat and broad, with its encampments of striped tents on the white sand. Barbara Hutton and her husband of the era, the Dane, wore matching bathing suits and had their hair dyed the same color. Everyone tried to get invited to the Cole Porters' parties when they rented the Palazzo Barbaro from the Curtises in the summer of 1923. The following year the Porters had the Papadopoli palazzo, and for three summers after that, the enormous Rezzonico, where the Brownings had once lived.

After World War II, a millionaire who said his money came from Mexican silver mines, Debeisteguy, turned up in Venice, rented the Palazzo Labia, and began to throw huge parties. Movie stars paid hundreds of dollars for an invitation. But Venetian society never wholly liked Debeisteguy, and people told each other, as one told me, that "the last really elegant party ever held in Venice was the Cole Porters' red and white costume ball at the Palazzo Rezzonico." And that is quite a reputation to leave in any town as snobbish as Venice.

At that famous ball, gondoliers in red and white lined the palazzo's marble staircases with flaming torches in their hands, and the Porters supplied their guests with four kinds of red and white paper costumes beautifully made to represent Venetian dress of the past. There is an anecdote attached to the ball, concerning a friend of the Porters', a frequent houseguest who was left off the invitation list. Outraged, he showed up anyway and stalked into the kitchen, where the help knew and greeted him. When they were distracted momentarily, he seized the trays and pots containing much of the midnight dinner and heaved them into the Grand

Canal. Then he rushed into the ballroom and shouted, "Ladies and gentlemen, dinner will *not* be served."

Whether this particular story is true or not, food-throwing and object-throwing is part of Venetian lore. After all, it is the one city in which to throw yourself out the window in a fit of depression. Another such story, this one guaranteed to be true, concerns the Curtises' Palazzo Barbaro, where the butler and one of the gondoliers hated each other. The gondolier delighted in wearing his fancy traditional uniform, which he kept spotlessly clean. After lunch the butler would come into the dining room, and if the gondolier was at his post on the landing below, he would carelessly heave the remains of the Russian salad out the window. "I don't know why it was always Russian salad," said the person who related the story, "but it was."

Many American celebrities wandered in and out of Italy in those years. Scott Fitzgerald was one. Another was Gary Cooper, who walked out of his studio in 1930, went to Rome, and stepped into the arms of Dorothy Frasso, a New York heiress estranged from her aristocratic Italian husband. She owned the splendidly frescoed Villa Madama in Rome, now used by the Italian government for high-level meetings and as a guest house for foreign visitors. Marchesa Terry Canevaro remembers meeting Cooper at Dorothy Frasso's lavish parties: "He was incredibly beautiful and a little foolish, with so many Italian girls flocking around him and he replying to their conversation in bits of broken Italian." Rome society believes that Cooper was "polished up" by Marchesa Frasso, and she allegedly took him around to the best Italian tailors and introduced him to a great many polished people, including a dozen Italian cavalry officers who invited the "cowboy" to a steeplechase contest. It was a tough course, and Cooper, at one water jump over six feet of rocks, found himself staring down at what he later described as "a lake bordered by the north rim of the Grand Canyon." He made it to finish second in a field of four, eight of the cavalrymen having gone down.

Not even Cooper, however, quite matched the elegance of the Cole Porters, whose Venetian summers ended in 1927, when police raided the Palazzo Rezzonico. Linda Porter was away, and the cops reportedly found her husband and various friends with a flock of young Venetian boys, including the police chief's son. Porter, upon being asked firmly to leave Italy, did. By then, Bernard Berenson was bruiting about the story of his love affair with Linda Porter, but since it was generally believed that she was unresponsive to men, many people suspected B.B. of embellishment. Said one longtime expatriate, "Berenson had this extraordinary ability to make others take him at his own evaluation. It's a very special gift that few people have."

Berenson had become a celebrity himself by then, and the visitors' book at I Tatti was always thick with distinguished names. When the Wall Street banker Thomas Lamont went to Italy to negotiate a loan to Mussolini's government, he first stopped at I Tatti, and Berenson tried to talk him out of it on the basis that U.S. money shouldn't be backing the regime. Lamont replied realistically that big banks loan money to any government able to repay it, and that, moreover, American policy aimed at the stabilization of European currencies, including the lira.

Berenson continued to live in Italy because of its art and beauty, but he made no secret of his antipathy toward the regime. John Walker, who lived at I Tatti in the 1930s, recalled: "People always imagine I Tatti as a place where we sat around discussing paintings with the master, but Berenson was bored of talking about art. He was far more interested in politics, in what Roosevelt was doing, in the dictators. By the time I lived there, I Tatti had become an antifascist hotbed. Moravia came there often, and so did a lot of known opponents of the government. If you'd had a really repressive regime in Italy, I Tatti would have been blown sky high. Ciano protected Berenson, who was everything he shouldn't be politically — a Jew by birth and an outspoken anti-Fascist."

Walker, born in Pittsburgh and a boyhood friend of the Mellon children Paul and Ailsa, had studied art at Harvard and, upon graduating, was sent to I Tatti by the Department of Fine Arts so that he could study with Berenson. "I lived with the Berensons almost as though I were their son for three years," Walker said. Offered the post of Professor of Fine Arts at the American Academy, he moved to Rome and became engaged to the daughter of the British ambassador, Sir Eric Drummond.

They were married in February 1937, but not before an Italian embassy employee had committed the perfect crime at their expense. He was a spy for the regime, and as Ciano wrote in his diaries Il Duce was privy to all the most secret British reports.

DAVID LEES

*A legend in his own time, Harvard-educated art critic **Bernard Berenson** was still absorbed in this Bellini Madonna in his villa, I Tatti, as an old man of ninety. The son of a Lithuanian immigrant, Berenson revolutionized art history with his brilliant concepts and meticulous research.*

Shortly before the wedding, Walker's mother arrived from the States with a very valuable gift for her future daughter-in-law, a superb diamond necklace. Fearing theft, Mrs. Walker asked Sir Eric to keep it in the embassy's safe. When the spy found the necklace in the red leather dispatch box along with papers he intended to read, he realized that there, sparkling before his eyes, was a flawless case for larceny. Even if Sir Eric denounced the theft, the Italian government would never prosecute so as not to admit it had a spy in the British embassy. The employee confirmed everyone's suspicions by promptly building a showy villa on the Appian Way.

Walker believes that Mussolini kept the Italians poor and thus, "incompetent and bombastic" as he was, preserved the country's beauty. "Oh dear, it was such a beautiful country then," Walker told me nostalgically when we met in London. "But then, B.B. always said, 'You should have seen it when I came here in 1910. Then it was really beautiful.'"

The beauty of Italy, the pleasure of living there, held Walker so spellbound that when he was offered the post of chief curator at Washington's new National Gallery, he almost turned it down in favor of becoming an expatriate in Rome. His wife argued for Washington, however, and so did Berenson. The master of I Tatti was not about to follow his own advice, however, and even when the regime stepped up its anti-American bombast and began to lace it with anti-Semitic attacks to please Hitler, B.B. stayed right where he was.

Many of the second-generation American expatriates were real fellow-travelers of fascism. The Fascist *podesta* (roughly, party chief) of Florence was Beppino della Gherardesca, whose mother was American. If he was able to strut around at the Cafe Doney, it was thanks to her money, yet he seems to have felt no loyalty to America. The mixed parentage had a lot to do with it, particularly if the father was an Italian aristocrat. The children became members of the aristocracy at a time when Italy was still a kingdom and having a title meant something. Older Italians bowed to you, and that privilege was hard to shake off or resist. Maggie Fergusun remembers that when she returned to Florence at the end of the war, one of her old half-American aristocratic friends sought her out and apologized. "I was wrong to believe in fascism," he said. "I hope you'll forgive me." Charitably, she did.

Though she was born in a Florence hotel, Maggie had never considered herself Italian because both her parents were American: "It never occurred to me that I was ever anything but a pure, unadulterated American." A lot of her friends who were "half this and half that" had trouble deciding what they were. To the children of Italian fathers, who had grown up in Italy, the American legacy was often tenuous. Princess Jane's lovely daughter, Virginia, married Edoardo Agnelli, the heir to the Fiat empire and the only son of the company's founder, Senator Umberto Agnelli. When Edoardo was forty-three, he was killed instantly in Genoa Harbor after landing in a seaplane. He stood up to get out of the taxiing plane when it struck a log, and he was hit in the head by the propeller.

His widow was still a beautiful and interesting woman, and her being half-American contributed to a restless, stormy independence of character that would be better understood today than in the lingering Victorian puritanism of northern Italy in the 1920s. "My mother felt enormously the fact of being half-American," Suni Agnelli told me. Suni, Virginia's daughter and the sister of Fiat chairman Gianni Agnelli, is a handsome, vigorous woman who is a parliamentary deputy in Rome. "She was not at all conventional, as Americans are not."

In the 1920s Princess Jane would spend her summers on the enormous beach at Forte dei Marmi, north of Pisa, at that time one of Europe's most fashionable resorts. Society girls would bring their American boyfriends to meet her, as Dorothy Frasso did when she was Gary Cooper's lover. One summer Princess Jane told the beachboy to summon an exotic, attractive man who walked along the shore every day and was said to be a political prisoner, confined to Forte dei Marmi and forced to report to the police every day. "Aren't you Malaparte? Come here. I want you to talk to me," she said.

Curzio Malaparte, the journalist and novelist who would one day write *The Skin,* sat and talked with Princess Jane at the foot of her striped beach tent. So Virginia Agnelli met Malaparte. She was a lonely, beautiful thirty-five-year-old widow, and she had a love affair with the writer at the house where he was under semidetention. This and other indiscretions caused the old patriarch Senator Agnelli to claim custody of her seven children. When she later tried to take them to Rome from Turin, police boarded the train in mid-journey and hauled them off. All this has been charmingly and sensitively told in Suni Agnelli's book *We Always Wore Sailor Suits.*

It is never easy in Italy to go up against powerful establishment figures, and it was doubly so in the 1920s and 1930s, when Mussolini set the tone. In one of his essays, Luigi Barzini told a wonderful anecdote about Mussolini stopping to pee by the roadside and everyone else in the official party — generals, diplomats, ministers — lining up against the same wall to pee whether they felt like it or not. Mussolini sought to be a twentieth-century *condottiere,* but at heart he was a peasant and not a very bright one, corrupted by the marble statues that abound in Italy. (American correspondents in Italy called him "The Duck," a sardonic phonetic transliteration of the grandiose Il Duce.) Countess Alicia Spalding Paolozzi, an American married to an Italian nobleman, went to a state reception in Rome in 1939 for Halifax and Neville Chamberlain, and she recalls the indelible impression of going down the reception line, which was "mannered and lovely," and then coming upon Mussolini in an inner room of Palazzo Venezia pacing back and forth surrounded by a circle of brown and black uniforms. "He would point to somebody and that person would come up and speak to him. He was so coarse — and he looked like a buffoon."

Another American woman married to an Italian, Aileen Flannery of New York, was very much in the thick of Italian society and on good terms with the royal family. She was about to return to the United States for a short visit in the summer of 1939 and was in Rome calling on friends, when Crown Prince Umberto asked her to deliver a private message to FDR. Both Umberto and his wife, Maria José, according to Aileen, were anti-German and dreaded the Pact of Steel, which Mussolini had signed in May. "They wanted Roosevelt to help them break the pact if possible. Prince Umberto asked me to have Roosevelt invite him and Maria José to the World's Fair as official guests, which would give him an opportunity to confer first hand with American leaders and explain the true feelings of the Italian people. It wasn't possible for him to go to the fair as a private citizen because of Italy's special relations with Germany, but since other royal families were being invited he hoped to be able to get to the United States that way."

Aileen wrote to her friends the Astors explaining that she needed to see the President, and soon after the ship docked she was invited

In a great portrait of regal matriarchy, showing four generations of the Agnelli family, appear, from the left: baby Clara; Virginia Agnelli, a half-American beauty despite her Italianate appearance in this photograph; the baby's great-grandmother, the Princess of San Faustino, enthroned in her chair as head of the female household; and, standing behind the chair, the baby's American grandmother, born a Campbell in Kentucky, Jane Bourbon del Monte, also Princess of San Faustino.

to the White House for lunch. "When I got there," she recalled, "I realized it was impossible to speak openly since the other luncheon guests included the president of a South American republic and about ten other people. I'd almost given up, but as we were leaving, Roosevelt said to me, 'Look here, young lady, I want to talk to you about Italy. Come back tomorrow at teatime and we'll be alone.' That night I couldn't sleep. I drank cognac and took Benzedrine and every kind of thing and was nervous as a cat, but the next afternoon I saw the President alone and gave him Prince Umberto's message."

As she recalled it, "Roosevelt told me that he'd been trying to pry Italy out of the Axis, too." She remembered him saying, "I've admired Mussolini at times and I've been interested in some of the things he's done, particularly the corporations, but now he's become a slave to the Germans. He should stay away from the Axis." Roosevelt told her that he'd written several private letters to Mussolini, offering to meet him in the Azores or anywhere else the Duce wanted (a well-known fact), and that it would be unwise to make overtures to the royal family until Mussolini had at least replied.

She tried to see the Duce as soon as she returned to Rome. That proved impossible, but Mussolini's son-in-law, the Italian Foreign Minister Count Ciano, was a close personal friend. Ciano said he would deliver her message to Mussolini and get back to her. The next time she saw Ciano he was crestfallen. Ciano told her that as soon as he'd brought up the Roosevelt letters, the Duce had harangued him coarsely, shouting, "You're a fool, you've always been crazy about Americans and their stupid jazz. They're drunk all the time! They won't lift a finger to go to war!"

Very few American residents in Italy played jazz or were drunk all the time, so Mussolini must have picked up these superficial impressions from the movies. They were an index of his fatal provincialism. If anything, the long-established American expatriates in Italy and their children had become part of the establishment, and, in some cases had become enthusiastic black shirts themselves. Giorgio Nelson Page, who wound up in an Allied concentration camp at the end of World War II, was the grandson of a Confederate naval captain who sailed his ship to Cuba at the end of the Civil War and consigned it to the Spanish administrators of the island "so that it wouldn't fall into the hands of the damn Yankees." Soon there were Pages in Florence and Rome, and Giorgio's uncle, Thomas Nelson Page, was the American ambassador to Italy during World War I and resigned in protest when President Woodrow Wilson refused to accept Italy's claims on former Austrian territory. Year by year, various members of the Page family were more Italianized as they became part of the Roman aristocracy and its circle. Giorgio, who grew up in the twenties and thirties, went riding and played cards with young Italian bloods fired by the idea of conquest and empire. The Fascist and Nazi concept of a European elite was, after all, a debased version of the aristocratic assumptions of Europe in the nineteenth century, when upper-class white men bore the burden of ruling the world and enjoyed the spoils of colonialism. Though an American citizen by birth, Giorgio Nelson Page chose to become a naturalized Italian in 1933. He worked at the Fascist Ministry of Propaganda during World War II and, picked up by the occupation authorities after the liberation of Rome, he was imprisoned.

Just such a debased notion of aristocracy may have led Ezra Pound to commit treason. The poet had moved to Italy more or less permanently in 1924, and the following year he and his wife, Dorothy, bought a house in Rapallo, on the Italian Riviera. Pound's personal life had by then grown quite complicated. In Paris, twenty-three-year-old George Antheil had introduced him to a young violinist from Boston, Olga Rudge, with whom he conducted a love affair for the rest of his life while remaining married to Dorothy Shakespeare. He also had unconventional ideas politically. In 1922, while still in Paris, he had begun to take stock of the changes set loose by World War I and came to some very pessimistic conclusions: "There is no organized or coordinated civilization left, only individual scattered survivors. . . . Aristocracy is gone; its function was to select. . . . No use waiting for the masses to develop, they aren't moving that way."

Had these ideas remained abstract, the reactionary streak that surfaced in them might have been dismissed as an expatriate poet's nostalgia for a vanishing or vanished world. But Pound had something of the country bumpkin's belief that there had to be a simple answer to things. He tried writing to Roosevelt, who ignored him, and to Mussolini, who gave him an appointment at Palazzo Venezia and heard him out. The Fascists, too, believed in simple solutions,

DAVID LEES

Brought back to the United States in disgrace, after World War II, and threatened with death for his wartime treason, poet Ezra Pound was instead committed to an insane asylum. Released after an international campaign in his behalf, Pound returned to Italy and lived as a virtual recluse in Venice where photographer David Lees took this evocative picture in 1969.

like all authoritarians, and from that point on Pound was openly pro-Fascist. With it went an ignorant anti-Semitism, which held that Jews had destroyed the economic system of feudal times through commercialism. Why one would want to return to the economic system of the Middle Ages wasn't quite clear, and Pound's closest friends seriously worried that he was losing his mind. Joyce wrote to Hemingway that he had met Pound for lunch in Paris and had been physically afraid. Pound — who had helped Joyce publish *Ulysses* — seemed to the Irishman berserk, shouting out his theories vehemently and forcing everyone else into an uneasy silence. Yeats, who had taken a house in Rapallo near the Pounds, was disturbed at the changes in his old friend, and during the late 1930s their relationship began to cool. In 1940, Pound began making pro-Fascist broadcasts over Radio Rome, arranged by a half-American aristocrat. Pound was then on the threshold of treason. The war would push him across it.

CHAPTER NINE

t five o'clock in the afternoon of June 10, 1940, one hundred thousand uniformed Fascists, soldiers, and ordinary Romans streamed toward the Piazza Venezia, which was already heavily guarded by police and carabinieri. The word was out: Mussolini was going to declare war on England and France. At six o'clock, wearing a black uniform, Il Duce appeared on the balcony as the crowd broke into frenzied cheering. Alicia Spalding Paolozzi was in the crowd, listening with dread to Mussolini's emphatic bellows and the booming roars of approval: "I was shocked at the easy joy of people who couldn't project the event into the horror and tragedy and suffering that I knew it would be." She went home and cried for days, she remembers.

For weeks, Mussolini had been tormented by the thought that Hitler would collect all the spoils. The panzers had ripped through Belgium and the Netherlands, turned the Maginot Line, and were racing for the Channel. The war appeared already all but won; Germany, unstoppable. Mussolini's decision was cowardly and rapacious. He knew the Italian army was unprepared for war. The country had barely any steel, little gasoline. Gambling everything on a quick finish to World War II, he attacked France across the Maritime Alps, a decision that FDR stigmatized forever a few hours later in his famous radio broadcast when, with scathing patrician contempt, he drawled: "The hand that held the dagger has stuck it into the back of its neighbor." The phrase, full of implied racism, raised the ghost of the scheming, sly, and Machiavellian Italian, and it cost Roosevelt votes among Italian-Americans. Yet it was the perfect definition of the dirty deed.

After June 10, the U.S. consulate in Rome was jammed with American citizens wanting to get home — and quickly. For others, however, it wasn't possible to go back. They had been in Italy so long that they no longer had a home in the States or they had married Italians and had to stay with their husbands and children. It was no fun being an American, particularly in the cities where even among Italians there was widespread fear of the plainclothes police. Miss Flowerton, who had come over with her mother for the winter season in 1925 and who married a Neapolitan banker, remembers that Italians called these agents *orecchini* — "little ears" — and she recalls that "when we walked around the Via Veneto, Italians would point to their ear and that meant, 'Look out, you're being tailed.'" Among themselves, Americans called these plainclothesmen "guardian angels," and she remembers meeting someone from the consulate near the Hotel Flora who said to her, "We'd better go our different ways; my guardian angel is across the street." America seemed then a safe but faraway haven.

The real blow for the Americans still in Italy fell on December 7, 1941. Reynolds "Pack" Packard, the UP bureau chief in Rome, who, with his wife Eleanor, would beat Mark Clark into the city three years later, was having dinner with Ezra Pound at the San Carlo restaurant on the Corso when a waiter came over and said he was wanted on the phone. It was Eleanor, and she broke the news about Pearl Harbor. Packard rushed back to the table and demanded the bill at once.

"What's the trouble?" asked Pound.

"The Japs have bombed Pearl Harbor, and according to my wife, they've knocked the shit out of the U.S. Navy."

"My God!" gasped Pound, "I'm a ruined man."

Bill Rospigliosi, then the bureau chief of INS in Rome (the Hearst wire agency, now no more), has a slightly different version of that evening. He was in the office when the bulletin announcing the Japanese air strike came in and, realizing at once that it meant confinement of one sort or another — he was later interned in Perugia — he was trying to compose his thoughts when the phone rang. On the other end was Duchess Elena Lante della Rovere, an Italian noblewoman who worked as a stringer for Packard at the UP. "You know," she said to him, "Packard was out to dinner and he just telephoned me from the Cafe Greco. He asked me if there was any news and I said yes, the Japanese had bombed a place called Pearl Harbor. He seemed very upset. He shouted, 'Why didn't you call me immediately?' and slammed the phone down. Bill, why can that be?''

And Prince Rospigliosi, reluctant to bring the duchess down to earth too abruptly and a little dazed himself, full of the sensation that another age was passing when things would never be the same, replied gently, "I have no idea."

Many Americans, the men at least, had already been under police surveillance. Now they were enemy aliens. A few days later Mussolini made it official by declaring war on the United States from the balcony at Piazza Venezia. Again, the same festive, black-shirted crowds turned out by the thousands. They carried denigrating posters, one of them showing Mrs. Roosevelt wearing a toilet seat as a necklace. Mussolini appeared on the flag-draped balcony between the towering German ambassador Hans von Mackensen and the tiny Japanese, Zembei Horikiri. Then he drew his head back and began to shout into the microphone in his stentorian, strongman manner: "The powers of the Pact of Steel . . . participate in this war . . . on the side of the heroic Japanese against the United States!" Italy was already losing the war, and now it was taking on the most powerful nation on earth and one where millions of Italians had relatives. Marchese Emilio Pucci, later to revolutionize sportswear and put women in pants but then a flier stationed on Rhodes, remembers the deep dejection of his comrades as they listened to Mussolini. His squadron was flying planes that were already outclassed and obsolete, three-motored Savoia Marchettis with canvas-covered wings. "A nation with no steel declaring war on the world's greatest steel producer. We all knew it was madness." Pucci had studied at Reed College in Oregon just before the war. He knew the Americans and sensed he'd be seeing them soon in his native Florence — if he lived that long. Other Italians felt the same way and hardly bothered to conceal their emotions.

Before their repatriation to the U.S., Pack and his wife spent eight days at Rome's Grand Hotel, where they would have a nightcap with Pietro the barman and toast their return to Italy.

"That will mean the end of fascism and the war," Pietro would whisper. "Here's to your return."

And when they were driven to the Ostiense Station outside

Rome, built for Hitler's visit, one of the carabinieri accompanying them gave Pack his brother's address in Brooklyn. "Tell him I'll join him after the war," the policeman said.

Like other American newsmen, including the *New York Times*'s Herbert Matthews, Packard had been picked up immediately after the declaration of war and locked up in Rome's Regina Coeli (Queen of Heaven) prison. The Fascist government had heard a report that Italian reporters had been taken into custody in the United States, and it decided to reciprocate. Also arrested was a tall, statuesque American beauty, Teddy Lynch, the former wife of millionaire Paul Getty, Sr., who had been studying opera in Rome. "I hope prison hasn't ruined my voice," she said wearily when she was finally released and allowed to join the correspondents in their internment at the Pensione Suquet. Two days later the group was moved to Siena and put up at the Hotel Excelsior. Obligingly, friendly cops accompanied the male detainees to the local brothel a couple of times a week. "I must say it was a pleasant change from the hotel," Pack wrote in his racy book, *Rome Was My Beat*. "It was warmly heated and the girls didn't hesitate to show preference for the Americans as more carefree spenders."

The newsmen, Teddy Lynch, U.S. consular officials who had been expelled on May 7, 1942, and seminarian John P. Boyle of the American College, who had stayed on in Rome and managed to obtain early ordination at the Capranica, were sent in a sealed train to Lisbon, where the Swedish exchange ship *Drottingholm* took them home to New York. Still, hundreds of Americans stayed put in Italy. It has been impossible to determine the exact number, since no precise records exist; it may have been in the thousands. The American women who had married Italians and who had decided to stick it out learned to cope with the black market and a constant sense of danger in a country that was losing a war. Fortunately, the Italians themselves remained kind and tolerant, and particularly so toward women.

Rosemary Sprehe (pronounced *spray*), still an attractive, willowy blond today, had married a Milanese engineer in 1939. They had met on a private seaplane that broke down in the Bay of Naples, and after living on Capri with her husband, she moved to a house on the Via Appia a few miles from Rome because enemy aliens were not allowed to live on the islands. "I could show you the spot in my house where I was standing when I heard Mussolini announcing that he was declaring war on my country," she remembered. "Having an Italian husband and an American brother, I couldn't take either side. I was completely divided and crawled into my shell."

During air bombardments, she, her mother, and her baby son would take refuge in the ancient Roman catacombs located conveniently beneath the house. They could always tell when the bombers were coming because their two dogs, an Afghan and a sheep dog, would quietly get up a few moments before the sound of the motors could be heard and walk down into the catacombs. She and her American mother had converted all their cash into jewels, which they cunningly hid in geranium pots that lined a wall outside the house. Unable to get any money from the States, they were in a constant state of anxiety over the jewels, which represented their total capital — whichever way the war went. After the eighth of September, 1943, when Mussolini fell and Italy began its lurch toward the Allied side, bringing the Germans in force to the peninsula, they emptied the geranium pots and buried the jewels, their silver, jade statuettes, and old coins in a suitcase in a corner of the garden, beneath a rhododendron bush.

Though Rosemary Sprehe stayed on in the house on the Via Appia, raising her son and waiting for her husband to come back from the front, her mother, Mrs. Kimmel, was eventually repatriated. It was then quite late in the war, and the moment the ship docked in New York she was shadowed to her hotel, the Alrae, in the Sixties between Madison and Fifth, by FBI agents. Mrs. Kimmel is still bitter over this treatment. "In Rome I was constantly followed around, and when I got back to America they thought I was a spy." On her second day at the Alrae, she was visited by two FBI agents. "They even took the pictures off the wall and tore the rubber out of my fountain pen." Mrs. Kimmel also had with her two checks, of $25,000 and $3,000, which a famous Roman jeweler had entrusted to her. The jeweler had been unable to deposit the checks in his account in Switzerland, and he had asked the American woman to send them to Geneva from New York. They were certainly compromising, and the FBI agents at once confiscated them. At the end of the war Mrs. Kimmel wrote to J. Edgar Hoover asking that the checks be returned, and they were.

Well before Mrs. Kimmel's reimpatriation, however, Americans had begun returning to Italy. They were not exactly on a Grand

Tour and they were reluctant visitors to Arcadia. On the night of July 10, 1943, the American Seventh Army, led by General George Patton, landed on the southern coast of Sicily roughly where Hannibal had invaded the island two thousand years before. The weather was terrible. Breakers thundered among the landing craft, and the wind howled over the bubbling white wakes. One unit, the Second Battalion of the 157th Infantry, lost forty-five men by drowning. In the morning, while drowned men and overturned landing craft still bobbed in the heavy swell, the GIs found themselves in an arid, sun-scorched land of stone walls and prickly pear bushes. The villages they entered were stupefyingly poor, the people ugly in a broken-toothed, biblical way. All dreams or notions of beautiful Italy vanished immediately and for most American troops never returned.

The Italian soldiers in Sicily were often glad to be captured and put up little resistance. The German Afrika Korps veterans fought a delaying action with mines and 88s before scooting over the Strait of Messina so they would not be trapped on Sicily by an enemy with superior naval forces. Preparations were made for a landing on the mainland that would knock Italy out of the war and send the Duck into early retirement. At that point, Patton was replaced by the youthful Mark Clark, who emerged from the war as the most highly criticized of the top U.S. battle commanders, blamed for the slowness and bloodiness of the Allied advance up the Italian boot.

I met Clark when he returned to Rome in 1974 to celebrate the thirtieth anniversary of the liberation of the city by the Allies. It was a strangely depressing occasion. He was in the basement of the Hotel Excelsior in an overstuffed and dusty lounge, waiting to be interviewed by an Italian television crew, while outside, on Via Veneto, a vast army of protesters in long rows marched down the street from the Aurelian Wall. The protesters had come from Naples to condemn firings and plant closings in the area, and they were carrying red flags and shouting slogans against American multinational companies. Clark sat on the sofa, looking fit and erect for a man in his seventies. His eyes, however, were anxious. In the years since the war he had been castigated over and over as a vainglorious fool who had strutted around the vast Bourbon palace at Caserta while his Fifth Army bled before Cassino in the hills to the north. So many men of so many nationalities died in the Liri River valley before the ancient Benedictine monastery that, after the war, when Harry Truman tried to appoint Mark Clark his personal envoy to the Holy See, Sam Rayburn would have none of it. In Texas they still accused Clark of having mismanaged the Forty-fifth Division, one of the first two National Guard divisions activated by President Roosevelt in August 1940.

As we sat on the sofa in that overheated basement lounge, the faint rhythmic chanting of the marchers coming down the Via Veneto vibrated in the hotel's vents like the murmuring of a distant offstage chorus. Clark asked what the noise was. After a moment's embarrassment, one of the Italian TV crewmen replied, "Just strikers."

Clark nodded and went back to his reveries of the 1940s. To the rest of us, the savage certainties of those anti-American protesters contrasted strangely with the sad ruminations of this old warrior, who, in a remote, bygone era barely remembered by the village elders with their long white beards, it seemed, had given those people up in the street their country back. *Sic transit.* They had certainly picked a funny day for an anti-American demonstration, but fortunately Clark remained unaware of it.

I asked the general if he had been conscious of all the other commanders who had fought in Italy, and he replied, "No, I really wasn't. I was rather young when I was picked for high command. I never dreamed of Hannibal." We talked about the Mediterranean, which was being shaken in the early seventies by the end of fascism in Spain, Portugal, and Greece, by turmoil in Italy, and by socialist Islamic experiments in northern Africa. Did Clark feel that the tides of history had slipped from the grasp of the victorious United States? He replied, "I think history is made up of events, and crises, which have to be met as they come along. I saw change coming in Northern Africa then. Colonialism was beginning to go out. People were beginning to demand independence. It's just continued to build." Then I asked him about the criticism that has attached itself to his record. "I was told to attack, attack, attack," he replied with some annoyance, "to eliminate and kill Germans and bring them into the Italian battle so that Ike could go on with the main mission. The cost was heavy."

In those terms, Clark's army accomplished its mission by drawing thirty-seven German divisions into the Italian peninsula. The high ground, however, always seemed to be in German hands, and the Germans could defend their lines with fewer men and much less equipment than the attacking Americans, Britons, New Zealanders, Canadians, Poles, French, Moroccans, Brazilians, and pro-Allied Italians of Clark's polyglot army. In strategic terms, as everyone has always pointed out, it made no sense to land in southern Italy and then fight one's way up the interminable mountain ranges of the boot in rain, mud, and ice when a landing could just as well have been made on the plain before Pisa or along the Adriatic south of Venice. The Italian campaign, however, was planned largely on political, not strategic, terms. After the loss of Sicily and the Allied bombing of Rome, the Fascist grand council met in a night-long session and forced the resignation of Mussolini, who was arrested as he emerged from a heated meeting with King Victor Emmanuel at the Quirinal Palace and driven to the mountain fastness of l'Aquila. Marshal Badoglio took over the reins of government and, to the dismay of most Italians, announced that Italy would continue to fight at Germany's side.

The landing at Salerno, code-named AVALANCHE, was designed to put Allied troops on the Italian mainland swiftly and take advantage of the widespread desire in Rome for a separate peace. As Clark wrote in his book *Calculated Risk,* "The Nazis obviously were going to fight for Italy regardless of the action of the Italian government, but there was always the possibility that we could seize Naples with Italian assistance before the Germans could act." Air support was another factor in the decision to land at Salerno. Clark suggested an invasion north of Naples, in the area of Gaeta, which was strategically and tactically more sensible, at least on paper, but British Air Marshal Sir Arthur Tedder said that the proper air support could not be given at Gaeta because of its greater distance from Allied bases, and so the choice fell definitively on Salerno.

An ancillary plan was being bruited about at the same time that might have changed the course of the Italian campaign and perhaps shortened it by months. Representatives of Eisenhower and Badoglio were meeting secretly in Lisbon. Since the Italian negotiators wanted the Americans to drop a division of paratroopers on Rome itself to protect the capital and bolster their own forces at the moment Italy left the Axis, Brigadier General Maxwell D. Taylor, then an assistant division commander to Matthew Ridgway of the famed Eighty-second Airborne Division, made a daring secret trip into Rome to meet with leaders of the armistice movement. Ike told Clark on September 3 that it had been decided to drop the Eighty-second on Rome, but Taylor's meeting with Badoglio had convinced him the Italians could not provide the assistance they had promised in Lisbon, and the dramatic parachuting of American troops into the Eternal City was called off.

On the night of September 13, three days after the Salerno landing, Ridgway's paratroopers were dropped on the beachhead instead to help Clark's desperately hard-pressed American and British forces. Clark had put thirty thousand British and twenty-five thousand American troops ashore against about twenty thousand defenders, but the Germans were well dug into the mountains ringing Salerno, and Kesselring, their seasoned, able commander, had another one hundred thousand men in reserve in Italy. By the third day, AVALANCHE was in deep trouble.

It was also obvious that the Germans were going to fight for every inch of ground. One hopeful theory widely shared among Allied intelligence officers on the eve of the Salerno landing was that, to avoid being plastered from the air, the Germans would pull back to northern Italy and not contest the South. U.S. and RAF planes continually worked over enemy communication lines, hitting bridges, tunnels, and the Brenner Pass itself, but the theory was a dud. The Germans continued to move supplies southward successfully, and they contested nearly every valley and river crossing.

By late September, the Allied forces broke out of the Salerno bridgehead, and on October 1, British and American patrols entered the outskirts of Naples. Above Eboli, Forty-fifth Division troops found one thousand political prisoners from southern and eastern Europe, most of them Jews. No one knew of Hitler's extermination camps yet, and this was only a small inkling of that inhuman tragedy. Dr. Peter C. Graffagnino of Columbus, Georgia, a battalion surgeon with the Forty-fifth Division who was later captured in the caves at Anzio, recalls that "it was a strange experience to be surrounded by a weeping, clamorous crush of cadaverous humans whose gratitude was overwhelming and whose needs and hunger were so acute." In the streets of Naples, meanwhile, GIs were being mobbed by cheering crowds. The Neapolitans had been accustomed to receiving conquerors for centuries, and this time the conquerors were rich and good-natured.

Sir Alec Guinness, as a young naval officer with the British forces, found himself in the midst of imploring urchins in the Naples suburb of Pozzuoli. They noisily beseeched him and other Allied officers for food and candy. Years later, he was relating the incident to co-star Sophia Loren when her beautiful face lit up and she suddenly mimed the gestures of those imploring children. "I was one of them," she told him gaily. Guinness was rather stunned, but there was no shame or sadness in her recollection, and he had been given another insight into the exceptional endurance of the Neapolitans.

The liberated city's human carnival had its torrid and unsavory side as well. Naples turned into a bazaar of peddled flesh and black market goods. Slum-dwelling *scugnizzi* (as small boys are called in the local dialect) soon became expert at stripping drunken GIs and selling their clothes and weapons. The city's baroque imagination reeled with the mingled stimulus of freedom, of so many men under arms and so much loot. In Curzio Malaparte's savage novel of Naples during the liberation, *The Skin,* there is a scene in which a mermaid, supposedly netted by fishermen and placed in the city's aquarium, is boiled and served to General "Cork" and his staff. In the superheated emotional atmosphere, the city's women, like the unfortunate mermaid, were served up — or gave themselves — to the young warriors. More romantically, thousands of GIs fell in love, and Italian war brides began sailing to new homes in America. Meanwhile, the war continued, and the advance north of Naples was slower and more bloody than anyone had expected.

The Germans dug in their 88s on the mountain ridges, and before retreating to the next range of hills, they sowed the ground with plastic SHU mines the size of a large matchbox, which would shatter a man's leg up to the knee so that it had to be amputated. They also booby-trapped everything, particularly the water tanks on toilets, before evacuating a village. Winter rains, whipped by icy winds, made the advancing troops miserable.

Frank Melville, a Canadian who fought with the Eighth Army on the Adriatic front as a twenty-one-year-old in the Toronto Scottish infantry regiment, remarked recently that "people talk about the bloody trench warfare of World War I, but they don't realize that Italy in the winter of 1943 was just as awful and bloody, in the mud and the slush."

Clark, in his book, admits to "a general feeling of discouragement in the final months of 1943 as the Fifth Army took one strong point after another, only to see, through the rain and mud, still another mountainside on which the enemy was entrenched in pillboxes and well-protected artillery emplacements." The inevitable price was being paid for the decision to invade Italy from the south and fight uphill all the way up the boot, but as morale sagged, the men took out their frustrations on Clark and pined for the already legendary Patton. One officer confided bitterly: "It was evident that the leadership of the American Fifth Army [by command, always identified in press releases as "General Mark Clark's Fifth Army"] lacked the imagination and purpose of the Seventh Army under Patton. Things were just confused, and stayed that way. The Germans retreated at will. We seemed to stumble along in inordinate fashion, advancing when we should have been regrouping and holding when we should have been advancing."

In its inordinate fashion, the Fifth Army stumbled into one of the most effective fortified points in the history of warfare. The best brains of the French general staff had labored for twenty-five years to construct the unbreachable Maginot Line, and the Wehrmacht went around it, over it, and through it in a week. The Japanese tunnels and caves on Iwo Jima were hell to go against, but the island fell to the Marines in a searing amphibious attack. With only a few short weeks to prepare a winter defensive line, dubbed the Gustav Line, the German Todt organization constructed an underground bastion through the mountains between Naples and Rome that proved to be impregnable for longer than anyone could have imagined. Its cardinal point was the ancient Benedictine Abbey of Monte Cassino, overlooking the Liri River valley (renamed Purple Heart Valley by the men of the Fifth Army).

If you go to the Monte Cassino Abbey, now rebuilt, you will see why it was a stronghold in World War II. That destiny was probably incorporated into the abbey's history, since St. Benedict had undoubtedly chosen to build this premier jewel of the monastic movement on the site of an ancient Roman fortress. The abbey is on top of a great dome of a hill, rather barren, with white stones and lichens showing among patches of coarse grass, which dominates the Liri Valley, and in that winter of 1943–1944 the U.S. Fifth Army, and the British Eighth Army, having tried to go around it, were forced to storm it over and over.

Once a platoon of the 135th Infantry fought its way to the very

walls of the abbey, only to be thrown back. The U.S. Thirty-sixth
Division took 1,681 casualties in three days trying to cross the
Rapido River south of Monastery Hill. The U.S. Thirty-fourth
Division did cross the Rapido north of the hill and bent back the
Gustav Line, but at a terrible cost. By the first week in February,
the British were called in. General Alexander had secretly moved
the New Zealand Corps from the Eighth Army front on the Adriatic to Cassino. The corps included the Second New Zealand Division, the Fourth Indian Division, and the British Seventy-eighth Infantry Division. On February 12, with the Indian Division due to
attack, British General Bernard Freyberg, a much-decorated World
War I hero, asked for an air strike on the abbey itself. The message
was taken by Clark's deputy, General Alfred Gruenther, who told
Freyberg, "The monastery is not on the list of targets." Nevertheless, when Freyberg persisted, apparently supported by various
commanders in the field and by General Alexander, B-19 Flying
Fortresses bombed the abbey to rubble on February 14. Henry
Cabot Lodge, then a major attached to the Fifth Army, remarked:
"It was a great mistake militarily, because the abbey was not a good
observation point. There were better ones around it." He can remember the bombing raid, which began at eight A.M. and involved
a total of 255 Allied bombers. Many of them dropped short, however, and their bombs fell within the Allied lines. "The bombers
damn near killed us all," Lodge recalls. "I was thrown to the
ground and my mouth was full of gravel."

After the air bombardment finished, the artillery opened up and
shelled Monastery Hill until three P.M. By then, a pall of gray dust
and smoke hung over the ruined abbey. When Freyberg's New
Zealanders attacked, however, the Germans popped out of their
holes and began firing back. Lodge told me: "You would have
thought there wouldn't have been a German alive, or in his right
mind. But they came out of their cellars firing. It was unbelievable.
They must have given them pills, or something, to keep their
nerves together." Blasted into rubble, moreover, the abbey itself
now became a fortress from which the Germans fired down on attacking forces. Nearly every nationality in the Fifth Army had a
try, including Italians themselves. A few regular units of the Italian
Army had begun fighting with the Allies, and one of these was sent
up against the abbey. "I'll never forget the Italians singing as they

went to attack," a Fifth Army veteran told me. "They went past our positions, singing and joking, but when they came by again they'd lost maybe half the unit and they weren't singing."

The anguish before Cassino was matched by the agony of Anzio. The U.S. Third Division and the British First Division had gone ashore there, on January 23–24, to circumvent the Gustav Line and lead the drive for Rome, thirty miles to the northeast. Unlike the previous year's landing at Salerno, the one at Anzio caught the Germans by surprise. The troops, pushing inland, camped under the tall, cool umbrella pines of the area's woods in relative quiet. One of the first patrols to be sent out got within sixteen miles of Rome. Because of timid leadership at the top, unfortunately, this initial advantage was not exploited. Hitler, raging that "this abscess at Anzio" had to be eliminated, sent Kesselring reinforcements from as far away as Yugoslavia and France. And, as always, the Germans made excellent use of the high ground, placing their artillery in the Alban Hills just south of the Eternal City, which looked straight down on the Anzio beachhead. They brought in huge cannons mounted on armored trains, which GIs dubbed the Anzio Express. By the seventh day, the landing forces were in serious danger of being annihilated, a disaster that would have cast a pall not only over the Italian campaign but over the imminent invasion of Normandy, OVERLORD. On February 18, after having driven a wedge between the British First Division and the U.S. Forty-fifth, the German commander Mackensen threw everything he had into a desperate attack. At some points German panzers and U.S. Sherman tanks fought almost muzzle to muzzle, so that curious Italian civilians prowling over the battlefield weeks later found these charred monsters locked in death grips, with their blown, twisted plates nearly touching. Between January 16 and March 31, the Fifth Army took 52,130 casualties, but the Germans had expended everything they had without eliminating the Anzio beachhead, and now the balance shifted decisively in the Allies' favor. On May 11, the Fifth Army broke through on a wide front from Cassino to the sea. A week later, General Anders's Polish Corps finally took Monastery Hill and the ruins of the abbey. The race for Rome was on.

To the civilians awaiting liberation, the sound of distant artillery fire and the roar of Allied bombers overhead had become commonplace. The Rome railway station had already been leveled, though the bombing was absolutely accurate and, as Lodge remarked, "not a peanut was ever dropped on St. Peter's." More harrowing to the civilians were the vindictive last-minute reprisals being carried out by the SS and what remained of the Fascist secret police, the OVRA. A relative of my wife's, a seventeen-year-old boy with no desire to fight for Mussolini or the Germans, was hiding from the draft board at home. The family lived on the fifth floor of an old building in the Prati neighborhood, near St. Peter's, with tall windows and huge, vermilion shutters. When the SS raided the building looking for partisans and draft-dodgers, the boy's mother had him crawl out on the ledge and fasten his fingers and toes on the slats of one of the shutters, which was flat against the window. Then she pushed it open. He hung there for half an hour until the Germans, finding nothing, got back into their trucks and drove away.

Rosemary Sprehe, still in her house on the Via Appia, also lived through one of these raids. "When the Germans came, everybody was absolutely terrified," she recalls. "We all hid in a cave where we stored wine, but the Germans soon caught on that we were down there and shouted that unless we came out they would drop a grenade down. Everyone filed out. I came out last and saw the others standing with their arms over their heads. It wasn't funny at all, but certain things are always funny. I had my son, who was very small, in my arms, and so I could only raise one arm." The Germans checked their papers and left.

On June 4, there was fighting along that same stretch of the Via Appia, where a single German tank held up the advance for several hours. Finally it was hit, and the U.S. jeeps and tanks went past the burned-out wreck, with its smell of roasted bodies. At Piazza San Giovanni, Italians were running out of the doorways to shout, "Americani, bravi, bravi," and wave handkerchiefs. As the crowds thickened later, women and girls would embrace and kiss the Allied soldiers as they drove slowly past in their vehicles. In the afternoon of that June 4, however, the Germans were still evacuating the city from the north as the Allies came in from the south. Ferdinando di Bagno, a great Italian playboy of the twenties and thirties, recalled how strange it was to watch the last German truck columns go roaring past and then, not a half-hour later, see a perky little jeep come up the street with an American officer studying a map, his booted legs casually draped over the hood. Reynolds Packard and his wife had been urged by the UP to be the first American correspondents to file from liberated Rome, and though they had Matthews, Homer Bigart, Jim Kilgallen, and a dozen others for competition, they daringly drove in with the advance troops and made straight for the Grand Hotel. As they entered the lobby, a group of German officers, including a general, were checking out. After celebrating with Pietro, their barman buddy of two years earlier, and a lobby full of enthusiastic Italians, they drove back to the press camp in darkness to send this classic dispatch:

04220 DATELINE ROME WE TOASTED THE FALL OF ROME TO THE U.S. FIFTH ARMY TONIGHT AT THE BAR OF THE CITY'S SWANK GRAND HOTEL AMIDST THE CHEERS OF ITALIAN GUESTS WHILE OUTSIDE THE TRIUMPHANT DOUGHBOYS WERE BEING KISSED AND HUGGED BY THOUSANDS OF ENTHUSIASTIC ITALIANS PARA WE ENTERED THE GRAND HOTEL AS HIGH GERMAN OFFICERS INCLUDING ONE GENERAL WERE LEAVING STOP WE TRIED NOT TO SEE EACH OTHER PARA

An even stranger encounter took place at the American Academy, where Henry Rowell, a former Fellow then in Army intelligence, rushed in to liberate it. The Academy's librarian, Albert Van Buren, who had remained at his post throughout the war, looked up distractedly at the sight of the excited officer and said absently, "Good morning, Henry," before going back to his reading. Later, however, Van Buren's composure broke. He broke into tears at the sight of mashed potatoes in a Fifth Army mess.

That same day Clark and Al Gruenther and other officers drove into the city in their jeeps and got lost, wandering around aimlessly looking for the Capitoline Hill, where Clark intended to hold a meeting of his corps commanders. They wound up at St. Peter's, where a priest called out, "Welcome to Rome. Is there any way in which I can help you?" The priest turned out to be from Detroit, and he gave Clark's driver the needed directions. An INS photo shows Clark being driven down the Corso, where Margaret Fuller once lived. An Italian girl has rushed out from the sidewalk to take Clark's hand and looks as if she is about to kiss it. Clark is smiling and, in the back seat, Generals Gruenther and Harry H. Johnson are also smiling. Margaret Fuller had watched Italian crowds in the same street cheering Garibaldi's name and cheering the liberation of Milan against the Austrians, a cause that had received the wholehearted support of the American people. A hundred years later, an

American commander was leading his polyglot army into a Rome liberated from a popular Italian tyrant and his more awful German ally. There was plenty of irony underlying the widely enthusiastic cheers of the Romans, and the GIs could not be blamed for being a little skeptical. On the road to Rome the Allied Army had suffered 124,917 casualties in Italy, including 20,389 dead, 84,389 wounded, and 20,139 missing. Of the dead, 11,292 were Americans, 5,017 U.K., 3,904 French, and 176 were Italians from the First Motorized Group.

Clark had hoped to lasso Kesselring's forces in a noose somewhere north of Rome in the relatively flat country around Orvieto or in the Val di Chiana. Two days after the fall of Rome, however, the landing craft hit the Normandy beaches, and OVERLORD naturally became the focus of the Allied war efforts in Europe. In order to mount a second landing in southern France, code-named ANVIL, the Allied high command stripped the Fifth Army of the Third, Thirty-sixth, and Forty-fifth divisions, plus the French Expeditionary Forces, commanded by General Juin. The diversion of these troops had a considerable strategic consequence, since it buried forever Churchill's wish to strike into the "soft underbelly" of Europe and deny parts of Eastern Europe to the Soviets. The quick pursuit of Kesselring's battered German divisions into northern Italy might have put the Allies in a position to move into Yugoslavia, into Austria, and beyond it into Czechoslovakia. While the decision to drain the Fifth Army of its strength in favor of ANVIL reflected what was probably a realistic reading of the postwar balance in Europe, in terms of the relative contribution of the big powers and the national liberation movements like Tito's to the defeat of Nazi Germany, it meant the anguish of a longer war for Italy.

The peninsula was now split in two. In the south the war was over; the occupation was in force. There was a curfew, and Fascist officials were still being rounded up. In and around Naples, hundreds of Allied deserters had formed gangs and had gone up into the woods like Ninco Nanco, Crocco, and the other bandit leaders of the Kingdom of Naples just after the Napoleonic wars. The same thing occurred in the woods around Pisa, where it took the MPs months to clear them out. The discipline of rear-echelon troops was often lax, and the opportunities for graft were enormous. Master sergeants in supply, some of them Italian-Americans

Lieutenant General Mark W. Clark (left front), controversial commander of the Fifth Army, enjoyed his moment of greatest triumph on June 4, 1944, when he led Allied forces into Rome to liberate the first Axis-held capital of the war.

with compliant relatives in southern Italy, managed to establish themselves like feudal lords for several years.

In the north, Italy was under the Gestapo and the rump government established by Mussolini after the daring raid on his l'Aquila prison by a hand-picked unit under the command of SS lieutenant Colonel Otto Skorzeny. The soldiers of Mussolini's Republic of Salò were often as ferocious toward their fellow Italians as the Germans, deporting Jews and hunting down partisans in the area they still occupied. In the northern cities, already half-skeletal from bombing raids, Italian families surreptitiously listened to the BBC and sweated out the arrival of the Allies. Tens of thousands of Italians took part in the resistance, and in the winter of 1944–1945, the Allies began dropping arms and ammunition to them from the holds of darkened C-47s. The cooperation between the Allies and the *partigiani* was slow to develop because the Germans naturally took advantage of it to send in fake requests for air drops. "Once we could get a *partigiano* commander we could trust," Clark said, "we'd start to work with him. It was always a risk — flying in low, parachuting jeeps and equipment." By the winter of 1944, however, the Fifth Army was issuing precise instructions to the partisans: Block such and such a road, capture or blow up a bridge.

For Iris Origo, running a Red Cross hospital for children near her estate at La Foce, the waiting seemed eternal. Being in the liberated countryside meant that the front passed over you, and she had transferred her hospital to a cellar, but the German commander requisitioned it from her for his men. For hours, she led the children over dust-choked roads while Allied fighters prowled overhead, looking for targets to strafe. "German soldiers, busy laying mines, looked in astonishment at our passing." Finally, on the outskirts of Montepulciano, a crowd of refugees and partisans came toward them. "They lifted the children and their knapsacks up on their shoulders, and, overjoyed by so much goodness, we climbed up the road to the town." Many of the partisans at Montepulciano, as elsewhere, were Communists or Socialists who had hidden their red flags for three decades and would go to meet the weary GIs waving them exultantly. Iris Origo was a marchesa and the daughter of an American patrician. Yet, looking back on those days, she told me, "It was exciting and interesting, and there was a strong sense of hope. We thought, perhaps naively, that there was going to be a great sense of freedom, and we cherished the illusion that the harmony between classes would continue."

In Florence, Suni Agnelli worked in a hospital while awaiting the Allies. It was dangerous to walk around in the streets during the last few days because some two hundred Germans and Fascist snipers had barricaded themselves at windows on the upper floors of buildings. Her brother Gianni was in the hospital. When he and Suni were being driven to Florence, the car overturned into a ditch and his anklebone had to be removed. The first Allied soldier Suni saw was a Scottish officer wearing a kilt. A sniper shot him, and he was carried into the hospital. "I was madly curious to see this Allied Army that I had waited for with such anxiety," she wrote in her book. "It was like a blind date with a boy whom you are expecting to be fabulous."

One afternoon recently in her elegant apartment near the Quirinal Palace, she enlarged on the impressions set down in her book — the overwhelming one being that the Allied Army smelled differently, that it smelled of soap, of cleanliness. War on the Allied side, she felt, "was like a movie set" in comparison with the privations, the hunger, the fear, the executions she had lived with. "They would offer us these slices of white toasting bread that we hadn't seen for years, with butter and jam. These cars everywhere — the ambulances! We had little, low ambulances that were converted Fiats into which you could slide one stretcher. They had colossal ambulances, like trucks. How I envied them! I would have given anything to have an ambulance like that!" And later, when Turin had been liberated, she recalled GIs who had been invited to her house walking in "and shaking the butler's hand, calling him senor. Now it wouldn't strike me at all, but then it seemed amazing."

Her impressions reflect those of millions of Italians. The Allied Army *was* fabulously well equipped by their standards; it did smell differently; and the GIs often behaved simply and spontaneously toward the civilian population. An atmosphere of civility and peace began to settle over the Italian peninsula while hard fighting still continued in the North.

Senator Robert Dole of Kansas, who had joined the Tenth Mountain Division in November 1944 as a replacement second lieutenant, was hit by shell fragments at 9:45 A.M. on April 14, 1945, two weeks before the end of the war in Italy. "We were on the last

ROBERT CAPA

Italy's defeat in World War II was a bittersweet experience for millions of its citizens. While they were grateful for having been liberated from a dictatorship, they had to serve their conquerors cheerfully, like this "shoeshine" in Palermo. The Allied troops paid their own heavy price: 31,886 dead and 189,000 wounded in the Fifth Army.

big push for the Po Valley," he explained. "We had walked some distance and had gotten up into the mountains. I was up on a hillside when a German shell landed nearby. My arms were in front of me when it happened, and when I was turned over I couldn't move anything and I couldn't tell where my arms were."

Dole lay near death for several hours, watched over by one of the men in his platoon. Finally the medics arrived with a stretcher, and he was brought to a field hospital, then to Pistoia. The shell fragments had shattered his right shoulder and arm, damaged his left arm, broken five cervical vertebrae, and destroyed a kidney. He was hospitalized for the next thirty-nine months and all but lost the use of his right hand.

A few days later, during the climactic drive to the Alps, one of the great soldiers of the Fifth Army was killed on Lake Garda. He was Colonel Bill Darby, who had led the Rangers ashore at Salerno. He had returned to Italy with Army Air Force General "Hap" Arnold on what was intended to be a field visit, but he asked to be reassigned to a unit. He was killed instantly by a German shell.

On May 2, Clark's headquarters intercepted an order from the German commander in Italy that his remaining troops should lay down their arms at two o'clock that afternoon. The Italian campaign was over. The Fifth Army had suffered 189,000 casualties since the landing at Salerno and 31,886 men had been killed, 19,475 of them Americans.

CHAPTER TEN

espite the wreckage of the war, the grimy poverty, the broken-toothed skyline of bombed cities, Italy just after the war was beautiful. It retained, for the last time, the pastoral stillness of the preceding centuries. Gore Vidal, who had been in New York and Guatemala since his discharge from the Merchant Marine in 1946, reached Rome in 1948 to find a city immersed in a pastoral silence that belonged more to the nineteenth century than to the twentieth. "I always thought of Rome in the late forties as the most quiet city in the world," Vidal told me when I went to see him a few years ago in his Rome apartment. "There was no sound, ever. You'd just hear the human voice, never the sound of machinery. There was a beautiful kind of golden stillness about it."

With Tennessee Williams, who had never heard of the philosopher, Vidal went to visit George Santayana at the Convent of the Blue Nuns up on the Aventine Hill. The old man in a blue bathrobe had lived out the war in a tiny cell. "Discreetly dying," in Vidal's phrase, Santayana was reading Toynbee and had torn the covers off the volumes. After finishing each bound segment of pages, he would rip it up and drop it into the wastepaper basket. It was his solution to the problem of keeping too many books — and indeed, Vidal said, there were only six in his cell. "Robert Lowell had been to see him. I went to see him four times. He had no idea who any of us were, but I felt I was communing with the nineteenth century, since of course he was a friend of Henry James and of Story, and had known the Rome of that era." To Vidal, the contact with

ROMA'S PRESS

American playwright Tennessee Williams listened to Italian actress Anna
Magnani in one of Rome's excellent restaurants where dinner was often eaten at
midnight, and, in summer, outdoors, in the most relaxed atmosphere anywhere in
Europe. Ten years before this 1958 photograph was taken, Williams had explored
Italy in a secondhand jeep with Gore Vidal.

Santayana seemed a "laying on of hands." It would be convenient
to live in Italy, Vidal perceived, using it as a kind of studio, not getting too involved with the country, yet drawing from its rich culture, and thus carrying on, in his own way and in the consciousness
of a new generation, the expatriate tradition of Crawford and
Story, James and Santayana.

A great many young veterans just out of uniform headed for Italy
in those years, intent on doing something valuable in the arts.
Many of them had gone home after being discharged only to discover they had picked up the Henry Adams sickness — the young
man returning to America and feeling European, or at least
"foreign." Home, moreover, represented ties, responsibilities, ca-

reers, marriages, mortgages — all of which the young artist wants to defer to a later time. Italy was wonderfully accessible and cheap. Other artists had flourished there, in its great atelier of history and art, for hundreds of years. "In our minds," recalls Robert Cook, "there was the idea that Rome could become the Paris of the twenties for our generation."

Cook, a first-rate figurative sculptor who still lives in Rome, found that his veterans' benefits could nearly cover his expenses when he first arrived in 1948. "It was a charmed life. I had seventy-five dollars a month from the GI Bill, and only needed ten dollars more to balance my budget." He rented a little apartment near the Via Margutta, then a wonderfully picturesque pink and yellow street just off the Piazza di Spagna. It was the artists' quarter of Rome in the twentieth century, only a few hundred yards from the Spanish Steps and the buildings where the Freemans and Morses and Storys had lived. Cook could not afford a car on eighty-five dollars a month, but that was all right because so few Italians had one in those early postwar years. "We'd hop on buses to get around," he recalls. "There was a little shop on Via Margutta where you could rent a pushcart and a man to take your stuff around if you had anything heavy to carry."

One of the other Americans who hopped those same buses and lived in a studio in the same area was a lanky, black-haired Italian-American, Bob Guccione, the future publisher of *Penthouse,* who was trying to establish himself as an artist. He eventually abandoned the effort, but he remembers his struggling Roman period with great fondness.

Up in Florence, Curtis "Bill" Pepper was living in a pensione and writing a first novel about the experiences of a young man in the war. Pepper had had an exciting war in Italy. With Professor Dick Lewis of Yale, Edith Wharton's biographer, he had served in a secret, hand-picked intelligence unit called MIS-X, attached to the British Army. The MIS-X specialized in "escape and evasion," and Lewis and Pepper, and a Mexican-Englishman, had the whole front between the Eighth and Fifth armies, opening "rat tunnels" across the German lines so that Allied pilots who had been shot down and hidden by the partisans could get back to the Allied side of the front. After the German surrender, the unit was put to investigating war crimes of Fascist officials. Pepper told me, with undiminished awe, "We had a hundred fifty-three war crime trials to investigate, and never once did we come across an instance of an Italian being cruel to a prisoner."

It was one of the reasons that persuaded Pepper to return to Florence, a city he had loved since 1936, when he had first ridden into it on a bicycling tour of Europe and, in his excitement to see the Masaccios, crashed into another cyclist. Florence was home to him now. He spoke the language and mixed easily with the international set. He could go to a cocktail party and run into Sinclair Lewis or drive over to Settignano and call on Berenson at I Tatti — the stimulation and sense of tradition any young, would-be artist or writer longs for. When he gave up the novel and went down to Rome to get a job on the *Daily American* as a fledgling journalist (he would become the *Newsweek* bureau chief in Rome for many years before returning to full-time book writing), it seemed to him perfectly natural to pick up the phone, call the Royal Danieli Hotel in Venice, and get a quick exclusive interview with Ernest Hemingway, who had just returned from Africa and a near-fatal plane crash. The other reporters' eyes popped a bit, Bill remembers. He had only come to work a few hours before, and here he was chatting with Hemingway.

In Rome and Florence, the least battered of the major Italian cities, the cosmopolitan spirit was again at hand. Up at the American Academy on the Janiculum, scholars barely out of uniform strolled jauntily through the broad shady atrium, and Rome had never been more receptive to their presence. Here were Americans cradling books, not sidearms, at their hips, to partake rather than command. The cocktail party given at the Villa Aurelia by the new postwar director, Laurence P. Roberts, and his charming wife, Isabel, attracted a distinguished Anglophile group that included Iris Origo, Harold Acton, and the Princess Caetani, whose "little magazine" *Botteghe Oscure* would be Rome's version of the *Paris Review*.

Isabel Roberts, the director's wife, had run the Brooklyn Museum while her husband was in the Army. She was a brilliant, active hostess, and it was widely surmised that the Robertses paid for their elegant soirees at Villa Aurelia largely out of their own pockets. They were generous, and their generosity inspired that of others. Among the friends the Robertses made in Florence was a wealthy retired U.S. diplomat, Lewis Einstein, who had a huge villa and a celebrated art collection. On his death, Einstein's relatives discovered that he had left the bulk of his fortune to the academy. They contested the will, but the settlement still left the academy richer by about a million and a half dollars.

The Robertses' tenure, which lasted until 1960, brought the academy to a high point of influence and luster. Anthony Hecht and William Styron received the first two fellowships in literature. Van Wyck Brooks researched *The Dream of Arcadia* while a writer-in-residence. By increasing the stipend for married couples, Roberts was able to attract older, established artists to the academy, where they remained for six months or a year in close daily contact with the students. The director could look down the long refectory table and see young Fellows and Fulbright scholars talking to musicians like Samuel Barber, architects like Nathaniel Owens, writers like Elizabeth Bowen, poets like Archibald MacLeish and John Ciardi. Big, gruff Henry Rowell, the Army officer who had rushed into the academy during the liberation of Rome to find Van Buren hunched over his book in the study, was installed as head of the Classics Department. Every summer the wartime colonel would lead some twenty high school teachers through battlegrounds of fallen marble and make the fragments of history take on substance and form.

Though Rowell became a postwar institution, loved or detested according to one's taste, classical studies were no longer the unifying linchpin of the academy. McKim had envisioned a high place on one of Rome's seven sacred hills where budding architects would draw side by side with archaeologists. But no one designed buildings in the classical style any longer, and the ornamentation of Renaissance Rome had little to do with the simple geometric look of a steel and glass skyscraper like Lever House in New York. This dispersion had its good and bad side, like so many changes. The old unity was gone, to be replaced by an academy where an abstract painter rubbed shoulders with Rowell or Van Wyck Brooks or a pioneer electronic musician like John Cage.

"The case that can be made for such an academy," says its current director, classicist John H. D'Arms, "is that you have a great many activities under one roof, on a small scale. You're living together and eating together, and sharing ideas all the time."

When they descended from the peace of the Janiculum into downtown Rome, members of the academy found themselves immersed in a bewildering human tapestry composed of Roman ruins and of Roman citizens trying to emerge from the ruin and shame of

war. The Italian social fabric seemed an even richer and more con-
fusing kaleidoscope than it had been before 1940. Men with push-
carts jogged beside crammed buses and the occasional old-style luxury automobile. Ragged-looking political demonstrators marched
beneath towering, indifferent palazzi. Rome was ancient and modern, marble columns shadowing a people who were painfully sorting themselves out after the debacle.

It wasn't easy for an American — and even for many Italians —
to read this society, wounded and in flux, where jeeps scurried
through storied roads and signs reading OFF LIMITS TO MILITARY
PERSONNEL hung on sun-drenched walls beneath studios where left-
wing Italian artists and writers voraciously read such hitherto unac-
cessible fare as *For Whom the Bell Tolls* and *The 42nd Parallel.*

Educated Americans who tried to make Italian friends were often
drawn into flattering contact with the aristocracy, as Americans had
been for over a century. The aristocracy, however, was now a trun-
cated, if still gilded, class. The war had not swept away its possessions. The upper-class Americans who returned to Italy somewhat
apprehensively after the war to renew ties with noble relatives
found, to their relief, that things seemed superficially unchanged.
Even while peasant refugees lived in caves and shacks on the outskirts of bombed-out cities, the aristocrats were still a privileged
caste in a poor country, carrying on in the grand manner. They
were still waited on by old family retainers who turned down beds
in the evening and appeared at the tinkling of a silver bell, seeing to
it that fresh-cut flowers were in their appointed vases. Up and
down the peninsula, nobles still possessed vast estates worked by
peasant labor, as in time immemorial. Nor was this inequality altogether resented. Ordinary Italians, who had bowed and scraped
before pushy, ill-mannered Fascist officials, arrogant Germans, and
often inebriated Allied occupation soldiers, found it less onerous to
bow before a native count or baron who was at least a gentleman.
Old traditions live on in ancient cultures, even in modern times. I
remember, as late as 1965, going with my wife to pick up our car in
downtown Rome and seeing Prince Torlonia riding out of his palazzo on horseback, a weird, marvelous sight, and the parking attendant practically falling on all fours as if we had been in deepest
feudalism, crying out, "Good day, my prince."

A sea change had washed over the peninsula, however, when the
young King Umberto had been sent into exile in Portugal. The

royal family's cravenly flight before the German occupiers of Rome in 1943 had not been forgotten, and three years later, in their first major vote after the war, the Italian people elected by a narrow margin to abolish the monarchy and dwell in a republic. At one stroke, the nobles were disinherited as a power center. This was a seminal event. For centuries, Italian aristocrats had been the sometimes brilliant, often fickle, custodians of power, from the Medicis in the Renaissance to Count Camillo Cavour in the Risorgimento. The new republican constitution specified that "Titles of Nobility are not recognized." Many individual nobles reacted to the crisis with elan and energy and stepped into positions of power in the postwar industrial elite, taking advantage of their money, international connections, and command of languages. They were absent, however, from positions of power in Rome and, with few exceptions, from intellectual life. Who would replace them?

Italy's institutions, sapped by twenty years of fascism, had all but been severed by the war. The great pre-Fascist political parties were largely gone, vanished into the dust of a more stately era. An American looking over the political graffiti littering walls up and down the Italian peninsula could only scratch his head at the proliferation of names and symbols. The most ubiquitous of all was also the most puzzling to the untrained Anglo-Saxon eye. This was the letter W, which preceded fiery undulating messages of all sorts; in Italian it stands for the two *v*'s in viva. An upside-down W, also a common sight, stood for "down with."

As the wall slogans testified, two new political forces had emerged from the war to begin a long, hard-breathing wrestling match for power. One was the Communist party, whose hunted and persecuted members during fascism had formed the backbone of the wartime resistance. At war's end, the Communists had turned in their weapons to the Allies but preserved their carefully nurtured reputation as heroes in the Garibaldi tradition. The Communist hammer and sickle was a prominent part of wall art, and when the 1948 elections drew near, the Communists and their Socialist allies unveiled a superb poster showing Garibaldi's stern but beloved face and exhorting the people to vote for their Democratic Popular Front.

A few weeks later a counterposter appeared: Garibaldi's face had been turned upside down, revealing the stern but unloved image of Joseph Stalin. This clever turnabout was the work of the Christian

Democrats. Like their Communist rivals, the DC (Democrazia Cristiana) had barely come into being when Mussolini seized power and put it out of business. The Catholic party's founder, a tall jut-jawed Sicilian priest named Don Sturzo, fled to exile in London and then New York. His successor, a craggy-faced scholar from the northeast of Italy, Alcide De Gasperi, found shelter in the Vatican Library and was safe from the Fascist police so long as he did not step outside St. Peter's Square. The territory of Vatican City, which includes the square within Bernini's colonnades, was and is as neutral as Switzerland.

The 1948 elections — Italy's first true political poll since 1924 — pitted these two antagonists together in a classic battle of opposites. Neither the Soviet-backed Communists nor the "Vatican" party had existed as a national force before the twenty-year Fascist interlude, which made the outcome that much more uncertain. The Communists looked strong, as they always do. Red flags sprang up like tulips in the piazzas as Communist orators cried out against age-old social injustices. The Christian Democrats were no less dramatic. Squads of electioneering "flying priests" raced around the countryside to energize the piety of Catholic church-goers and back the Christian Democrats' nonpriestly candidates. Loudspeakers mounted on church belfries blared out electioneering sermons by village priests, often in cacophonous competition with scratchy renditions of "Motherland" and other red marching hymns at Communist Sunday "folk festivals." Priests warned the faithful that Communist voters risked excommunication, a sly draconian threat aimed at the conventionally Catholic wives of Communist workers.

The American embassy became deeply involved in the election, reflecting Washington's fears that a Communist victory would wreck Europe's still fragile peace and rip the Yalta agreement apart. Secretary of Defense Lovett, Marshall, and other leaders in Washington held anxious meetings. "This was before the CIA had really started up," one veteran U.S. diplomat explained. "So those officials got together and passed the hat around in the government, and among Italian-American organizations." Papers recently released under the Freedom of Information Act show that Monsignor Montini, then Deputy Secretary of State, was in close touch with Washington on strategy. Lest anyone get too indignant at this American "interference" in Italian domestic affairs, Italian Commu-

nist leaders today freely admit that their party was then heavily fi-
nanced by Moscow.

The most effective U.S. stratagem was the letter-writing campaign mounted among Italian-Americans, who were urged to be-
seech their relatives in the old country to vote for the Christian
Democrats and against the heathen Communists. A militantly pa-
triotic ethnic group, the Italian-Americans responded by putting
pen to paper. Groaning postmen staggered up Calabrian mule paths
with bulging sacks of personalized campaign literature. By election
day, April 18, 1948, ten million pieces of mail had crossed the
Atlantic, and they undoubtedly helped to fashion the Christian
Democratic triumph. The Vatican's party took nearly half the vote,
with the Communists and Socialists lagging far behind in second
place.

When the astute and principled De Gasperi was sworn into office
as Italy's prime minister, the country moved into a phase of recovery that was swifter than anyone had envisioned. For the Christian
Democrats, however, the great victory of '48 would gradually turn
into a gnawing problem, for there was no one else to replace them
in office. The small lay parties at the center were too weak, and the
Communists too strong, to allow for the normal transfer of power
that must occur in any democracy. Italy would become a democracy without democratic change at the top — an anomaly. The
desire to "sweep the rascals out" became the perennial issue in Italian life, and the Communists upset all the predictions by slowly
continuing to increase their vote at the same time Italy enjoyed a
prosperity unmatched in its history.

All that, however, was in the future. Before anyone was quite
prepared for it, Italy suddenly blossomed into the radiant Cinderella
of Europe. This swift if ragged transformation came when Americans were just discovering the neorealistic movies of Roberto Rossellini, like *Rome, Open City* and *Paisan*. These were revolutionary
movies because they had no real hero, no happy ending, none of
the Hollywood stardust. They were appallingly human, and sad,
telling the heart-rending, pathetic stories of people tormented by
war and poverty. When Americans thought of Italy in those days,
they did so with pity. But already the reality was changing, and
Italy was emerging into a great era, a new *Umanesimo* that came to
be a magical twilight of the arcadian Italy of the past.

CHAPTER ELEVEN

lmost overnight, in the early fifties, Italy changed from a country of muddy privation and misery to a land of startling, sensuous vitality. At first the change was visually incongruous, since old and new existed side by side in a socially disassociated human intimacy. In Milan sleek apartment houses and office buildings were thrusting upward from the dusty holes of bombed-out buildings. At the factory gates of firms like Fiat in Turin and Pirelli in Milan, ill-paid, shabbily dressed workers left their bicycles parked in rusty ranks to work spanking new press forges and lathes bought with Marshall Plan money. Within a few years, these workers would be driving their first car, and traffic jams would begin to clog some of the world's most beautiful cities.

When Gina Lollobrigida started her career as a starlet, Cinecittà, the movie lot east of the city, was still a refugee camp, and she married the camp doctor, a Yugoslav. Within a few years she became an international sensation, even more alluring because her beauty conserved something of the earthy, domestic Italian peasant girl, newly glamorous and yet womanly in a traditional Latin mold. "La Lollo," as Italians called her, was a symbol of a fantastic regeneration. All of a sudden, Italian movie actresses had the most luscious, ripe smiles and full breasts in the world, as if the old soil of ruins and woeful history had been fertilized by blood into another spectacular spring.

The first tourists to Capri and the Italian Riviera found the restaurants stocked with fresh seafood, the wine plentiful and good,

Gregory Peck, who starred in the heartthrob comedy Roman Holiday *with Audrey Hepburn, vacationed with his wife and a group of friends at Santa Margherita on the Italian Riviera. In the 1950s and 1960s the hilly, wooded coastline between Genoa and La Spezia, with its many picturesque fishing ports, was one of the most carefree playgrounds of Europe.*

the waiters polite and cheerful, the population eager to show its best face to the world. A British woman recalls visiting Italy on her postwar vacation in 1950: "I couldn't believe it. In London we still had rationing; we couldn't get enough bread; life was still very, very grim. Going to Italy was like going to another world. Italians seemed well dressed, and they were having fun. It occurred to me, 'My God, we've lost the war and they've won it!' "

Nineteen fifty was also the first postwar Holy Year, and it brought hundreds of thousands of Catholic pilgrims to Rome. Boatloads of Americans crossed the Atlantic to attend mass in St. Peter's and stroll through the sunlit streets of the Eternal City past operatic-looking carabinieri, with their black dress uniforms, long swords, and Napoleonic hats. A few discovered ruefully that despite the dressy cops, presumably Catholic pickpockets were not loath to commit sin under the stern gaze of Pope Pacelli and Bernini's marble saints.

In August 1951, after an engrossing visit with Bernard Berenson, who talked to them about the nature of love, Jacqueline and Lee Bouvier arrived in Rome. The Bouvier sisters, aged twenty-two and eighteen, were touring the Continent for the summer. They went to Via Margutta to look up American artist Bill Congden and instead found Italian sculptor Pericle Fazzini presiding at a sort of outdoor atelier in a leaf-shaded courtyard. The two young women made it their Roman headquarters during those hot August days, when the city was half deserted. They would tour museums and go shopping in the morning, coming back to the studio in time for lunch at a nearby trattoria. In the afternoon Lee made ceramic jewelry while Jackie posed for Fazzini, who drew portrait after portrait — all of them abstract. As the sisters wrote in a wry couplet:

> *Jackie so plump and full of attraction*
> *Posed for Fazzini and came out abstraction.*

In their recollections of the journey (later published as *One Special Summer*), they remembered those Via Margutta days affectionately. "Such a gentle Via Boheme," Jackie wrote. Perfect strangers would wander into the courtyard studio — some of them ex-GIs or tourists — and Fazzini would talk to them. If he liked them, as in the case of the Bouvier sisters, he would take them to lunch, give them drawings, teach them to paint or sculpt. Jackie didn't speak

Italian and Fazzini didn't speak English, but, she recalled, "we talked together incessantly." When the sisters left for Naples, Fazzini and his whole gang of artists and onlookers tumbled out into the Via Margutta to shout and wave good-bye.

American tourists who stayed in Italy long enough to really "do" the country — and one could get around very well on five dollars a day in those years, including chilled martinis at Harry's Bar in Venice and outdoor suppers at the Tre Scalini in Rome's Piazza Navona — found the peninsula ever more bisected into two cultures. The pastoral, often beautiful south, dazed into a stubborn yet violent lethargy by the hot winds of Africa, was barely changed from its millennial past. Feudal *signori* still ruled the people with an iron hand, their domination in Sicily and Calabria often reinforced by the local Mafia. Romantic banditry still flourished, and when a young Sicilian named Giuliano took on the Italian state in the early postwar years, espousing self-rule for the tormented island, the authorities hunted him for months until, as most people believe, the Mafia decided he was a hindrance and disposed of him, turning his bullet-ridden body over to the police. In Naples, American tourists and naval officers dining at Zi' Teresa on the crumbling waterfront could still experience the sultry heat and abandon and ripe odors of the Levant, and, strolling into the U.S. consulate, they would encounter hordes of anxious Southerners crowding the waiting room in hopes of being granted visas to immigrate to the States.

The north, by contrast, was cool, self-sufficient, and industrious. The hard-working Milanese saw American economic aid, which would total three and a half billion dollars, as a God-sent chance to rebuild their personal fortunes first of all but also as something more.

Industrialization on the American model offered them a way of resolving Italy's underlying problems, which had roots deep in the peninsula's long and divisive history. Every Italian inescapably looked back to the four centuries when Rome's legions had ruled the world with unchallenged power. Since then, Italians had been forced to compete against one another for survival — Florentine against Genoese, Genoese against Venetian, in a dreary, petty series of cabals and plots, compromises and betrayals, extending even to the papacy, which had left a gaping emptiness at the center of their society and made Italians more loyal to their families than to each other.

ROMA'S PRESS

As the United States' First Lady, Jacqueline Kennedy holidayed along the Amalfi coast with one of her hosts, Fiat Chairman Gianni Agnelli, whose own mother, Virginia, was half-American. Mrs. Kennedy and her sister Lee had toured Italy in 1951, seeking out Bernard Berenson at his Florentine villa, I Tatti, and Italian sculptor Pericle Fazzini on Rome's Via Margutta.

The idealistic patriots of the Risorgimento, like Margaret Fuller's friend Mazzini, had struggled to reconstruct the social fabric through national unity. They had failed because the social classes had still been riven by the gulf between wealthy landowners and the roughly twenty-five million shoeless immigrants (half the country's current population) who had been forced to abandon their native soil in order to live, as they said, "like Christians." Mussolini had sought to resurrect the power of Rome, and the failure of that doomed, vainglorious endeavor had covered the Italians with shame and ridicule. A poor Mediterranean country that had briefly gloried in the heady sense of administering colonies in Africa found itself, at war's end, prostrated, defeated, helplessly small in power and prestige, at the mercy of decisions made in remote and mighty capitals.

Work, in the eyes of northern Italians, appeared as the last chance to dig themselves out of this pit. America, more than just furnishing money to a defeated nation, offered an inspiring model for the solution of Italy's centuries-old failure — poverty, inequality, and the cutthroat, antisocial competition of one Italian against the other for a morsel of food, a suit of clothes, a house, an education for the children, all of these the basic vital ambitions of a family. America had resolved the problem of a fairer distribution of property to all its people, freeing their energies for larger concerns. More than that, the United States had taken in poor, half-illiterate immigrants from all over the world, including some six million southern Italians, Irishmen, Poles, Russian Jews, fiery German socialists, Africans, and even Chinese and Japanese, and had somehow, groping past the ills of slavery and exploitation, fused these people together into a harmonious, productive whole. To Italians, the ideal of harmony had always been the most elusive — and most precious. America seemed a society that northern Italians could, by temperament, admire and emulate. When intellectuals like Milan's celebrated architect Gio Ponti spoke of their city as "a little New York," they were not referring to the skyline, still bare of skyscrapers, but of Milan's capacities to transform Italy. More than Rome, with its baroque, sun-washed, and indolent grandeur, gray Milan emerged in the postwar years as the most representative Italian city and the capital of the nation's astounding "economic miracle."

Italian aristocrats, disenfranchised from political power in the new republic, turned to business with an almost missionary zeal at the moment when the entrepreneur was a national hero. Count Giannino Marzotto, the head of one of Italy's largest textile firms, won the Mille Miglia auto race in 1950 at the wheel of a Ferrari — wearing a gray flannel suit. "I am a businessman," he explained proudly, "not a professional driver." In Milan, Count "Miccio" Borletti rebuilt his Rinascente emporium to bring into being Italy's first American-style department store chain. Supermarkets followed, and cheaper mass-market shops, selling everything from crockery and hardware to blue jeans. At a time when salesgirls in these new department stores were still wearing ugly black uniforms like orphans in an institution, superbly dressed Italian aristocrats were flying on TWA Constellations to London and New York to get a feel of the world market and adapt themselves to the acceptable executive mold. "We've got to cut out long lunch hours and afternoon naps," one of them reported sternly. "It's not the style in which business is done over there."

Italian entrepreneurs and workers were anything but lazy, and their products were blessed with style. Emilio Pucci, having survived a dangerous and difficult wartime service — which included torture by the Gestapo after having smuggled Ciano's secret diaries to Switzerland — caught the eye of American buyers in Florence when he began to design fashions in the early 1950s. Tuscany had always been blessed with skilled artisans, and Pucci hired them to make superb, colorful textiles, but he was unsure how to market his radiant, inventive products until a troop of acquisitive Americans walked up the grand staircase of Palazzo Pucci, on Via dei Pucci, a few blocks from Giotto's campanile, and fell all over themselves with enthusiasm. He recalls the experience with genuine gratitude: "I didn't know what a checkbook was, I had no idea what prices to charge." His visitors — Carmel Snow, *Life*'s Sally Kirkland, Laurence Marcus and his wife, Hannah Troy, and many others — were willing to write out their own orders and help the elegant, slender marchese decide what items to push for the American market.

"All these people," Pucci told me, "were discovering Italy with glee, happiness, kindness, and this meant suddenly an economic possibility to an agrarian country. By coming over to Italy, looking around feverishly for talent, exchanging information with us, and setting standards, they caused our country to burst out in thousands of initiatives."

Aristocrats like Pucci were not the only innovators. In Turin, a former bicycle mechanic named Pininfarina and his two handsome sons were designing automobiles so beautiful that the big manufacturers in Detroit, and in Europe, began secretly ordering mock-ups of prototype cars. One of Pininfarina's creations, the 151 Cisitalia, would be exhibited more than once by New York's Museum of Modern Art.

Postwar Italian design extended to the utilitarian as well as the luxurious. The stubby, graceful Vespa motorscooter, powered at first by spare military engines, replaced the bicycle on Italian roads before becoming an international hit. Its popularity lay in its style as well as in the particular Italian consideration for women that it conveyed. Prewar motorcycles had been vehicles of male machismo — fast, dangerous, oily, as noisy as machine guns, a vehicle on which a lady would mount only for the thrill of wrapping her arms around a knight's shoulders and hang on for dear life. The Vespa was a ladylike vehicle, small, dainty, and quiet, its plump, flared rear fender concealing the motor and protecting a woman's skirt against splatterings of oil and eruptions of smoke. One of the epochal sights of Italy in the 1950s and 1960s was that of a pretty girl, elegant in nylon stockings and heels, perched sidesaddle on the back of a Vespa with one arm casually embracing her boyfriend's or husband's waist.

The entrepreneurs who produced these sought-after products, transforming Italy in the process, were not ascetic saints. They retained a handsome share of the profits for themselves and their families, in the time-honored Italian tradition. A very wealthy, fun-loving class of Italians emerged, dazzling their rich American visitors. Consuelo Crespi, who had been a deb in New York before marrying Count Rudi Crespi, remembers how enchanted the Rockefellers, the Mellons, the Paleys, were with the summer life at Portofino, on the Italian Riviera, where stupendous seaside villas nestled luxuriously among groves of maritime pines and yachts rode at anchor in a picturesque fishermen's port.

"The summer style of the Italians made Americans go wild," Consuelo recalled when we talked recently in Rome. "They fell in love with that Mediterranean relaxation and the fantastic Italian *savoir vivre,* sleeping late, going on yachts to islands like Capri and Sardinia, dancing shoeless in nightclubs."

A stunning, lithe brunette, Consuelo was Irish on both sides of her family. At eighteen she had been one of the most photographed debutantes in New York, and at that very young age she had married Count Rudi Crespi, whose grandfather had immigrated to Brazil and made a fortune. The dashing couple went to France on their honeymoon, then drove over the Alps and went to lunch at the Agnellis' in Turin. "My first day in the country I was having lunch with Gianni Agnelli," Consuelo said. "I loved Italy immediately. Everybody looked at me curiously because I was the only American girl who'd ever married an Italian aristocrat without being an heiress."

The Crespis settled in Rome, where they became the most visible and talked-about couple of Italian postwar society. Unfailingly polite and seraphically calm, the lovely Consuelo was more ambitious than American society women married to Italian noblemen of the preceding generation. She had children, went to all the parties, and entertained, but much of her energy went into a career in fashion. In 1963 she began reporting for *Vogue,* whose editor, Diana Vreeland, was one of the great movers in making Italian style known to the world. Every issue of *Vogue* in the late fifties and early sixties had six, ten, twelve pages devoted to Italy, introducing American readers to the elegance of Valentino, the Missonis, Simonetta, Pucci, Gucci, and a tall young American named Ken Scott, who had settled in Milan, near the old silk weaving and dyeing center of Como, and designed spectacularly colorful fabrics. With Diana Vreeland as editor and Consuelo in Rome, *Vogue* not only covered Italian fashion, but served as a showcase for upper-class Italians, with color spreads of their villas and castles, boats, parties, and, above all, their zest and gaiety.

"It was a marvelous time," Rudi Crespi said. "It started in those wonderful, crazy fifties. Everything had gone wrong for so long. The Italians had been repressed under fascism, beaten in the war, humiliated, occupied, then the Marshall Aid money came in and there was a lot of money. Upper-class Italians were suddenly the gayest and best-dressed people in the world."

Italian males recovered their confidence and sex appeal, and one of them, a paunchy, balding Neapolitan, stunned the world by seducing the most beautiful woman in Hollywood and luring her

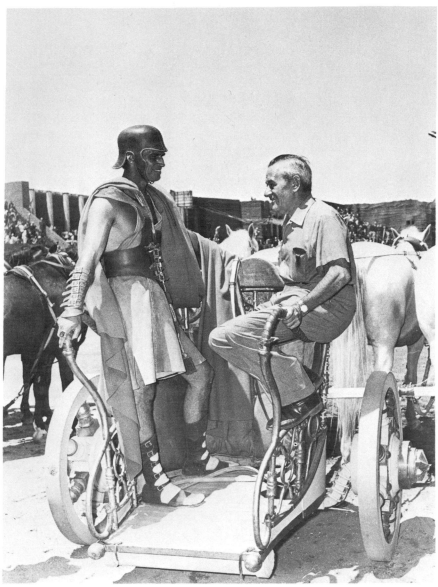

Star Charlton Heston and director William Wyler conferred in a working chariot constructed by studio carpenters at Cinecittà, outside Rome, during the filming of Ben Hur *in 1958. Heston, who returned to Italy to star as Michelangelo in* The Agony and the Ecstasy, *was one of the Hollywood stars who most steeped himself in Italian history and culture.*

ROMA'S PRESS

The late Gary Cooper, arriving at Rome's Excelsior Hotel in 1959, was an idol of Italian movie fans. He had a number of friends among Italian socialites, dating back to the years before World War II, and engaged in a widely publicized love affair in the Italian capital with the American wife of an Italian aristocrat.

away to a volcanic island. The affair began quietly enough in 1949
when Ingrid Bergman, by then a naturalized U.S. citizen (though
everyone thought of her as Swedish), wrote Rossellini an innocent
note from Los Angeles saying how much she'd enjoyed *Rome, Open
City.* Rossellini was on virtually the next plane to Hollywood,
scribbling the synopsis of a movie script on the back of an envelope. It was the sketch for *Stromboli,* the movie that Rossellini made
with Bergman on the island of the same name off Sicily. By then,
Bergman and the heavyset Italian director were lovers, and there
were tacky photographs in the gossip magazines of their tooth-
brushes side by side in the same water glass.

Hollywood's real involvement with Rome began quietly enough
with accountants' reports, when the major studios discovered in the
late forties that royalties on their movies, which had been blocked
by the war, were on deposit in Rome but could not be exported
because of Italian government restrictions. To put those funds to
use, they decided to make a few B movies in Rome, but their interest leaped when *The Prince of Foxes,* shot in Italy and starring
Tyrone Power, became a box-office hit. Suddenly the men who
lunched at Hollywood's Brown Derby awoke to the possibilities of
making historical or biblical spectaculars in Cinecittà, where costs
were enticingly cheap because of low labor costs. The first big-
budget spectacular was William Wyler's *Ben Hur,* with Charlton
Heston and a script partially written by Gore Vidal. What the *Hollywood Reporter*'s Sam Steinman was to call "Hollywood on the
Tiber" came into being with that movie, though it was never anywhere as ruthless as the original.

American stars began to perch at the tables along the Via Veneto
in the evening, spawning a typically Italian sideline business — that
of the paparazzi. The paparazzi were quick-shooting, agile news
photographers skilled in shadowing movie stars and other celebrities, waiting for the moment when a beautiful star was kissing her
co-star or the wind had blown her skirt up or she was sitting beside
a glowering prince in a Ferrari. Rome's showy vulgarity erupted
like another Vesuvius, splattering the hot lava of publicity on anyone within reach.

Being a paparazzo involved hours of waiting followed by breathtaking chases through Rome's narrow streets. Because movie stars
traveled in limousines driven at high speeds by expert chauffeurs,
the paparazzi became expert chase drivers, and whenever one saw a

ROMA'S PRESS

In the late 1950s and 1960s, the most exciting, sexy (and sometimes the most vulgar) street theater in the world was performed every evening in the Roman-circus atmosphere of Via Veneto, where swarming photographers, dubbed "paparazzi" by Federico Fellini, pursued the stars. Among the most beautiful of Rome's women in those years was Ava Gardner.

ROMA'S PRESS

A youthful Jack Lemmon took directions from a look-alike vigile urbano (*Rome traffic cop*) *on Via Veneto, epicenter of the phenomenon that Sam Steinman of the* Hollywood Reporter *dubbed "Hollywood on the Tiber."*

big car, sometimes even a Cadillac, being pursued recklessly by a swarm of little Fiats, motorcycles, Vespas, and Lambrettas, it was probably a movie star. There was even a "king of the paparazzi," who was able to slip through any security screen, climb any wall, wait patiently for any number of hours, in order to get his shot. In the movie *La Dolce Vita,* ex-journalist Fellini drew on the experiences of the paparazzi to create the marvelous scene where Anita Ekberg goes wading in the Trevi Fountain in a long, low-cut black dress with Marcello Mastroianni, only to be slapped across the face by her half-drunk Hollywood husband (played by Lex Barker, the former Tarzan) when she finally turns up early in the morning at the Excelsior Hotel on Via Veneto to the popping of flashbulbs.

Most American stars had a marvelous time in Rome, despite the hazards of the paparazzi. Shelley Winters recalls the evenings that would begin on Via Veneto before midnight and end at dawn: "We used to go to a nightclub near the Tiber, in a cave. We used to dance all night, and sleep all day on the set of *Mambo* when we weren't shooting. Dino [De Laurentiis] used to wonder what was wrong with us all." Gregory Peck turned into a soccer fan when he was in town for the shooting of *Roman Holiday*. On Sunday he would go down to the big stadium built for the 1960 Olympics, and his presence escaped neither the press nor the public. The players played better knowing he was watching, and the spectators were so tickled by his presence that they once chanted Gre-go-rio, Gre-go-rio, as if they were crowning an emperor. Charlton Heston, who was successively Ben Hur and Michelangelo, became such an art scholar, and in particular an expert on Buonarotti, that he had involved technical arguments with the director of *The Agony and the Ecstasy* during the preparation of the dummy Sistine Chapel. Few other stars took their craft that seriously, and some made a veritable business out of fountain-wading and other publicity tricks. Jayne Mansfield had a famous dress that came undone at the top, accompanied by a great deal of astonished squealing on her part and the paparazzi vaulting over restaurant or nightclub tables to catch the magic moment.

Fellini, who is a keen observer of everything despite a deceptively vague manner at times, remarked that "for American actors and actresses, making a movie in Italy represented a kind of vacation within a privileged colony, amid all the cultural and historical seductions that Italy has always represented for Americans, the land of culture, of art, of the popes, of the Renaissance, of monuments. For them, it was like a working vacation." By 1960, Hollywood people had indeed created a little colony along Via Veneto. Producers had suites at the Excelsior or the Grand Hotel. Publicity flacks virtually lived at the tables of the Cafe de Paris, across the street from the Excelsior, and one American, Charlie Fawcett, a bit player, even proclaimed himself "the mayor of Via Veneto." He would be there every evening, greeting celebrities or people in the trade and holding court. Most stars, surrounded by the Hollywood colony, did not have much to do with Italians. With the exception of Anthony Quinn and Richard Basehart, who married Italians and lived in Italy on and off for years, very few Hollywood people broke into the snobbish, inward-looking society circles of Rome. The Hollywood stars, as Fellini added dryly, saw mostly Italians who were waiters, maids, drivers, "a people anciently accustomed to deal with foreigners."

Most other American professional men, and their families, lived in a similar, semicolonial style, as they would have lived in almost any other foreign country. (The exception is Britain, because of the common language and similar outlook.) Italy was a sunny, beautiful country in which to reside and fairly calm politically in those postwar years, but it was unmistakably foreign, and the tight family structure of Italians was hard to penetrate socially. "I couldn't understand why the Italians, who are so warm, are so impenetrable," remarked a longtime American professional in Rome. "You're on friendly terms with dozens of people, but they rarely become close friends. Then finally I figured it out. Italians aren't just impenetrable to foreigners. They're impenetrable to one another."

By the mid-sixties, there were some fifty thousand American residents in Italy, including diplomats at the big American Embassy on Via Veneto, movie people, lawyers, Americans working for the Food and Agricultural Organization of the United Nations in Rome, some thirty American foreign correspondents who spent much of their time in the Middle East, businessmen, artists, scholars, photographers, and the occasional celebrity who didn't quite fit any category. Henry Luce was one. He kept an office in Rome for a while when his wife was the U.S. ambassador. American playwright Robert Ardrey was another; he wrote best-selling books on paleontology while living in Rome with his wife, a beautiful South African actress.

One saw these people occasionally because most Americans moved in an international set. An "interesting" dinner party in Rome might include the Ardreys, an Italian actress, photographer Roloff Beny (a longtime Canadian expatriate in Rome), one or two FAO officials, a few diplomats (American and foreign), a cardinal or a theologian from the Gregorian, perhaps a Washington journalist passing through Rome on a fact-finding trip, and an artist or two. In Florence, one tended to see a greater number of American art scholars; in Milan, more businessmen; and in Naples, more high-ranking Sixth Fleet officers.

Though they grumbled, naturally, as one does in any short-term foreign assignment, American executives and other professional people lived glamorously in Italy. They usually rented big apartments with panoramic terraces or lived in the historic center of town in old but picturesque settings. They dined out pretty much whenever they wanted to at first-class restaurants. Those who cared to went to La Scala or the Rome Opera, or the concerts at the Baths of Caracalla. The ones who lived in Naples and Rome usually belonged to beach clubs, and residents of Milan could whip up to the Italian lakes within an hour for sailing or be skiing in Switzerland within two or three hours. The wives studied art and Italian history, took tennis lessons or yoga classes, and went to PTA meetings at the local American school much as they would have at home. The language barrier was a bore for them, complicating shopping and making relations with the maid more emotional. Still, many of them had full-time, live-in maids, whom they griped about at the time and lamented afterward, for it is difficult to disabuse oneself of that luxury. "What gave our life its substance and gloss was the availability of live-in servants, cheaply," said a hard-headed, practical American woman who has lived in Italy for years.

Outside the cities, where the transient executives or officials tended to be, one was more likely to come across the new generation of American expatriates. Some of them still lived in villas or, like Peggy Guggenheim, in a Venetian palazzo, but they no longer tended to live in hotels for very long because it had become too expensive. There were also more American expatriates living close to the ground, in rustic farmhouses or country houses, cultivating a few friends among other foreign residents and getting to know their neighbors and the tradespeople, the postman, the carabiniere. Contact with ordinary Italians in the countryside remained the great attraction it had always been because of their open-faced kindness. Robert Cabot, a retired U.S. diplomat who lived for some years in a rustic villa outside Florence, told John Bainbridge, "I would say that the peasants in this part of Italy are the kindest and most understanding people of any social class that I have found anywhere in

(Right) *Rome's grandly handsome American Academy, founded in 1894 with funds partly contributed by J. P. Morgan, has become the rendezvous of American artists and scholars in Italy. In this 1954 photograph, the Academy's most celebrated postwar director, Laurence Roberts, escorts U.S. Ambassador Clare Boothe Luce and Henry Luce to their car after an Academy function.*

the world." Caresse Crosby, who had edited *Black Sun Press* in Paris and published some of Hemingway's earliest work, bought a gigantic castle in the late 1950s that dominated the little village of Rocca Sinibalda in Umbria. The castle had something like three hundred and fifty rooms, some of which were found to contain good frescoes of Michelangelo's school under the whitewash on the walls, and a terrace over a precipice so deep it was one of the few places where guests could have cocktails while observing a hawk circling *below* them. Caresse, a great believer in one-worldism, designed a universal flag, which she flew from the battlements of her castle, and now and then she would summon the villagers to pledge allegiance to the ideals of one world. They cheerfully consented, accepting the American lady's eccentricities for what they were — well meaning.

The desire to be master, or mistress, of one's time, to be selective about seeing people, to be able to work quietly on a long project — all these motives continued to draw reflective Americans to Italy. The poet Robert Fitzgerald lived with his wife and numerous family in a big villa overlooking the sea at Levanto on the Italian riviera during the late 1950s. He was translating *The Iliad* from the Greek, and the relative isolation, the lack of external pressure, and the beauty of the sea and pine-covered hills made the loneliness of the place more bearable. Friends periodically came to visit from the States. The children went to village schools and learned Italian. The Fitzgeralds could go to town in less than five minutes for shopping or to call on the local nobleman, Baron "Jeppe" Massola, who spoke perfect English, had a beautiful Genoese wife, and had hidden an escaped English officer in his villa during the war.

Italy is so much smaller than the United States — three quarters the size of California — that it was not considered unusual by any of these new expatriates to board a train and go to Milan overnight, in order to hear an opera or a concert at La Scala, or to Florence for a particularly interesting exhibit. Two events were on almost everyone's list sooner or later: the Venice Biennale, a huge exhibit of contemporary art from all over the world, and the Spoleto Festival. American artists were heavily involved in both events.

Venice and Spoleto are both theatrical places: the towns themselves become a stage where everyone meets — players and spectators. I can remember a Biennale in the early sixties when Peggy Guggenheim's low, tasteful palazzo at the foot of the Grand Canal was part of the show. She had loaned it, and it held the then-startling works of American "pop" artists, like a huge toothpaste tube and a fluffy cheeseburger by Claes Oldenburg. You'd come out of her palazzo, cross the Grand Canal in a gondola, walk into St. Mark's piazza, and someone would point out Oldenburg, Rauschenberg, Lichtenstein, sitting and having coffee and reading the Paris *Trib*. If you had the gall, you could go over and talk to them about their exhibits.

Spoleto had the same stagelike atmosphere, only even more collected and compressed. Gian-Carlo Menotti, the Italian-born composer and adoptive American, inaugurated the festival in June 1958, with the conductor Thomas Schippers, as a place for young artists to play professionally. Menotti also felt that the concert stage had isolated performing artists from ordinary people, and he wanted a place where art could be practiced as an everyday activity. Spoleto was an ideal site. The half-forgotten Umbrian town, only a two-hour drive or train ride from Rome, had two beautiful seventeenth-century theaters and a dramatic piazza for outdoor events.

His Festival of the Two Worlds, as it was originally called, wowed Italians (and everyone else) with its superlative mix of art, show business, and high society. It had enormous class mixed with the quicksilver inventive casualness of a happening. Though the festival's hard-pressed organizers were often in a state of panic, the atmosphere around them was pleasingly indolent. The festival ran from mid-June to mid-July, when the days were long and sunny and the nights cool. International society would meet at the piazza during the day and gather at night after the last performance at Menotti's or at Countess Spalding's palazzo for midnight suppers that lasted into the wee hours. There was never enough hotel space in Spoleto during the festival, and Menotti, already hard pressed for time, had to undertake a third career as a hotelier. His Albergo del Matto (Madman's Hotel) was naturally the best place in town.

Dress was casual during the day, smart in the evening, when Roman aristocrats would stroll through the beautiful, ancient streets in black tie, their partners in evening gowns by Valentino and Galitzine, while sweatshirted locals gawked. Many of the Spoletini women had box seats of their own at their windowsills, and the performance they watched was the one put on by the socialites and celebrities who came in droves to opening nights. It was said that the people of Spoleto hadn't had as much excitement since

August 14, 1499, when the last Duchess of Spoleto, Lucrezia Borgia, had stopped in town overnight with a retinue of forty-three coaches, ladies-in-waiting, and bejeweled attendants.

Though Sophia Loren was probably more of a sensation in Spoleto than Lucrezia, to say nothing of Elizabeth Taylor and Richard Burton when they were in Rome filming *Cleopatra,* the Italian aristocracy lent the festival a particular social glitter and showed once again how deep an affinity there had been between upper-class or artistic Americans and the Italian nobility. Many of the aristocrats at Spoleto, like Princess Letizia Ludovisi-Buoncompagni, were themselves children of American mothers. "I am regularly faced by an avalanche of princes, dukes, and duchesses who swarm over my house in their wonderful clothes," Menotti told a reporter, "eating, drinking, and cooking spaghetti in my kitchen."

He would groan about these invasions, but only halfheartedly, since he was a keen enough showman to know how valu.   *hat glitter and excitement was to his brilliant initiative. "I'll tell you what I need," Menotti would say. "One million dollars. One." He was forever facing a money crisis, only to be saved by the generous support of Alice Tully, Mrs. Angier Biddle-Duke, Countess Spalding Paolozzi, Mrs. Henry Heinz III, Mrs. Robert Tobin, Mrs. Ernest Boissevain, the Browns of Brown University, and other American sponsors.

For all its social panache, the festival's success rested on electrifying art. More than any other event, it introduced the best American creative talents to Italian audiences. Chief among them was Thomas Schippers, a radiantly handsome young conductor from Kalamazoo, Michigan. Still in his early twenties when he first appeared at the festival, Schippers quickly became its artistic director and built up an international reputation as one of the world's best conductors of Italian operas and music. He was so esteemed in Italy that shortly before his premature death in 1977 he was offered the post of resident conductor at Rome's Accademia Santa Cecilia.

Extraordinarily attractive and gifted, Tommy Schippers seemed a man blessed by the gods. His lovely wife, Nonie, was the daughter of a steel executive, and together they were one of the most dashing and sought-after couples in the world. Alas, the gods who had given so much finally withheld all. Nonie Schippers died tragically young of cancer in 1973, and Tommy of the same disease four years later.

At Spoleto, American dancers and choreographers helped to revitalize the weakest of Italy's performing arts, as season after season Italian audiences saw the works of Jerome Robbins, John Butler, Paul Taylor, George Balanchine, and Merce Cunningham. More recently, Arthur Mitchell and his all-black Dance Theater of Harlem (a company formed after Martin Luther King's assassination) showed Italians an example of militant art of the highest professional caliber. Two other black groups, the Gospel Singers and the company that brought *Black Nativity* to Spoleto, had a great influence in launching the present boom in Italian "folk" music, much of it historical and political in tone.

The festival not only influenced Italian taste year after year, but also gave young American artists the chance to perform under directors like Luchino Visconti, Franco Zeffirelli, and Louis Malle. Shirley Verrett was little known when she first sang at one of Charles Wadsworth's Noon Concerts in 1961. The following year she sang the title role in a splendid production of *Carmen,* directed by Menotti and conducted by Schippers, and the critical acclaim helped launch her international career. Along with such theatrical stars as Arthur Kennedy, Rod Steiger, and Claire Bloom, relatively unknown youngsters like Al Pacino and Jill Clayburgh appeared in stage productions, and the Open Theater and Ellen Stewart's Cafe La Mama Theater introduced Off-Broadway to Italy.

Nureyev and Fonteyn danced at the festival, as did Vassiliev and Maximova. Charles Wadsworth's Noon Concerts, which lasted an hour and were often reason enough for going to Spoleto, introduced Hungarian pianists and Japanese violinists. In 1965 a dozen world-famous poets came to the festival, including two Nobel Prize winners plus the greatest of all living poets, Pablo Neruda, who happily lapped up the sunshine in the piazza and flirted with all the pretty women, and Yevtushenko, who was irritable and arrived late. Ezra Pound was also persuaded to make an appearance that year. Caresse Crosby shepherded him to Spoleto in her limousine and sat him down in the piazza, where Pound, by then a virtual recluse, reposed with a wary defiance.

His admirers made a fuss over him, however, and soothed the old man's anxieties to the point where he lingered on, then moved in with Menotti and could be seen going to all the performances. As he shuffled with his delicate footwork over the cobbled street, Olga Rudge and Caresse Crosby hovering over him and strangers

Though Ezra Pound often would not speak to visitors, in the summer of 1965 Caresse Crosby prevailed upon the poet to go to the Spoleto Festival where poets of the stature of Pablo Neruda, Ted Hughes, Rafael Alberti, Evgenij Yevtushenko, and Allen Tate were reading their works. Pound seemed revitalized by the experience, though his vocal output remained spare. The festival's founder and director, Maestro Gian-Carlo Menotti, stands behind Pound in this press-conference photograph, while one of Menotti's most indefatigable staff members, Nadia Stancioff, is on the Maestro's right.

In 1968, the artist Christo "packaged" some of Spoleto's ancient stones. Though the fish-eye photograph is contrived, with dancers undulating in their leotards for the camera, it did capture one aspect of the festival, which was to situate avant-garde art within the stagelike confines of a medieval Italian hill town.

A youthful and not-yet-famous Al Pacino played the part of Murph in Israel Horovitz' one-act play The Indian Wants the Bronx, *in 1968. The Spoleto Festival was a great proving ground for dozens of young American actors and dancers.*

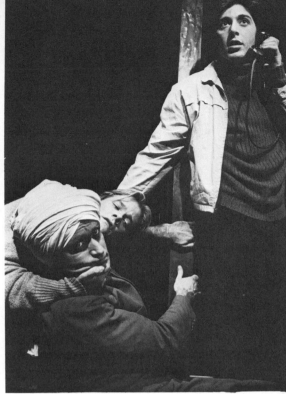

FESTIVAL DEI DUE MONDI — SPOLETO

Jerome Robbins presented "Ballets U.S.A." at the very first Spoleto Festival in 1958, which also included Eugene O'Neill's A Moon for the Misbegotten *and Verdi's* Macbeth *staged by Luchino Visconti and conducted by Thomas Schippers. Here, Robbins rehearses* The Concert, *a ballet set to Frederic Chopin's music.*

FESTIVAL DEI DUE MONDI — SPOLETO

of many nationalities asking him for autographs, it seemed like Pound's homecoming into the company of his artistic peers, with the wartime treason ignored, if not forgotten.

The previous year Menotti had invited the world's leading sculptors to show their work at Spoleto, outdoors, among the ancient stone palaces and walls, and the citizens had liked some of the statues so much they became permanent acquisitions. Alongside such sculptors as Henry Moore were some younger Americans, among them Beverly Pepper. A New Yorker, Beverly had met Bill in Florence when he was writing his novel and she was starting her career as an artist. They had married and gone to live in Positano, where Beverly painted and Bill wrote a television cooking series based on escape and evasion for an American producer, who added the final inappropriate touch by skipping out on the project. Bill went to the *Daily American,* then *Newsweek,* and Beverly turned from painting to metal sculpture. When she first went to make full-size pieces at the steel foundry at Terni, the Italian workmen couldn't get over this good-looking, stylish woman in her overalls bending enormous sheets of steel. She became successful, then celebrated.

After leaving *Newsweek,* the Peppers bought an old tower at auction, near the Umbrian town of Todi, which they transformed into a beautiful and luxurious residence. Yet they remain Americans despite their more than twenty years in Italy. "We think that being an expatriate is a state of mind," Bill told me at Todi. "There are people who come here, it doesn't matter how long, who separate themselves from their country. We've lived here for years and continued to be Americans."

The increasing speed of travel had made it easier, naturally, to maintain residences, ties, friendships, in America and in a foreign country. By the end of World War II, the three-tailed Connies made Milan or Rome a long overnight flight from New York, with a stopover in Shannon. "When the first 707s touched down at Ciampino," recalls Bob Edwards, a Fifth Army veteran who settled in Rome and became a movie producer (*Night Porter, Beyond Good and Evil*), "that was the real revolution: New York was eight hours away." By then, charters and package tours were bringing almost a million Americans a year to Italy.

These fortunate pilgrims were set down, with their heads still full of altitude and their stomachs a half-day behind, amid the bustling

American sculptor Beverly Pepper, who lived in Rome in the 1960s with her journalist and writer husband, Curtis "Bill" Pepper, bent huge pieces of metal in this foundry near Terni. When she first showed up, demure and attractive, and began twisting sheets of steel, the foundry workers couldn't believe their eyes.

confusion of Fiumicino Airport and then plunged into the jumble of antiquity and modernity called Rome that broke down into a different texture of colors from the familiar ones of home, a softer air, language and sounds that assaulted the senses. Once the change had been as gradual as the clip-clop of horses' hooves down the last hairpin curves of the Simplon Pass, and, in Henry James's lovely phrase, the slowly changing landscape "whispered in broken syllables that Italy was at hand." There was no whispered transition now, no restfulness. Outside the green blinds of a window in a Rome or Florence pensione, every motorscooter in Italy seemed to be racing by. Sightseeing and shopping had to be articulated into a single day's tour, like a map folded into one's pocket, and in the evening the new tourist sank gratefully into a little metal chair at a cafe along Via Veneto and watched Italian humanity going by, every face a picture.

If jet-age tourism made for quick impressions and raised complex questions abruptly, to be tasted like a tiny, savory cup of espresso coffee and then forgotten before they could be half-answered, it also broke down the remaining class barriers in travel. The flights from New York, Boston, Los Angeles airports unloaded a Via Veneto variotype of Americans — art-collecting millionaires, bearded or braided students with knapsacks on their backs, vacationeers from every profession and state, priests, nuns, Italian-Americans going to visit relatives, and returning veterans who visited the old battlefields and deposed flowers before the long, white rows of graves at the Anzio military cemetery. Most of these Americans worried vaguely about Italy's politics but took pride in the country's economic recovery. "We sure had something to do with that," beamed a Fifth Army veteran touring Italy on the thirtieth anniversary of Rome's liberation.

Italy's shiny new prosperity had now trickled down to the south. Poor, landless peasants were no longer mobbing the U.S. consulate for visas. For the first time within memory, the number of applicants was dropping steadily year by year. The peasants still pulled up roots and moved, but now they went north to Turin or Dusseldorf, to work in factories that were closer at hand. Yet the south itself, despite the age-old ills of unemployment, was changing visually, looking prosperous for the first time in centuries. There were new apartment houses in the villages, television antennas, and family sedans parked bumper to bumper.

The transformation was inconceivable to someone who had known the old south at the turn of the century. One immigrant returning from Brooklyn for his first visit home literally could not believe his eyes. He had left his native village near Naples in 1901 as a barefoot boy of twelve. As the taxi drove into the streets of that same village seventy years later and the driver said, "Here we are," the old man responded in a fit of fury. "You're cheating me!" he cried, pounding the floor of the taxi with his cane. "This isn't my village! I won't pay you a cent until you take me to my village!"

It took the chief of police to calm the old man, who sank into a daze at the sight of streets filled with cars and trim, new, three- and four-story buildings. He could remember the village when the streets were only muddy lanes, there was no electricity and hardly anything to eat, and bandits had been hung outside the battlements of the nearby castle. He had conserved those pictures of his village in his mind for almost seventy years, like fading but perfectly clear tintypes. And now everyone had television sets, and the "wash machine" — every family had one of those. The old man was in such a state of confusion he had to be put to bed for a day. "My God," he would mutter for weeks afterward, "these people live better than we do in Brooklyn." It was, for him, the ultimate shock.

Italian prosperity gave many Italians a second car and a slightly less amiable disposition because they had possessions to worry about. The social atmosphere, however, despite a constant rise in the standard of living and an increase in personal bank deposits of about 300 percent since the war, was like sunshine in the foreground with coal black clouds advancing over the horizon. There was something in the air that Fellini caught in his epochal movie, *La Dolce Vita,* which he would define as "a feeling of impending catastrophe that caused people to grasp even more tightly that spiral of pleasure and good times which had followed as a natural consequence to the war." In the early sixties, when the movie was released, these premonitions of a darker time were still faint. Italy had dug itself out of its pit. The country was changing dramatically, becoming urbanized, yet the old arcadian beauty still remained in many places. The days that passed were clearly moments in a rapid transition, yet they could be held, treasured, dipped in the dark-edged glowing sunlight, almost as Story had done with his *dolce far niente* hours in Bagni di Lucca and Castelgandolfo.

The twilight of this golden age reached its climax in the Catholic heart of Rome. In the winter of 1961, John Kennedy had two years of his brilliant life ahead of him. The papacy had been assumed a few months earlier by a peasant-born cardinal, Roncalli, who radiated goodness and hope from every cell. This Pope, so we have been told, was walking through the Oratory of St. Paul's Outside the Walls one winter day in 1961, worrying about the problems of the world and the troubled future of the Catholic church, when he turned to his Secretary of State, Cardinal Cicognani, and revealed something of a divine inspiration. "A council," he cried thankfully.

John's council, the second in modern times and thus quickly tagged by newsmen as Vatican II, opened amid matchless pomp and magnificence of show on October 11, 1962. A great procession of high prelates, glowing like a field of flowers in their colorful robes, wound through St. Peter's Square and into the vast basilica where they sat on tiers of seats erected on both sides of the central nave. The American cardinals and bishops sat rather glumly through the first weeks of largely procedural debate, as the various liberal and conservative factions felt each other out and polished up their theological battle equipment. The Americans were somewhat on the sidelines. After O'Connell, the true lovers of Rome had pretty well sunk out of sight except for Cardinal John Wright, and the American Church was ruled by a legion of dynamic Irishmen — the so-called brick and mortar bishops who excelled at raising funds and building churches but whose shrewd tongue could be tied in knots by theological debate. The council, particularly in those opening rounds, was made for European bishops, who excelled in Vatican power politics and who had lived cheek by jowl with Rome all their lives.

A second impediment to Americans was that all debate was conducted in Latin, a language familiar to most of them but one in which they were hesitant. Wonderful Cardinal Richard Cushing, a man of overflowing communicability, sat through a couple of months' debate in St. Peter's and then confessed, "Aw, I'm going home. I'm just wasting my time here." There were able Americans at the council, of course, among them Cardinal Joseph Ritter of St. Louis, and the shy, brilliant, Chicago-trained Cardinal Meyer, who was probably the most impressive and important American. He had studied at the Lateran, with Cardinal Ottaviani and Ruffini as his teachers, men from the very inner rank of curial barons. Meyer handled Latin capably and spoke Italian well, but his basic shyness made him reluctant to speak out in the council's early stages. Once, invited to lunch at Cardinal Cicognani's apartment, Meyer turned to the deeply conservative Ottaviani and said, "Your eminence, I'm going to speak in the debate on Dei Verbum."

"It's about time," Ottaviani rumbled.

"Your eminence," Meyer continued, "you may not like what I'm going to say."

"I don't care what you're going to say," Ottaviani replied, "whether you're for me or against me. Just speak, Meyer, speak."

It was perhaps indicative of the initial insecurity of American bishops in the Roman arena that Meyer always called the old barons like Ottaviani and Cicognani "your eminence," while they called him "Meyer," despite his equal rank in the College of Cardinals.

Ultimately, the Americans had a deep influence on certain council decisions, particularly in the area of religious liberty. Here, the United States possessed the most influential thinker to appear in Rome, the Jesuit theologian John Courtney Murray. A patrician-looking man who was actually the son of a Scots-born gardener, Murray had not been called to the council's preparatory sessions as a *peritus* (expert) because the Europeans who dominated these talks were generally unaware of American theology and suspicious of the liberal and predominantly Anglo-Saxon currents racing through the world's consciousness in the twentieth century. Cardinal Spellman, however, thought Murray the best living theologian and brought him to the council. The American Jesuit was hardly a stranger in Rome. He had studied at the Gregorian University and had been influenced by the liberal ideas of Leo XIII. He remained more of an intuitive thinker than a great scholar, however, and would query his brilliant former fellow student at the Gregorian, Bernard Lonergan: "Look, Bernie, you know how doctrine has developed, is there anything similar to this in Leo?"

Once he'd researched his ideas, Murray was forceful and persuasive in presenting them. Cardinal Wright brought Murray before the Theological Commission, which was presided over by Ottaviani, the prime papalist in Rome, who still thought largely in terms of the kind of absolute authority enjoyed by Pius IX. Murray was diametrically opposed. As he had argued in his book *We Hold These Truths,* Murray believed that the separation of church and state was a good in itself. To a curialist like Ottaviani, this was heresy of suspiciously Protestant origin. Yet in the reality of the mid-twentieth century, it was also a necessity. The Catholic church, Murray argued, could only remain healthy, particularly in Catholic countries, by admitting total religious liberty, because any denial of freedom was an attack on man's spirituality. It was an archetypal American view, brilliantly argued, and the debate between the persuasive, forward-looking Murray and the brooding Ottaviani, rooted in the past, was one of the dramatic high points of a council dedicated by Pope John to the *aggiornamento,* or updating, of the greatest of the Western churches.

John's luminous papacy marked the culmination of that marvelous golden age, almost a new Renaissance, that swept up Italy after World War II. His death in itself, coming so soon after the assassination of John Kennedy, seemed a portent of change, a dimming of the brightness. His death came too swiftly, but he clung to life. Along with other cub reporters, I remained entombed in the Vatican press room for about thirty straight hours as John went slowly into agony, in pain but lucid.

Finally, at about three A.M. the second night, we couldn't stand being cooped up any longer and burst out into St. Peter's Square, where the radio had said thousands were praying. We found only a few miserable-looking nuns from an obscure order kneeling in the square, praying, being bombarded by photographers' flashlights as if they had been movie stars. (That picture was in the next day's papers all over the world, the fibbing image of a prostrate Rome.) The square was otherwise deserted except for a knot of young men loudly arguing around the obelisk at the very center. Going over to check them out, I found about ten American sailors from a destroyer berthed in Naples arguing politics with about a dozen young Italian Communists. The two groups were going at it hot and heavy but peacefully, a bull session illuminated by the single lit window of the Apostolic Palace, where the Holy Father lay dying. Both the sailors and the Communists called on John's liberalism to justify and buttress their arguments, but the dying Pope was summoning the final reserves of strength to broadcast a universal appeal to the world while Rome slept, buried in the darkness of a million empty wineglasses and unwashed plates of pasta. Only the U.S. sailors and their antagonists wrangled below his window in a homely stew of politics and philosophy, while the great Pontiff called out over their heads to all humanity, but enfolding them also, "Et Unum Sint," And All Men Shall Be Brothers.

Whoever lived though the Joanine age in Italy will probably never see another like it. The era of John was a time of renewal, of *aggiornamento,* for all Italian society, and he will remain its symbol as no one else. Across the length and breadth of the peninsula people were on the move, exchanging a plot of land for an office desk, changing their social class, challenging each other's politics, ideas, and sexual roles.

"It was like a new *Umanesimo,*" Bill Pepper said. "How could it be otherwise, with millions of people coming off the land where they'd been imprisoned for centuries to reclaim their manhood. It was a time of renewal, and loss, just as Fellini told it in *Dolce Vita.*"

The Americans who vacationed in Italy in those years found a sunny, new, and burgeoning country risen phoenixlike from the ashes of war, and they felt proud at America's part in the renewal. Those who stayed longer, or came back often, found themselves enveloped in an atmosphere of polite cheerfulness that could hardly be found anywhere else in the world. It seemed Italians were endlessly tolerant. Even in the cities, inebriated tourists would stagger from one moonlit Roman fountain to another, making enough noise to wake the neighborhood, without being either arrested, mugged, or hit by a shoe. "What everyone loved," remarked Milton Gendel, the writer and art critic who has lived in Italy since 1950, "was the high gentility at all social levels typical of an ancient civilization, as in China — the feeling that in manners, in dealing with people, the Italians couldn't put a foot wrong."

To be an American was still to be a special person. Shortly before John Kennedy was killed, one of the Kennedy ladies drank a lot of wine over lunch at a Roman restaurant and decided on the spur of the moment to learn to ride the Lambretta owned by a waiter. The waiter obligingly started it up. She got on, gave it too much gas, and roared into the piazza, where she rammed a passing car. While she was unhurt, the car was dented. Ashen-faced aides from the embassy swarmed over the young driver, offering him money if he didn't go to the press. The young man drew himself up with dignity and said, "Don't worry, I won't tell anyone. I respect the Kennedys. And I'm grateful to America for what she did for this country."

That attitude would soon change, as the United States sank deeper into the poisonous swamp of Vietnam and smooth-talking politicians came to symbolize America's betrayal of its ideals. Yet Americans and other foreigners who lived in Italy between 1950 and 1965, those fifteen years of the golden age, will mostly think of Italy with well-deserved affection and loyalty. It was a marvelous time, when the polluting comforts of technology had not yet blighted the charm of the countryside, and the cities were still largely free of sophisticated, modern-day crime. It was a time that William Wetmore Story would have understood, for it approximated a century later that twilight age of papal Rome, and its passing.

And then everything changed, as it always does in Italy.

CODA

n the spring of 1961, President Kennedy's special assistant Arthur Schlesinger, Jr., flew to Italy to examine ways of breaking the country's deteriorating political deadlock. The Christian Democrats' crushing victory of 1948, engineered to some extent by Washington's intervention, had wedged them into power, and they had been in office uninterruptedly for almost fifteen years. Though their shaky coalition governments seemed to topple over every few months, the faces of politicians staring from wall posters and from the television screen were always the same. As one of the country's wisest postwar leaders, Ugo La Malfa, remarked bitingly some years later: "We Italians change governments often, and men rarely."

Democracies only remain healthy when political forces alternate, and by 1961 Italy was already turning into an anomalous, unhealthy democracy. It was sick because the most powerful opposition party, the one with some of the ablest men, was the Communist Party. It could not come to power without upsetting the Yalta agreements (which may be the Russians' view of what happened in Dubček's Czechoslovakia) and without being a minority government (as was Allende's in Chile), to say nothing of the internal repercussions.

The Christian Democrats' young turks, led by the late Aldo Moro, proposed a classically subtle Italian solution. Moro was then a rising young politician, tall, stooped, with a silvery streak in his hair that appealed to some women, ineffably levantine and master of such intricate syllogisms as his proposal for "parallel convergences." Moro's solution for the Christian Democratic impasse was to bring the Socialist party into the government, an "opening to the left" that he and others hoped would unleash new political energies in the country while keeping the Communists more or less isolated in opposition.

Schlesinger returned to Rome in 1963 and met with Freddie Reinhardt, probably the ablest postwar American ambassador to Italy. He talked to dozens of Italian leaders, often at the home of *The Reporter* magazine's correspondent Claire Sterling. At the end of his mission Schlesinger reported back to Kennedy that a center-left government, as Moro's formula was called, did not present a threat to Italy's role in the western alliance, that it was feasible and probably desirable.

The Socialists, halfheartedly shedding their romantic 1920s Marxism, joined the government in December 1963. They were immediately, and dramatically, dissatisfied. I remember visiting a newly appointed Socialist under secretary at one of Rome's ministries. He had been given a huge corner office, and as he sat at his desk he complained, only half-jokingly, that he felt like Horatius at the bridge fighting off hordes of smooth-talking Christian Democratic officials. "The corruption," he groaned, "you have no idea of its extent. It's like Naples under the Bourbons." Torn between his leftist ideals and party loyalty, he stuck it out for several months and then resigned. He was much happier in the role of combative socialist, an elegant, dark-suited maverick among the workers who raised their fists in protest and shouted against the government.

So were many other Socialist officials. Ashamed of sharing in the patronage, they were psychologically alienated from power. As a result, they continued criticizing the Christian Democrats as if they were still in opposition. They attacked governments in which they were serving and in doing so helped to create the climate of runaway protest that washed over Italy in the late sixties.

The "opening to the left" was probably an inevitable phenomenon of the Joanine era, when Pope John sought to establish a dialogue with all men of goodwill and to break down ideological barriers. Still, in retrospect, the center-left government was a questionable step. It crippled the Socialists and further diminished the possibility that Italy could develop its own variation of the two-party system. The resulting impasse gave young Italians — who were much more liberated and politically demanding than previous generations — the frustrating, ultimately deadly feeling that the country was always mismanaged by the same bunch of "crooks" in Rome, whether they called themselves Christian Democrats, Socialists, or Liberals. This pent-up frustration would help the Communists initially in the early seventies, but much of it would spill over into terrorism and widespread revolutionary attacks against the state.

The Italian crisis that began at the end of the 1960s was a more acute, more Latin version of the crisis of purpose that afflicted other Western societies and, ultimately, the United States itself. In retrospect, it is obvious that American planners in the postwar years missed a crucial opportunity to establish the Atlantic Pact as a kind of commonwealth of democracies, an exclusive club of free nations to which the only standards for membership would have been free elections, a free press, and a free judiciary. Had the presidents and prime ministers of the democracies been able to meet like knights of the round table, in a great body, mystical and practical, economically powerful and politically idealistic, they would have wielded a popular magnetism as great or greater than the "socialist" fraternity organized by Moscow. Third-world countries would have been motivated to develop democratic, two- or multiparty systems, and the addition of any genuinely free nation to such a commonwealth of democracies would have been a victory, a cause for the ringing of bells, of the same rejoicing with which the Communist bloc celebrates a new adherent to the "socialist" philosophy.

Instead, unfortunately, the Dulles brothers and other bleak establishment figures, thin-lipped men of wealth and power, as much at home on Wall Street as in Washington, adopted a narrower view of the Atlantic Alliance, construed to defend free enterprise principally and freedom only as a consequence. Thus, NATO became inimical to non-Communist European socialism, and even more so to democratic Western interpretations of communism. The first sign of this corruption of priorities was probably in Iran, in 1953, when a British and CIA coup overthrew Premier Mossadegh to bring back the shah from his exile in Rome, partly on behalf of the oil companies. By the late sixties, it became entirely possible for the Nixon administration to support a military dictatorship in Greece which tortured its democratically minded opponents — all in the name of freedom. Only, of course, it was not freedom that the men in dark glasses from the darker Washington agencies were defending; it was, in some dim, remote way, "our side," the free enterprise system, and embedded in self-interest the rationalization that democracy could return as it never does in Communist countries.

The American failure to value freedom above free enterprise hit Italy particularly hard. A country emerging from fascism, historically disoriented, an unstable democracy confused by its autocratic clerical traditions — Italy was the weak link in the Western alliance as Red Brigades founder Renato Curcio would argue with impeccable logic. It was a country where the wealthy had always oppressed the poor, where social injustice had reigned for centuries and where the left therefore had a much greater role to play than in an industrially advanced social democracy like the United States. NATO, by the late 1960s, had become for many young Italians a symbol of oppression rather than freedom, part of the American conspiracy — orchestrated, in the popular leftist view, by the CIA — which aimed at keeping the right-wing Christian Democrats perennially in power to defend the interests of multinational companies. Distorted and unfair as this view undoubtedly was, one could argue that America, which had liberated the peninsula in the 1940s together with its democratic allies, had never fully realized the precious responsibility attendant on that deed and had, like Dante's protagonist, at least temporarily lost its way in the dark wood of contemporary history.

By 1970, after union leaders had set off crippling strikes and right-wingers had replied with bombs, Italy was poised on the edge of "destabilization." Whether the subsequent terrorism was all internal, or some of it externally plotted, is still an open question. A difficult, tense decade was beginning for Italy and for the many Americans who loved the country and wanted to continue living there.

As always in periods when the central government has been weak and revolution is in the air, banditry reappeared. On July 10, 1973, tall, red-haired Paul Getty III, an American student who lived in Rome with his actress mother Gail Jeffries, was walking homeward in the vicinity of Piazza Farnese when he was kidnapped. Three months later his abductors slipped one of his ears into an envelope, which they dropped into the mail in Naples. The special delivery letter was stuck for eight days because of a postal strike but finally reached Rome two weeks later. Along with the ear was a note promising to send other pieces of the boy's anatomy unless the ransom was paid. In England the boy's grandfather, oil billionaire Paul Getty, Sr., had second thoughts and the kidnappers received nearly three million dollars. Though they were later arrested, that crime set off the vicious boom in body snatchings, until the papers were writing that kidnapping had become Italy's fastest-growing industry.

As the spiral of political and criminal violence tightened around them, many American residents concluded that Italy was no longer what it had been for so long, a haven from modern-day tensions, a land where life was humanly paced and the people friendly and good. Drug scenes became commonplace in some of Rome's most beautiful squares, like Piazza Navona and the Campo dei Fiori. Suddenly, people didn't feel safe after dark in these areas. "I never used to feel afraid in Rome," an attractive American woman said to me, "and it was such a wonderful, liberating feeling in a big city. Now it's changing and I'm beginning to feel I don't belong here." With her children and possessions, she moved back to New York.

As inflation and maddening "hiccup" strikes steered U.S. and British producers away from Cinecittà, hundreds of American movie people who had loved the glitter and good times of "Hollywood on the Tiber" decamped for the real Hollywood or found jobs elsewhere in the States. Farewell parties became commonplace.

The exodus of longtime residents was smaller in Florence, Venice, and in the countryside. Outside the industrial centers, Italy retained more of its arcadian quality. People were traditionally friendly, though even there Americans were losing their special status and prestige that had made it such a pleasure to be an American in Italy right after World War II. The TV news brought nightly horrors from across the Atlantic into every Italian household: Vietnam, political assassinations, racial hatred, drugs, American support for repressive regimes.

Like so many foreign residents in Italy, an American businessman living in Milan had failed to renew his official residence permit. When he was finally called in, he sheepishly pleaded an oversight and was stunned when a young police officer gave him fourteen days to get out of the country. The American, now thoroughly apprehensive, pleaded that he loved Italy, that he had lived there for years, that he had never meant to allow his permit to lapse.

The unsmiling young policeman remained unimpressed. "Give me one good reason why you should be allowed to remain."

"I — I bring in dollars," the American replied.

The policeman's face tightened. "We don't want your dollars," he snapped. He was too young to remember the 1940s. He had grown up on atrocity stories about Vietnam. He had no relatives in America and not the slightest intention of ever immigrating there himself. He was the prototype of a new urbanized Italian: middle class, tense, liberal with leftist tendencies.

The phenomenon of anti-Americanism in the early seventies was very complex. Gianfranco Corsini, a broad-minded and brilliant Italian Communist who spends a great deal of his time reporting and writing in America, told me: "In the 1960s, with Vietnam and the internal upheavals over civil rights, America ceased to be a model for other Western countries and for Italians in particular."

I would add something to that. The Italians had changed, too. It was not merely that their "love affair with America," as Fellini called it, was over. In some ways it wasn't over at all. The Italians were in the midst of one of their periodic, wrenching ideological adjustments. Millions of sober, middle-class Italians, from civil architects in Siena to shopkeepers in Florence, their wives and families, were rejecting the society to which they belonged.

They went sour on it, ironically, at the very moment when the postwar economic boom was reaching a climax. They saw that the boom had led chiefly to a mammonish orgy of consumption, not to social justice, and they felt guilty and troubled. Most of them had enjoyed the orgy, but when recession struck in the early seventies the orgy ended, and then what? As they looked around, these Italians saw that their country was like a mixed-up jigsaw puzzle, with smoke-belching factories set down casually among beautiful plains with olive trees, with penthouse terraces overlooking slums. Just a few miles from the Naples' *bassi* was a millionaires' row of villas where flowering patios overlooked the blue sea and the women tanning themselves were among the most self-seeking and stylish in the world.

Italy had always been like that, but it was late in the twentieth century now, and precisely because the economic boom had been an uprooting force, transforming peasants into lathe operators and lathe operators into white-collar union officials or even into small businessmen, the need for more schools, hospitals, stricter pollution controls, a reform of the bureaucracy, and all the more or less hidden backstage mechanisms of a modern society became that much more pressing. Granted, most citizens in industrial societies grumbled about inefficient services, but France worked, Switzerland worked. Even Yugoslavia worked, despite a legacy of regional disunity even worse than Italy's. A hundred years after the storming of Rome by the Piedmontese and the red-shirted Garibaldini, Italy was still not functionally united. It did not work. Italians were still competing against each other, and the free enterprise system — the middle class began saying — only worsened the problem because it kept raising the level of competitiveness artificially by creating new wants.

Even if the United States had not blackened its own eye with the war in Southeast Asia — and alarming little right-wing undercover operations by the U.S. Embassy in Rome during the Nixon years — anti-Americanism would have increased sharply during the late 1960s because it expressed the disillusionment of the opinion-makers, of the achievers, with the American model. The Communists were gratified with this change at the very core of the Italian consciousness, but basically they did not create it. Italy truly did lack unity. Nobody was bothering to fix the potholes in the streets over which the Ferraris rolled. Rome was degenerating into the corrupt never-never land that Emerson and other American puritans had criticized so sharply in the 1850s.

By 1975, it was respectable to be a Communist in Italy. It was even chic. Enrico Berlinguer was an attractive figure, a minor Sardinian aristocrat married to a churchgoing Catholic. He did not hesitate to preach the virtues of pluralism to Brezhnev while himself running a well-disciplined centrally organized party. Above all, he was a *gentiluomo*. The establishment increasingly trusted him. By contrast with the tediously familiar, corruption-tainted Christian Democrats, the Communists came across as Mr. Clean. The one city that they had governed uninterruptedly since the war, Bologna, was a model of efficient administration and social harmony. The Communists' greatest appeal was that they offered a new, and they claimed definitive, formula for attaining that vital, elusive goal of national unity.

The reason that Italy had not achieved it in the Risorgimento, the Communists taught, was because the capitalist system had not allowed for any widespread distribution of property following the breakdown of the old aristocratic and feudal order. Italy had not previously had a bourgeois revolution, like France, nor a Reformation, like Germany and England. It had only had the Counterreformation, and the Risorgimento did not compensate for this historic warp. Powerful landowners, often nobles, became powerful industrialists. Peasants remained peasants, finding themselves even worse off in the South, where they became redundant in Italy's primitive, nineteenth-century capitalist economy. Millions immigrated to America in a passive form of class warfare; others became anarchists and Socialists. The lack of social justice and unity among Italians led to the desperate retreat at Caporetto in World War I, to postwar strikes and violence, and to Mussolini. Fascism had led to Italy's "occupation" by the Americans and its subordination to American hegemony (including NATO). Sidestepping whenever possible the question of Italy's NATO commitments, the Communists proposed to bring about real equality within a socialist system but without altogether abolishing private enterprise. They would be flexible, tolerant, "Western," but the long-sought goal would be achieved through a planned, centrally controlled Marxist system. When the poor southern Italians, the unemployed students, the part-time artisans, had all become equal members of society with everyone else, then Italy would finally be united.

It was a plausible thesis, and it was particularly attractive in a Latin, Catholic country that had been steeped so long in an absolutist culture. Yet the resistance to communism was still very strong. In the 1976 national elections, the Christian Democrats actually increased their vote to nearly 38 percent while the Communists took 33 percent. The country was split — and as "ungovernable" as ever.

The most extraordinary thing about Italy's heavy flirtation with communism was that, in nonpolitical terms, America's influence on young Italians seemed to be increasing, if anything. In a head-spinning contradiction, the young fist-waving marcher who denounced "American imperialism" was likely to be wearing a University of Tampa T-shirt and majoring in American literature. The Italians' anti-Americanism had never run very deep, and many youths, like other young Europeans, felt a basic affinity with the movements of dissent that washed over the United States in the late 1960s and culminated in Watergate. Full of admiration for the protest by U.S. radicals against militarism and mindless technology, these mostly leftist Italians became stealthily, then increasingly, pro-American on the throbbing wavelength of *Hair,* Joan Baez, and rock and pop culture as a whole. America's sophisticated, rainbowlike output influenced most Italians, through the movies they saw, the language they used, the products they bought at the *supermercato.* As a reporter, I remember going to a huge, thundering Communist rally in Rome's Piazza San Giovanni after the 1975 elections and dropping my pen. As I knelt for it I saw, beneath a forest of blue-jeaned legs, crumpled Coca-Cola cans. In Milan, student revolutionaries trashed the box office of a movie theater because it wasn't showing first-run American movies at "proletarian" prices. They tossed out leaflets explaining that it was their intrinsic cultural right to see films like *One Flew over the Cuckoo's Nest.* Italian feminism sprang into being in the 1970s, taking a great deal from the American counterculture.

At Rome's foreign press club, a correspondent was once heard to moan ironically in a moment of crisis: "Have you heard the news? After two thousand years of continuous history, Italy's gone down the drain." It couldn't, of course, and in the late seventies, despite continued political terrorism, people began to lift their heads again and find that they were intact and the country was intact around them. It wasn't such a bad place to live, despite all its problems.

There were a surprising number of Americans left in Italy. Anthony Quinn was living in the Alban hills east of Rome with his Italian wife, roaming the Mediterranean to make Mustafa Akkad's *The Message* in Libya and *The Greek Tycoon* in Greece and Corfu. Bob Edwards, badly wounded during the war, had stayed on in Italy and become a producer. He was making probing, spiky films with Italian director Liliana Cavani, like *Night Porter.* Tyrone Power's pretty daughter Romina was living near Bari, married to Italian singer Al Bano.

Every summer, American archaeologists were working on a pastoral, windswept hilltop at Murlo, outside Siena, unearthing an Etruscan fortress. Most of them were students, working under the direction of Bryn Mawr professor Kyle Phillips, Jr. The dig, started in 1966, was so successful that the Siena city fathers (many of them Communists) decided to house the Murlo pieces in a new museum on the top floor of the majestic Palazzo Comunale. The most fascinating of the museum's bronze and clay pieces is a 2,500-year-old mounted horseman wearing a curiously familiar sombrero: an unmistakable Texas ten-gallon hat.

The American Academy's dig at Cosa, near Porto Ercole, about ninety miles north of Rome, was completed in 1978 after a quarter of a century. White-haired Frank Brown, a celebrated Yale archaeologist who was in Syria during the war, had picked the site in 1947. In recent years he had been joined by Dr. Anna Marguerite McCann, a beautiful and statuesque blond who had donned a rubber suit and an aqualung to explore Cosa's silty port. Over five consecutive summers, McCann and her team of divers explored the bottom of the port, discovering that even in the third century B.C. the Romans had used hydraulic cement that set in water to make jetties and piers and had built canal-fed fish farms back of the shore.

In the course of unearthing Cosa's stones and marble pillars, the academy's archaeologists concluded that the town had been built according to a master plan prepared in a sort of colonial office in Rome. A small frontier outpost girded by walls, Cosa had its forum, its market, its baths and rectangular grid of streets laid out with Levittown-like precision. "It is the best picture we have of a small Italian hill town in the third and second centuries B.C.," Professor Brown said proudly, "some three hundred years before Pompeii."

The academy itself was recovering from a glum, faltering hiatus in the early seventies, when the left-right combination of U.S. recession and Italian inflation had raised talk that it might even have to be closed down. The Prix de Rome fellowships were cut from two years to one, and the salmon-colored Villa Aurelia, where a succession of academy directors had entertained local and visiting intellectuals in white-gloved splendor, was rented out as the residence of the Indian ambassador. American artists, moreover, grumbled that New York was where it was at; Rome, a waste of time.

By 1978, the number of one-year Fellows at the academy had risen to a record level (Prix de Rome winners received $6,400, including air fare from and to the United States, $600 for travel around Europe, and extra stipends for married couples). Morale had recovered, and a new wave of young figurative artists were finding Rome far more pertinent than their predecessors. The inflationary spiral of the late seventies still menaced the academy's future, but its director in 1979, Michigan classicist John D'Arms, nevertheless hoped to have the two-year fellowships reestablished. The academy's turnaround had been guided in Rome by D'Arms's predecessor, art historian Henry Millon. A tough-minded but gracious man, Millon had carefully pared the budget while maintaining the academy's carefree, olympian atmosphere. "Millon did a magnificent job of keeping the place alive while instituting the necessary cuts," said trustee Henry Cobb, a partner in the architectural firm of I. M. Pei.

In New York, the trustees picked retired college president Harold Martin as the academy's first full-time president. Martin was an old hand at fund-raising, and in Washington he secured grants from the National Endowment for the Humanities and the National Endowment for the Arts. At the NEA Martin also found his successor, William Lacy, who continued to press for grants and corporate gifts. Thanks to those grants, an increasing number of older "mid-career" Fellows have been taking a three- to four-month break from their professional lives to fly to Rome and live at the academy. Michael Lax, a successful New York industrial designer who was a midterm Fellow in 1978, walked around Rome, studying its staircases with housing modules in mind and thinking of glass as a building material, letting his imagination probe the ancient and Renaissance architecture of the city for three months. "It's phenomenally valuable to have time to do that," he said at the end of the experience.

Thousands of American students were attending courses at the Italian campuses of universities like Stanford (Florence), Johns Hopkins (Bologna), and Notre Dame (Rome). In Florence, American support after the 1966 flood had helped to create the world's largest "art hospital," where damaged paintings are restored by an international staff of experts. With American funds, Professor John McAndrew was helping to save threatened buildings and artworks in Venice. One church on the island of Murano was so frequently awash during the city's highwater emergencies that the priest went down the aisle in a rowboat. A gift from an American woman (who prefers to remain anonymous) allowed the padre to have a new foundation put in, and he now uses the boat for other purposes. The Spoleto Festival was still vigorously alive, and Menotti established an American edition of the festival in South Carolina.

All over Italy, Americans were active in the arts and in business. The worst of the political crisis seemed to be over, or else they had adjusted to it. Anti-Americanism had grown boring. Italians who could afford it spent a great deal of time in New York. Some Americans who had loved Italy in the 1950s and 1960s would no longer put the Royal Danieli or the Hotel Hassler on their vacation itineraries because they did not feel safe in Venice or Rome. Yet, amazingly, tourists continued to pour into Italy. In 1975, when the country's disorders were at flood tide, over thirty-six million foreigners crossed the frontier — and this in a country of fifty-six million, which is said to have a population density six times that of the United States and twice that of India and China. No wonder the trains and buses were crowded.

More than a million and a half Americans toured Italy that year. They stayed in little pensioni in Florence, lined up to cash their checks at American Express. Many were youthful backpackers. Some of them slept on the Ponte Vecchio with the Italian hippies (known locally as *ippi*). Everywhere, Americans could hear Italians using startlingly familiar words. At the café, some people asked for "cappuccino" and others for "un baby" (a small whiskey). You could hardly go to the theater in Rome without going "off" (a term derived from Off-Broadway). Anything might be called "sexy," and for Americans many things in Italy were, particularly the late-night TV shows in which liberated housewives stripped to the buff. More traditional ladies talked about their plans for "il weekend" and hoped their husbands would not discuss "marketing" or "management." Every Italian tot watched *Happy Days* and religiously read *Topolino* (the hugely successful Walt Disney weekly magazine).

American tourists would note these "Americanisms" and return to their basic perceptions: the feeling of Italy, of the people, of sunlight and shade on a famous facade, of the quality of space inside St. Peter's, the smile on a wrinkled face, and the taste of mineral water. As always, they were fascinated by the oldness of Italy. A friend, visiting Rome for the first time, remarked, "I can't get over the amount of ornamentation on the princely buildings, where the aristocrats lived. You wonder about the relationships of these people with other Italians — or with God." As we sat on the Via Veneto watching people go by, he marveled at the variety of physical and facial expressions: "All you've ever wanted to know about humanity, and more."

How many Americans had had similar thoughts after a first exposure to Italy? The novelist and journalist Alberto Moravia once told some foreign correspondents: "On the whole, Italian culture is superior to Italian politics." In fact, the ties between the United States and Italy run in deep human and cultural channels. The intermarriages. The American Academy. The fifteen million or so Italian-Americans with special ties to the mother country. The artists, scholars, businessmen, musicians, industrial and fashion designers, and journalists who go back and forth regularly between Italy and the United States. The millions of American Catholics who fly to Rome and visit the Vatican because the Pope is there. Scientists and doctors trading papers, visiting each other's laboratories. All these links are probably more important, taken together, than political ones.

Allies in one war, enemies in the next, the United States and Italy have not always had smooth relations. One wonders, in fact, what would happen if the Italian Communists did manage to get a couple of cabinet seats. Alarm bells would ring in Washington and at NATO's Brussels headquarters. One hopes that cooler heads would prevail and that no one would be stampeded to action stations by the fear of "losing" Italy. It would be very hard for the United States to lose Italy in any way except by backing a right-wing coup. The human and cultural bonds are simply too strong.

American leaders seem undecided about the problem of having Italian Communists in power in what is, after all, a NATO country. Senator Dole, the conservative Republican who was so grievously wounded in Italy, told me: "I'm not saying Americans did it for Italians, but it happened and we were the liberators, and there was a special bond formed. Now, you don't understand what's happening in Italy. Several years ago only Bologna was in the Communist orbit; now it's spreading to most of the cities. Maybe it's a different kind, they talk about 'Eurocommunism . . . with a heart,' and I don't understand all that. You wonder if this is what the people want, or if this is best for the people. And I think the Italian-Americans wonder the same thing."

The wisest course might be to keep Italy a part of NATO's political arm, whoever is in the government, while moving the peninsula gradually and delicately toward neutrality once the Alliance has resolved its arms imbalance crisis with the East Bloc in the early eighties. We have only twenty years before the second millennium, and by the year 2000 all of Italy should be neutral ground, as the

Vatican is today. Whatever the outcome of SALT, the shadow of theater nuclear weapons should be lifted from the Venetian lagoon and the rooftops and cupolas of Florence. That is a concept of arms limitation the entire world would understand. Italy does not intrinsically belong to one side or the other. It is universal. Cities like Rome, Florence, Siena, Spoleto, and Venice belong to the world at large. That is, surely, in terms of the 1980s and beyond, the composite meaning of what Charles Eliot Norton, Story, Berenson, and so many other Americans perceived about Italy, that its stupendous legacy from the past was to be studied, and valued, and ultimately preserved because it belonged to all mankind. Military neutrality — not to be confused with "Finlandization" or any loosening of Italy's Western or EEC ties — would allow the country's political gordian knot to be cut and would favor the shift of political initiative from the national level, where every step has to be weighed in terms of the East-West power balance, to the local one, where initiative and energy abound.

Meanwhile living in Italy, or even visiting Italy, will undoubtedly continue to be an adventure for Americans. Poet John Peck, arriving in Rome with his family to start a year's residence at the academy, said, "I'm just getting a sense of the ground. What buildings and what stones! I have a feeling it's going to be very important for me, but in what way I can't predict." To be struck by the lived-in antiquity of Italy is natural, and for anyone coming from across the Atlantic it is a powerful discovery. The human and the timeless are mixed together in a way that produces a kind of beauty that is sharply different from the beauty of America.

I remember standing at the tall window overlooking the umbrella pines of Villa Borghese one evening about five years ago, when I was just starting the research for this book. I was alone in the office. Everyone else had gone and it was quiet, though the sounds of a family fight were faintly audible from one of the nearby apartments.

It must have been nearly eight o'clock, a time when many families are already pushing back their dinner plates, but the air was aglow with light, a twilight typical of Rome in the early summer when the setting sun strikes the upper floors of buildings and turns their stucco facades to a deep, deep yellow, orange, saffron — aflame — their galleries, balustrades, and deep windows full of shadows.

Below my window the bricks of the Aurelian Wall — now a mere traffic divider but once Rome's protective fortification —were already in deep shadow. Beyond the wall lay the dark green park of the Villa Borghese, its palmlike umbrella pines giving it a sensuous northern Mediterranean aspect somewhere between the tropical and the Nordic. A few tourists in shirtsleeves were strolling along the park's gravel paths, and the ice-cream vendor was still selling cones from a shiny aluminum freezer mounted on a three-wheeled bicycle cart. On the edge of the windowpane was etched the French Academy in the Villa Medici, and beyond it the *cupolone,* dark blue — the dome of St. Peter's.

Held by the magic of that interleaving of golden light and night-fall, a light that lingered and lingered as if this were the longest day of summer, I remained at the window gazing out, dazed and moved, over this city that conserved the imprint of so many generations who had shared these same intersections of space and time that had caught my own imagination. I stood looking out toward the hills of Monte Mario, where the Hilton is, and beyond them to the orange fire of the setting sun. There was no obstruction before my eyes, not a single skyscraper or high-rise building, nothing to separate the present and past but the muted sound of traffic occasionally vibrating against the windowpane.

How many Romans had looked westward at those same hills before the notion of America was even dreamed of? The same species of swallow might have been darting overhead, the shadows would have streamed through the pine trees the same way. There, in the Borghese, where the dark pools beneath the trees were spreading over the grass, the barbarian Alaric had once camped before this same Aurelian Wall with his Visigoth warriors, howling for loot and women. On these same gravel paths, where the ice-cream vendor now pedaled his cold cart slowly toward the exit, Hawthorne had walked with his boyhood friend Franklin Pierce, who had been President of the United States and had come to Italy to see the beauty of history.

INDEX